FOREVER A SOLDIER

UNFORGETTABLE STORIES OF WARTIME SERVICE

THE LIBRARY OF CONGRESS VETERANS HISTORY PROJECT

BY TOM WIENER

THE LIBRARY OF CONGRESS IN ASSOCIATION WITH

 NATIONAL GEOGRAPHIC

WASHINGTON, D.C.

Library of Congress Cataloging-in-Publication Data.

Wiener, Tom.
  Forever a soldier : unforgettable stories of wartime service ; the Library of Congress Veterans History Project / by Tom Wiener.
      p. cm.
  "The Library of Congress in association with the National Geographic Society."
  Includes index.
  ISBN-13: 978-0-7922-6207-7
  ISBN-10: 0-7922-6207-7
  1. Veterans--United States--Biography. 2. United States--Armed Forces--Biography. 3. United States--History, Military--20th century. 4. United States--History, Military--21st century. I. Veterans History Project (U.S.) II. National Geographic Society (U.S.) III. Title.
  U52.W54 2006
  355.3092'273--dc22

                                                              2006023125

Founded in 1888, the National Geographic Society is one of the largest nonprofit scientific and educational organizations in the world. It reaches more than 285 million people worldwide each month through its official journal, NATIONAL GEOGRAPHIC, and its four other magazines; the National Geographic Channel; television documentaries; radio programs; films; books; videos and DVDs; maps; and interactive media. National Geographic has funded more than 8,000 scientific research projects and supports an education program combating geographic illiteracy.

For more information, please call
1-800-NGS LINE (647-5463)
or write to the following address:

National Geographic Society
1145 17th Street N.W.
Washington, D.C. 20036-4688 U.S.A.

Visit us online at www.nationalgeographic.com/books

For information about special discounts for bulk purchases, please contact National Geographic Books Special Sales: ngspecsales@ngs.org

Printed in U.S.A.

TABLE OF CONTENTS

FOREWORD

BY TOM WIENER

After five years of collecting stories of men and women who served during this country's recent wars, the Veterans History Project has amassed an archive of over 35,000 individual stories. Selecting a representative handful—37, to be exact—to present between the covers of this book might seem like a daunting task. But it wasn't.

For one thing, I enjoyed the support of my colleagues on the Project, all of whom are listed in the Acknowledgments. In particular, I have to thank the people on our processing team, led by the inimitable Eileen Simon, who are on our front lines. They see all of the collections when they arrive, raw and unprocessed, at the Library of Congress. Every member of that team has become expert at spotting the "A" list interviews, memoirs, diaries, and photographs. Many of the selections in this book were their suggestions.

Also, in working for two years on the Project's web site (www.loc.gov/vets), I have become familiar with scores of outstanding stories. We regularly feature a group of collections on the site, tied to a theme such as Military Medicine or Prisoners of War. If you've been to our site, some of the stories in this book may look familiar. I am excited to share them with readers who still get at least some of their information from between the covers of a book and not just from a computer screen.

Conversely, you can access all of the collections in this book through our web site. There, you can hear Giles McCoy's voice eloquently describe how he survived four days in the shark-infested waters of the Pacific after his ship, the *U.S.S. Indianapolis*, was torpedoed in July 1945. Or you can read in full Jean-Marie Crocker's heartbreaking memoir of her son, Denton, Jr., and his service in Vietnam. Or you can watch Augustus Prince relate the story of how the Navy gave him his first break, and see how, sixty years after that moment, he still understands that it changed his life.

No one who serves in a war, whether on the front lines or stateside, can say the experience didn't have some profound effect on his or her life. The men and women in this book all had what I would call life-altering experiences, some of them more dramatic than others, to be sure. The veterans who were captured by the enemy, like Rhonda Cornum, a prisoner of the Iraqis in the Persian Gulf War, or José Mares, a captive of the North Koreans in the Korean War, suffered physical deprivations unimaginable to all but a handful of Americans. Moreover, their character was tested; maintaining a positive and hopeful attitude was as important to survival as physical endurance, as Roger Ingvalson, a Vietnam War POW, points out.

If there's any group of stories I have a personal connection to, it's the chapter titled The Healers, stories of doctors, nurses, and medical corpsmen who dealt resolutely with the casualties of war. My mother was a nurse during World War II, serving in Africa and Italy, where she met the man she would marry, a U.S. Army noncom. When I was growing up, neither of them were forthcoming with me about their experiences, but it didn't take much intuition to sense that they'd seen horrible things.

They kept few mementos of that time, but my father did have a scrapbook that contained one memorable photograph: a crowd taunting a woman who had been stripped of her clothing, her hair cut short. This, my father told me, was what happened toward the end of World War II to many women in liberated France who had been intimate with their German occupiers. What, I wondered as a young boy, could incite people to behave so brutally? I also wondered what the people not in the camera's view, the citizens in their homes and on the sidewalks of that town, who saw this procession might have been thinking. Did they feel pity for the woman or perhaps a shared sense of contempt for her?

Some of the veterans whose stories are told in this book were witness to similar episodes. James Dorris walked unsuspectingly in April 1945 into the concentration camp at Dachau, totally unprepared for the stupendous evidence of cruelty that was more unnerving than any battle scene he'd witnessed. Richard DeLeon was a medic in Vietnam who watched helplessly as a helicopter carrying a dozen new recruits crashed, leaving only two survivors. He was forced to extricate on his own the bodies of the victims and encase them in improvised shrouds made from poncho liners.

In selecting stories for this second volume based on the collections of the Veterans History Project (following *Voices of War*), I wasn't drawn necessarily to the most gruesome accounts of war. There are moments of levity and lightness here, even in the grimmest of circumstances, as when Milton Stern, a Jewish POW of the Germans in World War II, provides a list of Foods I Want To Eat when he gets free. Frances Liberty, an Army nurse with a reputation for toughness, was not above pulling a prank on the grounds of Walter Reed Army Medical Center in Washington.

"It would be wrong to say war is all grim," wrote the great correspondent Ernie Pyle in 1943. "If it were, the human spirit could not survive two and three and four years of it." Every veteran in this book, with one exception, survived his or her individual war. How they did so demonstrates the way we do rise above cruelty to a better place. It is perhaps the finest lesson any war can teach us. It is a lesson well learned by the veterans whose stories I have tried to tell.

INTRODUCTION

BY ANDREW CARROLL

RARELY DO THEY TALK ABOUT THEIR EXPERIENCES. Modesty prevents most veterans from discussing, especially in heroic terms, their wartime service, and for others it is simply too painful. The stories in this remarkable collection remind us why.

"On about the fourth or fifth morning," Raymond Brittain recalled of the December 7, 1941 attack on Pearl Harbor,

> we kept hearing a plopping noise in the water, most of it coming from our stern area. Then as it got light we could see what it was. It was bodies from the *Arizona* that had filled full of gas. They had been dead for four or five days and they were forcing up through the gangways and passageway. They were all face down in the water. Bad scene. Bad scene. Really bad.

Brittain added: "I try to forget things like that, but you can't. After 60 years, it's still there. I still think of it."

In the profile on Korean War veteran José Mares, who was captured and tortured by enemy soldiers, we find an even more graphic account of warfare. "A North Korean loudly asked the first man in the line for the size of his unit and what their mission was. When the GI barked out his name, rank, and service number, the Korean pulled out a .45-caliber pistol and shot the soldier in the head. Mares felt the man's blood splatter him, and he heard the corpse fall into the river." Mares was spared but savagely beaten, and the physical and psychological scars remained long after he returned home.

Although many of these veterans stood at the epicenter of history, witnessing firsthand such extraordinary events as the assault on Corregidor, the landings at Normandy or Iwo Jima, the sinking of the *U.S.S Indianapolis*, the fighting at Chosin Reservoir, or the invasion of Baghdad, the most vivid memories are the smaller details of combat that, although seemingly less momentous, sting like a splinter. For one serviceman it is the sight of a badly burned sailor being placed on a wire mesh stretcher, which stuck to his exposed skin and tore off small chunks of flesh when he moved. For another it is the unforgettable stench of dead animals and enemy troops rotting on the battlefield. And for an Air Force officer named Roger Dean Ingvalson who had been shot down over Vietnam and confined as a POW, it was an auditory memory that proved most excruciating. "Physical torture is tough," he recounted, "but mental is worse." To torment Ingalvson, who was the father of a young son, his captors repeatedly played a tape of a baby crying. (The recording was so realistic that Ingalvson initially thought he was hearing a real infant.) "To this day," Ingalvson remarked, "I can't stand to be around my grandchildren, my babies, when they cry."

As difficult as it can be for veterans to share these memories, many are increasingly recognizing the importance of doing so. On a personal level, the experience can be cathartic, allowing veterans to express feelings that have been pent up for years and even decades. Wendy Wamsley Taines, a medic in the Gulf War, was traumatized by the sight of young troops who had been burned, ripped apart by shrapnel, and mangled in combat. (Her very first casualty was a marine whose eye was hanging out of its socket.) "They need to talk about what they did, [and] make sense of what they did," Taines says of all servicemen and women who have encountered the horrors of war. "I say that from my own experience." There is comfort in knowing that they are not enduring the emotional aftershocks of battle alone. Even the most stoic and tough-minded veterans have found solace in hearing what their comrades in arms have undergone.

Not all of the memories are harsh or disturbing. Recorded here are instances of great daring and heroism, declarations of fierce patriotism and impenetrable faith, and examples of the honor and camaraderie that binds these troops together. "This isn't about politics or the people back home," a Lebanese-born American named Raffi Bahadrian said to his fellow marines, "This is about the person next to me, on my left and right. In the end, it is just making sure that the person to my left and right stayed alive." It is a sentiment that is expressed in war after war.

Some veterans even display flashes of humor. A U.S. Army nurse named Frances Liberty who cared for troops in World War II, Korea, and Vietnam was the embodiment of the fearless, no-nonsense New Yorker. When a high-ranking female officer from Washington, D.C., observed "Lib" using a water hose to wash off the blood and muck covering her patients at a field hospital in Vietnam, the officer was shocked. "Oh my, do you have to use a hose?" the officer asked.

"What would you suggest?" Lib retorted.

"Well, there must be something…"

"Well now, you go back to Washington and sit behind your nice desk and when you think of something, you tell us."

"I think you're being sarcastic."

"Yes, I am," Lib said. "Now don't get too close; you might get dirty."

Whether they are humorous anecdotes or horrific accounts of battle, the value of these stories ultimately lies not in their ability to shock or entertain but in their power to ensure that we never forget the sacrifices demanded of the troops who have served this nation. War, for the vast majority of us, is abstract and remote, something that has occurred in faraway lands and, with the exception of Afghanistan and Iraq, very long ago. These stories make it real. They infuse the impersonal facts of history with the individual personalities and perspectives of those who lived through these catastrophic events and have described them as only eyewitnesses can.

These veterans are not the generals, presidents, and military leaders who are highlighted in the textbooks; they are the men and women whose names frequently go unrecorded but who stepped—often voluntarily—into the maelstrom of war and bore the brunt of its fury. They are the young troops, many only teenagers at the time, who confronted head-on the most vicious and well-trained armies of the world during 1941 to 1945, braved the paralyzing cold of Korea, slogged through the sweltering jungles of Vietnam, and fought (and continue to fight) guerrilla warfare against terrorist forces in Afghanistan and Iraq. They are the war nurses who gripped the calloused hands of dying boys they deeply cared for and had desperately tried to save. They are the prisoners of war who sustained breathtaking cruelty at the hands of sadistic guards. And they are the courageous pioneers who, either because of gender or ethnicity, had to prove to the world that their service was as noble and impressive as anyone else's. The resilience alone of these men and women is an inspiration to us all.

"It's not sport or game any more but just terrible bloody slaughter," Eugene Curtin wrote to his mother on December 7, 1917, while in France during the First World War. Like so many troops, Curtin had gone off to war imagining it to be a "great adventure." But after being immersed in its brutality, his enthusiasm waned. In the same December 7 letter home he said: "The real details of the battle and the sights one sees are things I for one want to forget as soon as possible." For most veterans, forgetting would prove impossible. For the rest of us, it is imperative that we never do.

Washington, D.C.
August, 2005

Andrew Carroll is the author of Behind the Lines: Powerful and Revealing American and Foreign War Letters—and One Man's Search to Find Them. *He is the director of the Legacy Project, a national, all-volunteer effort that encourages Americans to preserve wartime correspondence before it is lost forever.*

CHAPTER ONE

ON THE FRONT LINES

WE LEAD OFF WITH A SERIES OF UNFORGETTABLE MOMENTS FROM WORLD
War II. For the men who were in Pearl Harbor on December 7, 1941, the
sights and sounds and smells would linger for the rest of their lives. One sailor,
Raymond Brittain, was luckier than many; although he was injured during the
bombardment, he was, as a gunner aboard a battleship, able to strike back at
the Japanese attackers. Immediately following are three stories among the
thousands that can be told of World War II's most momentous single day, June
6, 1944. John Sudyk landed on the beach at Normandy, Albert Hassenzahl
was a paratrooper who landed in France from the air, and Robert Powell was
a pilot who patrolled the skies above France to ensure safe landings by those
paratroops. For everyone who was still alive and unharmed on June 7, there
was relief tempered by the knowledge that the end of the war was still many
battles away.

In the stories that follow these memories of World War II the terrains
change, the face of the enemy may be different, but so much among these
stories, ranging from the trenches of France (Hillie John Franz) to the
jungles of Vietnam (Kenneth Ray Rodgers) to the deserts of the Middle
East (Rodgers and Raffi Bahadarian), has a familiar ring. There are the
physical hardships that can't be mitigated by advanced technology. There
is the noise, the confusion, the chaos, and the uncertainty of battle, no
matter how great the odds are in your favor. And there is the longing for
peace, for the calm of a day without bullets or bombs.

RAYMOND BRITTAIN:
PRESENT AT THE BEGINNING

"I could hear all the bullets ricocheting off the superstructure and off my director's chair about fifty feet above me. And Nash says, 'My God, the Japanese are bombing us.'"

RAYMOND BRITTAIN SEEMED ALMOST FATED TO BE A SAILOR. His father was a chief boatswain's mate in the Navy, but Raymond never knew him; he was killed while serving on a destroyer when Raymond was three months old. Raymond's mother married another sailor, and they had a daughter. He also was killed. The children were still young, and Brittain's mother worked as a nurse to raise them, paying whatever she could to friends to take care of her children. Raymond grew up in southern California, in Escondido, a small town north of San Diego, and then in Los Angeles, where he attended Torrance High School.

Given his father's death in the Navy and his graduation with a satisfactory scholastic record, Brittain was eligible for a full scholarship to any state university. He chose the University of California at Davis and a major in agriculture. However, in the summer of 1940, he and several buddies decided they were not going back to college. They were well aware that a war was raging throughout Europe, and "we decided that some day we were going to be in it." So he enlisted in the Navy and was sent to the Naval Training Station in San Diego.

About halfway through his scheduled training period, Brittain was

*After surviving the Pearl Harbor attack Raymond
Brittain, pictured here in San Francisco circa
1943, served throughout the Pacific.*

waked up one morning, told to pack his sea bags, and forbidden to
notify his family of the new assignment. Brittain was put on a boat to
Long Beach Harbor, where the carrier *Saratoga* was docked. Its deck
was empty of airplanes, but Brittain joined several thousand recruits on
a voyage to Pearl Harbor. Upon arrival, they were dispersed to the several battleships stationed there, "because," he recalled in a 2002 interview, "apparently they were undermanned at the time."

He was assigned to the twenty-one-year-old battleship *Tennessee*
(one year older than he was) and began his training at the Antiaircraft
Director's School. Brittain became an antiaircraft-director operator on
a five-inch battery; he got to practice his speciality on the *Tennessee* and
two other battleships, the *Oklahoma* and the *Nevada,* going out to sea
for several days at a time. The old-timers stationed at Pearl said that the
fleet always went through training maneuvers, but "they had never
seen anything like" the fall of 1941. In addition to longer and more
intensive training sessions, the ships in the harbor were completely
blacked-out every night.

Among his duties were three ninety-minute daily stints of mess cooking. On the morning of December 7, 1941, he was taking a load of garbage onto the boat deck to be dumped into a "honey barge," a boat that pulled alongside each ship to collect its garbage. The *Tennessee* was tied up adjacent to Ford Island, site of the seaplane base, at a mooring known as Battleship Row. She was berthed with six other ships: the *Maryland* in front of her, the *Arizona* to her stern, the *Oklahoma* outboard of the *Maryland*, the *West Virginia* secured to the port side of the *Tennessee,* the repair ship *Vestal* next to the *Arizona*, and the *Nevada* astern of the *Arizona*. The remaining battleship, *Utah,* was moored on the other side of Ford Island. Of that day, Brittain recalled,

"Standing next to me was an old-timer, a first class bo'sun's mate by the name of Nash. All of a sudden we heard a couple of loud reports from the seaplane base on Ford Island. We looked over and we saw smoke coming up, and Nash said, 'Oh, the crazy Army is practicing dive bombing on Sunday morning there.' We're standing there still looking at it, and all of sudden we hear a lot of loud humming in the superstructure of the battleship, right above us. And about that time, an airplane coming right flat across the airstrip on Ford Island come right above us. And Nash said, 'There's meatballs on that thing.' He said, 'Hell, Ray, those are Japanese planes!' I remember seeing the rising sun underneath the wing tip and the meatball on the fuselage. And what we were hearing, they were machine gunning our Battleship Row after they'd dropped bombs on Ford Island. They came right across Ford Island at a good right angle to Battleship Row. I could hear all the bullets ricocheting off the superstructure and off my director's chair, about fifty feet above me. And Nash says, 'My God, the Japanese are bombing us.'"

Nash ordered Brittain to go through the ship and to make sure everyone knew to get to his battle station.

"I went through real fast, yelling the Japanese were bombing, and everybody went, 'Ha, ha, ha.' Nobody believed it. And still general quarters hadn't sounded. I started to go up one flight of steps onto the boat deck, and I just got up onto the boat deck where the anti-aircraft guns were when all of a sudden I was knocked flat on my back. I remember looking up in the air, and several hundred feet above there was nothing but mud and water, which was coming from the *West Virginia*, tied up alongside us. She had received several torpedoes, and those first torpedoes broke just about every piece of glass on my battleship. Still, no general quarters had sounded on our ship. I started up more ladders to get to my director, and about halfway up there, general quarters sounded. But my director was locked up with a padlock, and I had to find what we call in the Navy a dog wrench. I started beating on the lock, and finally got it off and got into the director. When we came into Pearl Harbor after we'd been out practicing for a week, normally all our ammunition for our antiaircraft guns would be stored below decks, because it would get so hot, and the ready boxes, which would normally hold about 50 or 75 5-inch antiaircraft shells, would endanger the ammunition from exploding. But this time when we came in, they left them up in the ready boxes on the gun deck."

This was the only time Brittain remembered that had happened in the weeks of training that had led up to December 7th. When he and his crew got into the director, most of the naval officers were still "on the beach," that is, on liberty. The enlisted men were granted only Cinderella liberty, so they'd been back aboard since midnight. A Marine officer had to take charge of the antiaircraft gunners. Brittain began tracking bombers as they came in at a right angle to Battleship Row. He saw black dots falling from the planes and figured they were 150- to 200-pound bombs. The *West Virginia* caught fire from torpedoes, and then the *Arizona* was hit even harder. "There was so much smoke blowing," he recalled. "The oil coming down between the *West Virginia* and the *Tennessee*'s stern was setting us on fire."

Because of the fire on the *West Virginia,* she had to secure her starboard antiaircraft battery to prevent its shells from blowing up on the boat deck, and the *Tennessee* had to secure its port antiaircraft batteries, which were right next to the *West Virginia*. The only antiaircraft battery operating from either ship was Brittain's director on the starboard side, next to Ford Island. He was tracking the horizontal bombers coming in when all of a sudden ("I didn't see it") a large bomb hit the gun turret below Brittain. [Experts later figured it probably was a 16-inch armor-piercing battery shell, especially adapted as an aerial bomb and designed to do maximum damage to the heavily armored battleships anchored at Pearl.]

"When it exploded," Brittain recalled, "it blew me out of the director, and I hit onto the steel deck. It blew my shoe off my left foot, and I found out later it broke my left foot and ankle and the lower part of my leg. So I got back into the director, and we just continued our thing." Then there was a lull, as the first wave returned to their carriers. A lieutenant named Morris was checking in on everyone. He said, 'Brittain, where's your shoe?' And then he said, 'Oh my gosh,'" because by then Brittain's injured foot was turning black. The shell that injured Brittain also created deadly shrapnel that tore up the bridge of the *West Virginia* and killed its captain.

A second attack soon commenced. The *Tennessee* took another big shell, which went down through the main mast where there was a scout observation plane that could be launched with a catapult. The plane caught fire and blew up, and the debris killed several crew members below decks. Brittain thinks the *Tennessee* took two shells similar to the one that sank the *Arizona*.

Were they calm during the attack? the interviewer asked Brittain. "For weeks we had been practicing for something like this," he said. "But the word 'Japanese' was never brought up. We figured if we were going to war, we were going through the Panama Canal and get over into Europe." That morning, he recalled, everyone was doing his duty.

"When both of the attacks finished," he recalled, "everything was on fire, and ammunition was still exploding from the fires. The smoke was horrible. We could hardly breathe—that thick oil that battleships use is just like tar." He could see the *Oklahoma* burning in front of him; he went below deck for a moment, and when he came back up, the ship was rolled half over. The *Maryland* had received only a few hits, but the *West Virginia* was mortally wounded, and when she sank, she pinned the *Tennessee* against the big concrete mooring quays off Ford Island. "Meanwhile," Brittain recalled, "the captain of our ship did a marvelous thing. He started up the main engines on our ship, and he ran those engines full tilt, stirring up the water and pushing away that oil that was coming from the *Arizona* to us. It probably saved our ship."

The *Tennessee* was credited with downing six enemy airplanes that morning, but Brittain wasn't sure about the hits, because "everything was so smoky and confused." He also had no real sense of just how long the whole attack lasted. "I have no feeling about time that day. They say that whole thing was over in a little less than two hours." If Brittain had no concept of time during the attack, he also had no time to think about his injured foot. After the second attack, Lt. Morris told Brittain he was going to have to go to sick bay and get an x-ray and a cast on his foot. But, Brittain recalled, he couldn't bring himself to do it, "because all the time we were expecting another attack to come in. Too, the ship was fighting for its life with exploding ammunition and fire."

He ate no breakfast or lunch that day, but about six in the evening a cook came up with a bag of oranges, and the sailors had a couple of them apiece. About seven o'clock, Lt. Morris told him again to get to sick bay. He hobbled down from his director to sick bay, which was three levels below main deck. The room was "completely, completely packed with stretchers and people." The *Tennessee's* sick bay was taking injured from the *West Virginia,* the *Oklahoma,* and the *Arizona,* as well as its own men. What was most disheartening was that the stretchers were wire mesh. "So many sailors had burned so bad. They were laid in the stretchers on the bare wire, and when the medical personnel picked them up, the burned skin on the backs of their legs was left on the wire."

Brittain saw a corpsman he knew and asked him if he would x-ray and put a cast on his leg. The corpsman said tersely, "Look around you. Impossible." He gave Brittain a roll of three-inch-wide bandage and a roll of three-inch tape and told him to bandage and tape himself as best he could. He gave Brittain a shot of morphine for his pain, painted the letter M on his forehead with iodine, and gave him two more doses of morphine and a syringe to inject himself with "when it gets real bad." Brittain went back to sick bay a week later and saw another corpsman, who examined him. His toes were still purple. The man told Brittain to tape himself up again and not to worry as long as he had feeling in his foot and toes.

Brittain spent the night of December 7th up in his director. Not long after the two attack waves had rolled through Pearl, there was word that the Japanese were landing at a spot called Barber's Point. "As you're leaving Pearl Harbor," Brittain explained about the ship channel, "that would be to the right." The *Tennessee* turned its one operating battery, which could also fire at surface objects, toward Barber's Point in case they were needed, but the landing never came. About 7:30 or 8 o'clock on the night of the 7th, a flight of B-18s— U.S. planes—came in, and were fired upon. "All hell broke loose. Everybody was so jumpy. We expected anything—somebody floating up with a bomb, whatever." He recalled that if a small boat started to move around, somebody would shoot at it. Nights after the 7th were marked by the sound of small arms fire. Every morning, the ships would go to general quarters, all battle stations manned and on alert, a half hour or an hour before sunrise, "because that's when you're most vulnerable to attack at sea or in port."

As bad as the Japanese attack was, the delayed evidence of it proved to be devastating. Brittain recalled: "I remember on about the fourth or fifth morning [following December 7th] I was up in the director, and we kept hearing a plopping noise in the water, most of it coming from our stern area. Then as it got light we could see what it was. It was bodies from the *Arizona* that had filled full of gas. They had been dead for four or five days, and they were forcing up through the gang-ways and passageways and plopping up. All we could see was the backs

Brittain (right, holding shells) and his gun crew, aboard an LST-17, somewhere in the Pacific Ocean, 1944.

of white t–shirts. They were all facedown in the water. Bad scene. Bad scene. Really bad. I try to forget things like that, but you can't. After sixty years, it's still there. I still think of it."

A couple of days after that, he was assigned to a small boat as part of a work detail retrieving floating bodies, from the *Tennessee, West Virginia,* and *Arizona.* They looped white twine under the armpits, and then towed the bodies, four or five at a time, to a location east of Battleship Row called Aieia Landing. Personnel there eased the bodies out of the water, and Brittain's boat would go back for more. He thinks they recovered about thirteen to fifteen bodies that day, but there were other boats working as well, mostly from the *Arizona,* the ship that suffered the most casualties in the attack.

Raymond Brittain served in the Pacific through the early years of World War II, first in the Aleutians campaign, and then in support of action on Tarawa. He was taken off the *Tennessee* at one point (he admitted he's not too strong on what year or month things happened to him) and placed on a carrier heading back to the United States. The Navy wanted to train him for new duties as a fire controlman. From Washington, D.C., he shipped out to the Mediterranean on an LST filled with bangalore torpedoes, which were used to blow up booby traps and barricades on the beach during amphibious landings. His boat got as far as Gibraltar when they were ordered to turn around and head for the Pacific.

In August 1945 Brittain's ship was on its way from Manila Bay to the coast of Japan, in preparation for the invasion, when the Japanese surrendered. He then spent some time in postwar Japan with the occupation forces. It's difficult to imagine the emotions that a Pearl Harbor survivor would feel during that duty, even four years after the awful attack.

Brittain has seen the movie *Pearl Harbor.* "That's a good motion picture," he said. "It's a love story. But they can't duplicate it. No way possible that they could duplicate the noise, the smell, everything that happened." He was disappointed at some historical inaccuracies; "they showed 20mm and 40mm guns shooting, and we didn't have those." What upsets him much more are veterans who were at Pearl Harbor and talk about "things that never really existed."

He's a life member of the Pearl Harbor Survivors Association. Every five years the association has a reunion in Hawaii, and every other year they have one someplace on the mainland. He didn't want to go to the fortieth because it was being held at Pearl, which he had never revisited. He had been to Maui and the big island and liked them, "but I don't like Oahu because of the memories there." However, he was persuaded to attend.

He arrived on Oahu and read a newspaper article quoting a sailor who served on the *West Virginia* and still lived in Hawaii. The veteran claimed he was put on guard duty following the attack to prevent sailors off the *Tennessee* from looting side arms from the *West Virginia*. "I saw and heard what [really] happened," Brittain said. "I saw officers from the *West Virginia* come over to my ship and ask sailors if they could go down to their quarters that were almost filled with water and get their swords, which they graduated from Annapolis with."

In Hawaii forty years later, Brittain made a big fuss about the article; he wrote a letter to the newspaper, and he put out word in the reunion hotel that he wanted to talk to the veteran, who managed to make himself scarce. One day Brittain was walking through the lobby, and a bunch of sailors sitting around looked at him and said, "Oh, here comes one of those looters from the *Tennessee*." "And that didn't fare well with me at all," he recalled. He had a good talk with them and straightened them out.

After the *Tennessee* was freed from its position between the sunken *West Virginia* and the quay on Ford Island, it sailed with several other ships to a repair facility in Bremerton, Washington. As they approached the Strait of Juan de Fuca, which separates the U.S. from Canada and leads into Puget Sound and the port of Seattle, they found the area thick with Japanese submarines. Destroyers accompanying them were dropping depth charges, and the *Tennessee* was rolling from the undersea explosions. Had they survived the Pearl Harbor attack only to be sunk within sight of the United States mainland? During the voyage back to the mainland, Brittain and some of his shipmates talked among themselves. They wondered why they were still alive after the horrors of December 7th. "That was a puzzle that nobody could really answer, except the dear Lord willed it that way," he said in his interview.

They made it home, and the *Tennessee* later sailed out again, to serve in many more battles. Raymond Brittain survived, too, and sixty years later, he understands the value of the comradeship from that awful day, and the years that followed. "All of us," he said, "have been through a certain thing that nobody else has been through." His conclusion: "It's the old saying: You wouldn't go through it for a million dollars again. And you wouldn't take a million dollars for your experience."

ALBERT HASSENZAHL: FIRST INTO EUROPE

*"I thought that I was the only GI to land on
the coast of Normandy."*

I
N DECEMBER 1998, ALBERT HASSENZAHL SAT DOWN IN HIS STUDY,
alone, with a tape recorder. He had served in World War II and
witnessed some of the worst fighting in Europe. But for many
years he didn't discuss what he saw and experienced. Then something a neighbor said prompted him to record his memories for a
friend, George Gros, the son of Sergeant Leroy "Buddy" Gros, who
served in his company.

In the fall of 1941, Al Hassenzahl was in his junior year at the
University of Toledo. When the Japanese attacked Pearl Harbor that
December, he was determined to join the Army as soon as he could.
He finished out the semester and enlisted in February 1942. At Camp
Livingston, Louisiana, he qualified for Officer Candidate School as an
infantry officer and did his ninety days' training, earning a commission as a second lieutenant in the infantry. In town on leave he had
noticed the paratroops and "their excellent look," deciding "that was
the outfit I wanted to be in."

Hassenzahl applied to parachute school and underwent four rugged
weeks of training. He described it in four stages: Stage A was strictly physical, and the weak people washed out. Stage B involved learning hand-
to-hand combat, judo, and how to recover from a jump. In Stage C, they
went up on 250-foot towers and jumped with a parachute that opened

right away. On the first day, with a strong wind blowing, the first guy to jump broke his leg when he landed, and the second broke his ankle. Hassenzahl was next. The wind caught him and slammed him down on his right knee, aggravating an old football injury. He spent six weeks in physical therapy and finished Stage C later. In Stage D, they went up in an airplane to make five practice jumps. He graduated and got his silver wings, making him "a bona fide paratrooper from this point on."

He was posted to the 506th Infantry Paratroop Regiment, and was on a troopship in February 1943 crossing the Atlantic to England. For the next sixteen months, the 506th trained for the invasion of Europe—and managed to have a lot of fun, especially with weekend passes to London.

In early June 1944, he and the company were sent to a staging area. June 5 was "a special memory for me," Hassenzahl recalled. That afternoon, the troops in his area were called to assemble, and General Dwight Eisenhower and Prime Minister Winston Churchill arrived to inspect them. Hassenzahl happened to be in one of the front ranks when the two men came down the line; Eisenhower winked at him and told him, "Good luck, soldier."

They were taken across the English Channel late that evening in a C-47, which began flying in big circles, waiting for the drop signal. The paratroops were all wearing leg packs that were supposed to slow their descent, then release and hit the ground first. It didn't work that way; in some cases they came off right away, in others they didn't release. His unit jumped about 4 ½ hours before the first beach assault. He was the jump master, with seventeen men under him. They all hit the ground in pitch blackness, and he had the sensation that "I was the only GI to land on the coast of Normandy." Some of the men had trouble getting out of their parachute harnesses, because they were carrying more than the usual gear. Hassenzahl used a trench knife to free himself. Others got hung up in trees, and one came down smack into a German compound. Hassenzahl met up with other paratroops, and they took time to orient themselves, noting that many road signs were down. They ran into a few Germans, and there were minor exchanges of gunfire.

"Everything is in a fog in my memory," Hassenzahl admitted. He recalled a running fight with Germans along a hedgerow, and suddenly he felt a burning sensation in his right side and crumpled to the ground. "Punchy" Zettwich, a sergeant in his company, who got his

*Albert Hassenzahl in 1942, as a 21-year-old 2nd lieutenant and
a new member of the 101st Airborne Division.
Two years later, he parachuted into Normandy.*

nickname for his background as an amateur boxer, pulled him under cover and bandaged his wound. Their chaplain, Father Maloney, started last rites, and Hassenzahl told him to stop that, he wasn't go to die.

He was taken by jeep to Utah Beach and must have gone into shock because he had trouble talking. Lying there, he felt the wind blow off his blanket. Someone's arm reached out and tucked it all around him. He looked over to thank the man and saw a German POW on a stretcher next to him, his legs all mangled. Neither of them said a word; they just exchanged a look. Hassenzahl spent about a month recuperating from a damaged rib. He could have taken a limited-duty assignment, but he wanted to go back to his outfit. "Your company was your family," in this case, C Company of the 506th.

He spent August in England, training replacements. Their next mission was called Market Garden, on September 17, 1944, for which they were attached to the British Second Army. The plan was to jump behind the enemy lines into Holland and secure bridges that would allow the Allies to skirt the Siegfried Line, the Germans' solid defensive position, and speed the advance into Germany. The jump occurred in broad daylight at low altitude, about 600 to 800 feet, amid lots of antiaircraft fire. Tragically, C Company lost a planeload of men to ground fire. Hassenzahl and his cohorts assembled quickly in the drop zone, moved out to within thirty or forty yards of their targeted bridge, only to watch the Germans blow it up from the other side. Some of his men swam across, and as the Germans retreated, engineers hastily built another bridge. Cornelius Ryan's book and the 1977 film *A Bridge Too Far* showed how the operation was botched when British troops were decimated in the battle for Arnhem; they did not get re-supplied, and their tank columns never made it to the river.

In action after the drop, Hassenzahl lost his close friend Lieutenant "Bull" Winans. He was standing atop a dike when a tank gun blew off the top of his head. Hassenzahl almost caught him as he rolled down the dike. The fighting that ensued was especially fierce, some of it hand to hand. He recalled taking on a bigger soldier and with some help subduing him. Another American soldier took a Nazi flag from a tank they had immobilized with a bazooka; Hassenzahl traded him for it and still has it.

On October 6, they were ordered to attack the Dutch town of Opheusden. "That date will be imbedded in my mind forever," Hassenzahl said. It was a regimental effort that involved combing through town, house by house. The Germans were using their most deadly gun, the 88mm, which Hassenzahl described as "anti-tank, anti-aircraft, anti-personnel." His company's losses were staggering. They went in with 118 men and six officers and left with twenty-six men and Albert Hassenzahl, the only officer left. They rested that night, and the next day attacked Germans in an orchard, directing heavy rounds of mortar fire into the woods. They found fifty or fifty-five dead Germans amid the trees, and the battle was won. It was, Hassenzahl recalled, "probably one of the high points in my career in the military."

In early December, he got a pass to go to Paris, but it wasn't long before he was back in action. He was alerted to a new German counteroffensive in mid-December that became the Battle of the Bulge, the last large-scale battle of the war in Europe. The Germans had caught the Allies unprepared, and when he arrived in Bastogne, he said, "I'll never forget the spectacle of American troops streaming back to the rear." He became involved in the perimeter defense of a Belgian town called Noville, and he admitted, "I never thought we'd get out of that alive."

Sergeant Zettwich, who had helped him out when he was hit, was wounded badly during subsequent fighting. "It struck me that he was hit in just about the same area that I had been in Normandy in June of that year," Hassenzahl recalled. As they loaded him on a halftrack to take him to the aid station, Hassenzahl assured his pal he would be okay. "And he looked at me, and he could barely move. I'll never forget what he said. He says, 'Lieutenant, I don't think so.'" He died on the way back to the station. In 1994, Hassenzahl went back to Europe, thinking about his friend. He found Punchy's grave in a cemetery near Bastogne, and he "knelt down and had a little conversation with him."

The winter of 1944 in Belgium and France was legendarily cold and snowy. "You just couldn't seem to get warm," Hassenzahl recalled. The weather short-circuited the usual courtesies after a battle. One time they cleaned out a sector of the forest and took a lot of prisoners, but "we left a lot of Krauts lying in there. As a matter fact, their cries went on for hours after we pulled back."

In April, C Company of the First Battalion was one of the lead units into a town called Landsberg, where, in its prison, Hitler had written *Mein Kampf*. There were a dozen concentration camps in the area, and C Company came across one of them. Hassenzahl hadn't really believed the stories he'd heard of the atrocities against the Jews and Polish people and POWs. "But let me tell you, when we first approached Landsberg, you could smell it. The guards that were on duty just deserted the camp. When we went past that barbed wire and saw those poor, godforsaken human beings and the shape that they were in, they were walking skeletons."

Hours before the Americans' arrival, the Germans had stacked up corpses "like cordwood, one on top of the other, in huge piles. They didn't have time to put them in the furnaces they had there."

Hassenzahl and his men went into town, rousted out all the old men, women, and children, and made them dig three common graves in which to put all the corpses. He recalled, "We had to do something with them. We couldn't just leave them laying out there. I'll never forget that incident as long as I live. I believed everything now that I had heard in the past about the German atrocities. They did it, and they were responsible for it. How one human being can do that to another one, I don't have the answer."

Near the end of the war, they were in Bavaria in southern Germany. There was talk of diehard German soldiers resisting up in the Austrian mountains, but they never materialized. The 506th were the first troops to go up into Hitler's "eagle's nest" near the town of Berchtesgaden. Hassenzahl still has several books he took as souvenirs.

They also had the distinction of being some of the first troops to start the journey home. The requirement for points to ship back to the States was eighty, and with all his battle experiences, wounds, and decorations, he had accumulated well over 100 points.

"I guess I was much like many combat veterans," Albert Hassenzahl admitted in concluding his tape recording. "I didn't want to talk about it. Most people wouldn't understand it anyway. It's a different situation when we go to the C Company reunions. Civilians couldn't be expected to [understand]."

Much later, he became good friends with a neighbor who was a half generation younger than he, too young to have served in World War II. Hassenzahl said, "He's told me, 'Al, the experience of veterans like you should be disseminated to people as a matter of record.' And I think he's right."

ROBERT POWELL:
THE MODERN NEAR-ACE

"Learning to fly…was the foundation
on which I have built my life."

ROBERT POWELL FLEW EIGHTY-SEVEN MISSIONS IN WORLD War II over Europe. He didn't court danger, but he didn't avoid it; he loved doing strafing runs, which perhaps were even more perilous than air-to-air combat. He suffered battle damage five times, had his plane's tail shot off one time, but he only ditched his plane once, right after a takeoff in England. It was that moment, six weeks after he flew in support of the Normandy Invasion, when Powell could have become a footnote in the history of the war, killed in a meaningless accident, rather than shot down in glory after taking an enemy pilot with him. That moment defined him as resourceful, well-trained, and, like so many other pilots, not a little cocky.

He was born in a mining town named Wilcoe, deep in the hills of southern West Virginia, in 1920. In a 2003 interview, he remembered his hometown as a "great place to grow up," populated by immigrants from Poland, Italy, Hungary, and Ireland who all worked in the mines. In his first year in the town's five-year high school, the larger boys "liked to harass the smaller boys, including me," he recalled many years later. "They would throw a shoulder into you and knock you down when passing in the hallways. One day the fullback on the football team did this to me, and I got up and started trying to flail him with my fists. He grabbed my hands, laughing at me, and said, 'You're a feisty little bastard.

Why don't you come out for the boxing team? We need a flyweight.'"

A year later, after several high school matches, Powell entered the Golden Gloves tournament and fought the county champion to a draw. They both went to the state tournament. Powell won, though he broke both thumbs in the process. "I never boxed after that," Powell recalled, "but when I went to West Virginia University and was being rushed for a fraternity, one of my friends told his frat brothers that I was a boxing champ, and they started calling me 'Punchy.' It carried over to the military, and all who knew me in the service knew me as 'Punchy.'"

His love of flying had been kindled at the age of seven when his father took him to Bluefield—only thirty-five miles away, but a ninety-minute drive over the mountains—to see a barnstorming pilot. For the sum of two dollars the pilot would take anyone for a ride in the clouds. Young Robert's dad gave him a $5 bill, and the boy was so excited by the ride he forgot to ask for his change.

Powell was at West Virginia University on December 7, 1941. In January 1942, a buddy who was interested in joining the air cadet program talked Powell into hitchhiking with him to Pikeville, Kentucky, to take the program's entrance exam. "I sort of went along as his friend," Powell recalled.

"I passed the tests and was sworn in as a private and told that I would be notified when to report for duty. Meanwhile, the university decided to give credit to all of us who had a high grade level for that semester if we were going into the service." In late March he received his orders and took a train to Chicago and joined a group of recruits for a longer train ride to the Santa Ana Army Air Base in Orange County, California. He'd been in the ROTC program in college, so he adjusted easily to military life. Civilian instructors got him off the ground, but it was the West Point–educated upperclassmen he remembered best: "They would get right up in your face and say, 'Mister, why'd you join the Air Corps?' And we'd say, 'Sir, Pa beat Ma, Ma beat me, the food at home was p-poor, and my girl and my bank note were both thirty days overdue, sir! That's why I joined the Air Corps, sir!'"

Powell's next stop was Gardner Field, near Taft, California, north of Santa Barbara. He came under the tutelage of a Lt. Nelson, a hard case nicknamed "Nails" who taught lessons not easily forgotten. Once, when the two were riding together in a cockpit, Nelson told Powell his seat belt wasn't fastened. Each time Powell tried to buckle up,

Nelson hit the plane's stick and his pupil's head hit the hard canopy. This happened four times. Lesson learned.

At Luke Army Air Field in Arizona, Powell learned other lessons: formation flying, aerobatics, instrument flying. He went on cross-country flights and built up his flying time to 250 hours. During his training time, Powell lost a few comrades to accidents, but for most of the men it was the fear of being washed out that created the greatest tension. He estimates the washout rate for all three of his training assignments was about 50 percent.

On January 4, 1943, he got his wings and became an officer in the Army Air Corps. There was more training at Dale Mabry Field in Tallahassee, Florida, and in Cross City, Florida. "The first day we arrived [in Cross City]," Powell recalled, "there were P-39s lined up on the ramp, and we were really disappointed that we were going to be trained in those. However, before we ever got settled, a bunch of P-47 'Razorback' Thunderbolts were flown in and the 39s were flown out. This was the newest Air Corps fighter at the time, and we were delighted. During the next two or three months we got checked out in the 'Jugs,' and most of us got about fifty flying hours in one before we were shipped back to Tallahassee and readied for transport overseas." In April, Powell shipped out for England, via Camp Kilmer, New Jersey, and Halifax, Nova Scotia.

In England, he and his group were sent to a Reserve Training Unit at Atcham Airfield, near Wales, to learn to fly combat tactics. In the Air Corps, Powell noted, the RTU was one stage of training, usually a transition from training aircraft into combat aircraft, another stage of flight training before being assigned to a combat unit.

Powell recalled, "There we got some additional hours of flight training in the Jugs, i.e., formation crossovers, formation takeoffs, instrument flying, and finally, a week of gunnery [training] at an RAF gunnery school—actually very little gunnery training, just enough to qualify (15 percent hits in the target required for qualification)." The Army Air Corps began assigning the pilots to one of the three American fighter groups then in the UK: the 4th, 78th, and 352nd. Powell's pal, Fred Yochim, whom he had known all through training, was assigned to the 328th Squadron of the 352nd, and he talked up Punchy Powell to the Squadron CO, persuading him to get Powell assigned to the 352nd Fighter Group. Powell recalled arriving at Bodney, where that unit was stationed, in late August 1943.

His squadron flew its first training mission on September 9. Powell admitted in his interview to feeling "pretty shaky," mainly because the 352nd Fighter Group had all trained together in Connecticut, and he felt like an outsider who had to prove himself. The mission, a routine escort over the North Sea of B-17s returning from a bombing run, proved uneventful.

He didn't encounter any danger on his next two missions, and Powell was beginning to feel at ease on the fourth one. He was flying on the wing of Colonel Everett Stewart, who would later become one of the twenty-nine aerial aces in the 352nd. They were on their way back to England when Powell lost sight of Stewart's plane. He picked it up beneath him, flying upside down, having performed a Split S maneuver, and Stewart was headed in the opposite direction. Powell followed Stewart, careful to avoid overrunning him. Then he noticed Stewart's guns were firing and looked ahead to see a German fighter taking hits from the colonel's plane. Out of the corner of his eye, Powell spotted a second enemy plane, and he immediately began firing his own guns, downing that plane as well. Back at the base, Stewart wanted to know what model planes they'd downed. Powell had been so excited he didn't notice, but the gun camera on his plane revealed they were Messerschmitts. Powell kept that film as a souvenir and still has it.

The 352nd flew a variety of missions: escorting heavy bombers, performing reconnaissance, strafing German airfields to destroy as many planes as possible. Ground strafing was, in Powell's estimation, "much more dangerous than air-to-air combat," because the German airfields were ringed with guns. To avoid drawing fire, the strafing pilot flew very low—preferably under fifty feet—so that the enemy guns on either side of him, if they fired, would be shooting at each other. The danger came at the end of the run, when the pilot would have to pull up sharply to avoid drawing fire from the last line of defensive guns.

The 352nd developed a strafing technique involving three groups of planes. The first one would quarterback the maneuvers of the other two. The second group would simulate a dive bombing of the field, drawing the attention of the gunners, while the third group swooped in low on a strafing run.

In April 1944, Powell's group switched to Mustangs, at five tons a lighter plane than the seven-ton Thunderbolt, and with a longer range. The Germans had calculated out the limited range of the Thunderbolt, and their fighters began to hold back from engaging the Americans until the Thunderbolts had to turn around and head for home. Powell got a crash course in flying the Mustang; he recalled having only thirty minutes inside his Mustang before he took off on his first mission in it. "In those days, you could fly one airplane, you could fly 'em all," he noted, but it was still a little disconcerting to have so little experience with your aircraft before setting off on a mission.

At an Eighth Air Force Reunion in the early 1980s, Powell met the man he later described as "THE German pilot," Adolf Galland, commander of the Luftwaffe Fighter Forces. Galland was invited by the Eighth Air Force to speak on a panel of air aces, and with 104 victories, he more than qualified. Powell considers Galland "undoubtedly the top German fighter strategist of WWII." By the time American pilots would have encountered Galland in his Messerschmitt 109, he had put in over 2,000 hours in the air, including service in the Spanish Civil War, the Blitzkreig of Poland, the bombing of the Low Countries, and the Battle of Britain. "I got this information," Powell would later write, "when I asked him about his Me-109 time. And then he asked me how much time I had in the P-47 Thunderbolt when I flew my first mission over Europe. My answer: 'A little over fifty hours.' Then he said, 'You must have had some good training because you learned the tricks of aerial combat damned fast.'"

Galland's career was much longer than any American's, because the Luftwaffe required their pilots to fly for the duration, and America put limits on the number of required missions. Those limits got revamped in the spring of 1944, as plans for the Normandy Invasion took shape. Earlier in the war, there were no set tours of duty, but then it was established that once you flew 200 combat hours, you could be rotated back to the States. However, with the invasion, there was a need for as many experienced pilots as possible, and the fear was that too many pilots would reach their 200 hours before the Allies hit the beaches of northern France. So pilots were given two choices once they reached

Robert Powell, with the plane he flew over France
during the D-Day invasion.

200 hours: they could go home for thirty days and return to fly another 200, or they could simply remain in England and fly another 100 hours. Powell chose the latter option. He knew of some pilots who chose the first one but weren't able to make it back in time for D-Day.

The tip-off that D-Day was swiftly approaching came when orders went out to paint every available plane with black and white stripes around the fuselage and wings. This would make identification of Allied aircraft by naval and ground forces simpler. After dinner on June 5, 1944, Powell and his fellow pilots were told that there would be a briefing at midnight, that if they wanted to get some sleep, they should take a nap between now and then. The men were also encouraged to write letters to their loved ones.

The 352nd had never flown a night mission before. At the briefing, the flight surgeon was frank: "I have been instructed to keep you flying until the beaches are secured, even if I have to give you pep pills." Fortunately, as Powell recalled, it never came to that. Lights were set up around the perimeter of the field at Bodney, but a taxiing aircraft ran into one of them and knocked the whole circuit out. The first squadron took off in the dark at 1 A.M. The leader lined up with his compass, but the second of the four planes lined up slightly off, which created a domino effect with the third and fourth planes. The first two planes took off without incident, but the third never made it, slamming into a control tower that was under construction.

At the time of the crash, Powell's squadron was being briefed. "When this plane exploded," Powell recalled, "naturally, with the tension, we thought the Germans had found out about D-Day and were bombing the field." Some of the men hit the floor, "which was the proper thing to do," some ran out the door, and some dived out the open windows. On his way out the window, Powell stepped on someone. Later, Powell ran into Major Harold Lund, who was rubbing his neck. He asked, "Who was that SOB who stepped on my neck diving through the window?" Powell was only a lieutenant, so he didn't think it was in his best interests to reveal his identity. Many years later, at an Air Force–Navy football game in Colorado Springs, Powell was able to tell Lund, and they had a laugh over the incident.

Powell's squadron took off close to 2:00 A.M. by the light of the burning plane. Their assignment was to patrol an area south of the beachhead at Normandy. They were part of a wall of 1,000 planes that started at 50 feet and went up to 30,000. "No German plane got through there," Powell remembered with satisfaction. After they returned to England to refuel, their next mission was to watch for anything moving on the roads near the beachhead. The French Underground had been alerted to keep all civilians off the roads that day, so it was assumed that any vehicle—from bicycle to truck—was aligned with the enemy and was "fair game" for strafing. Each squadron was assigned to a certain sector. After a third mission, he was able to take a break. He had been in the plane for sixteen hours; flying in a Mustang, he recalled, was like "sitting in a tin can," and he was so stiff and jammed up that he had to be helped out of the cockpit.

For the next few days, Powell was assigned to fly over various sectors, supporting different tank and infantry groups. He was in radio contact with the tanks, which would direct him to strafe certain targets. "It was an exciting time," he recalled.

Six weeks later, on a routine takeoff, Powell came closer to death than on any of his other eighty-six missions. On July 18 he left Bodney on his second mission of the day. Shortly after takeoff, at about 300 feet, his plane burst into flames. He's still not sure how it happened, though he thinks a gas line broke loose, spilling fuel onto the hot manifold and igniting the fuel. His wheels were already up, he had cleared the open field, and he was over a stand of trees. From his training, he knew that "if you are ever crashing, not to try to turn the airplane because it'll stall, and you'll cartwheel and more than likely be killed. Whereas if you crash straight ahead you have a better chance of survival." Nevertheless, he broke that rule:

"I was going into these trees on fire, and I turned it a little bit to avoid them. There was an opening in the trees, and I turned it a little bit into that opening. And just about that time I felt it beginning to stall. We flew by the seat of our pants, and if you've had some experience in an airplane, you can tell if it's about to stall. You got the feel of it. And I felt it was about to stall. I rolled it back into a level position and bellied in on this farmer's field. Fortunately, he had plowed it the day before. As the plane slid along on its belly, the loose dirt coming back across the airplane knocked the flame down long enough that I was able to get out of it. I did have a little trouble getting the canopy loose—had to kick it loose. But I got out and ran like a scared rabbit—which is what I was. Of course, I didn't realize how scared I was until I got out. You know you do things under conditions like that—it isn't courage, it isn't bravery, it isn't intelligence, or anything else. You just react. And if you react properly, you might save yourself. And fortunately, I did."

He had crashed not far from the squadron huts, so he walked back to his unit. When Powell walked in, Dave Lee, the fighter group's intelligence officer, was on a field phone saying, "Punchy had gone over the trees on fire, and it looks like he's had it." Powell looked at him and said, "No, I haven't had it, Dave. I'm here." They got into Lee's jeep and drove over to the crash scene. Powell saw the flight surgeon and hailed him: "Hey, Doc, who was it?" "Punchy," came the reply, until the surgeon realized he was talking to a dead man. Powell was sorry to lose that plane; its nose had been painted with its nickname, "The West 'by Gawd' Virginian." But a mechanic was able to save that section and presented it to Powell. He still has it, and in his video interview he shows it off. Writing about the crash many years later, Powell ruefully noted, "I missed a big opportunity not completing that mission. My squadron got in a big fight on that date, and my butt was still back at Bodney."

His last mission came on August 4, 1944. He was escorting bombers to Peenemünde, a German research, testing, and assembly facility for V-2 rockets. He recalled, "After I belly-landed my P-51C at Bodney on July 18, I was given a P-51D-15 model to fly my final missions in, and on that flight to Peenemünde I developed a propeller oil leak, an oil seal that contained the light lubricant for the prop. It wasn't bad except that it left a light oily coating on my canopy, which was somewhat like liquid Vaseline, making it difficult to get a clear view. Had we encountered enemy fighters I would not have been able to see them. Luckily, we did not, but it was a very long mission, five hours, fifteen minutes, according to my logbook."

The 352nd compiled an impressive record, earning the nickname "Second to None." Powell estimated that they shot down five German planes for every one they lost. The Germans paid them tribute, calling this fighter group "The Blue-Nosed Bastards of Bodney," after the painted noses of their Mustangs. "We gave them a pretty hard time," is Powell's typically modest assessment. When an interviewer referred to him as an ace, he made sure that the record was set straight. His record reflected six aircraft destroyed on the ground and in the air combined; a true ace has to take down five in the air. (The top ace in the 352nd was George Preddy, who was credited with 26.83 kills, including six German airplanes in a single day.) Powell has spent much of his retirement working on histories of his fighter group; he has written two books and has been active in the 352nd FG Association, founded in 1983. He also began speaking to school groups about World War II after he heard a teacher refer to that conflict as "World War Eleven."

"Going into the service," Powell noted, "I was just a hillbilly from West Virginia. Learning to fly built up confidence in myself. I went from a boy to a man very quickly. It was the foundation on which I have built my life. It has stood me in good stead."

JOHN SUDYK:
THE SOLDIER OF 10,000 ROUNDS

"You're loaded with ammunition;
so one little stray bullet in a gas can, and away you go."

O N THE MOST IMPORTANT DAY OF WORLD WAR II, ARTILLERY-man John Sudyk was playing a waiting game off the coast of Normandy. The GIs who first hit the beach on June 6, 1944, at least found a release for their pent-up anxiety about D-Day. Sudyk and the men who manned the big guns had to wait until the beach was relatively secure before they could unload their cargo. And for Sudyk, D-Day was only the beginning of an eleven-month slog across Europe.

He was a nineteen-year-old young man from the small town of Hinckley, Ohio, when the U.S. entered the war. His first impulse was to join the Navy and see the world outside of Ohio, but, as he recalled in a 2001 interview, "things got kind of fouled up, and I didn't like the uniforms," so he wound up getting drafted into the Army. He did his basic training at Fort Bragg, North Carolina, after which the tests he'd taken steered him to gun mechanics school. His specialized training continued at posts in Vermont, Tennessee, and Virginia, before he shipped out to England in October 1943.

Sudyk was with the 18th Field Artillery, one of the so-called "bas-tard" outfits that were not associated with any single Army division. For the upcoming invasion of France, they were selected to support the 29th Infantry Division, which would eventually land at Omaha Beach.

On June 6, they found themselves sitting on their landing craft, scheduled to hit the beach the next day. He recalled, "There was no place to put us because of what happened on the beaches. So we're sitting out there watching the whole show, watching the planes strafing the upper hills, the beach, the bluffs, and the battleships shell the coastline."

He and his buddies felt vulnerable in their LST. "You're loaded with ammunition," he recalled, "so one little stray bullet in a gas can, and away you go. It was more treacherous out in the water than on the ground." Sudyk had unbuckled his boots in case they got hit and he had to go into the water. When he looked down into the roiling waters of the English Channel, he saw thousands of jellyfish and thought, If I go into the water I'll be stung to death.

The waiting continued through a long night of bombing by German planes. He remembered the scene. It was like the water was "raining up" from the impact of the bombs. Tracer shells from Allied ships were shooting up into the sky, but he and his buddies were thinking, "Those shells have to come down somewhere," so they hid under whatever shelter they could find on their boat.

Around 2 P.M. the next day, his boat nosed in to the beach, ready to drop its ramp. Mines were everywhere; they saw one in their path, which they had to bridge across to get to the beach. They started unloading the large artillery pieces, and the sixth vehicle off the boat hit a mine and blew up right in front of them. He recalled that as quickly as they were unloading their cargo, medics were reloading the boat with stretchers bearing the wounded from the first day. On the beach, he saw soldiers digging trenches to temporarily bury the corpses, the Americans first, then, if there were time, the Germans.

They were told the Germans might try to repel the invaders with a gas attack, so they had to impregnate all of their clothes and shoes with a compound that prevented mustard gas from seeping through. They were carrying heavy gas masks as well, though they didn't need them.

Sudyk's gun was a 155mm howitzer with a range of about 12,000 yards. It fired a shell that was 6.1 inches in diameter and weighed about 96 pounds. Sudyk was the Number One man on the crew; after the shell and powder charge were inserted into the gun, he put the primer in the breech block, closed it, and fired the gun. They moved inland, and the next morning were in position in front of a small French town. His lieutenant came around and asked for volunteers, then pointed to Sudyk and several others. They were given a bazooka, explosive charges, and told, because theirs was the "most forward element in that sector," they had to clear the way by ambushing German tanks. Sudyk recalled the officer telling them, "I'll be over here," indicating a position about 200 yards away, "and will let the battery know." Sudyk considered it a suicide mission, but he proceeded. Fortunately, the artillery battery fired at the tanks first, destroying a few of them, and the rest turned back. Of the action and his lieutenant, Sudyk noted bitterly, "He got a commendation, we got nothing."

It wasn't just tanks they had to worry about. At night, German planes flew overhead, dropping flares to see if they could get a fix on his gun's position, while Sudyk and his men would try to shoot down the bombers. In the morning Allied planes would take to the air to provide cover for the advancing troops. Early one morning they accidentally shot down a British Spitfire. The plane, he recalled, "came out a little early," and they assumed it was an enemy aircraft. Fortunately, the pilot was able to parachute to safety, but when they next saw him, "he was mad as hell."

Their daily advances were modest until late July when they busted out of the Normandy region. At that point, the 18th was transferred from the First Army to the Third Army under General Patton. The pressure picked up with Patton running the show. Sudyk recalled one sergeant in his outfit telling a colonel that the roads were almost impassable because of enemy small arms fire, to which the colonel replied, "You get down that road, or I'll have you shot in the morning."

As much as anything he saw in those first weeks in France, Sudyk remembered the smells. The odor of death was very strong, between the rotting corpses of enemy soldiers left behind by their retreating comrades and the bodies of farm animals devastated by artillery shells or stray bullets. Overall, he noticed the land had a "musty" smell about it.

Artillerymen like Sudyk never traveled light. "You always had to worry about that gun," he said. "When you go in position, the first thing you do is get your gun in position, dig your ammo in, then you dig yourself in. You're expendable, you're last." The vehicle that pulled his gun was a full-track prime mover, which was "dangerous as hell" to operate. When they went through a town in the rain or snow, it slid around like crazy on cobblestones. He recalled that during the Battle

"You always had to worry about that gun," said artilleryman John Sudyk, who landed on Normandy with a 155mm howitzer in tow.

of the Bulge, three soldiers in the 18th were killed when their vehicle turned over and their ammunition exploded.

They supported the 29th Infantry Division and had the honor of helping to liberate Paris in August. The 2nd French Armored Division, made up of soldiers who fled to England in the wake of Germany's invasion of their homeland and formed a special unit anxious to go back, were given the honor of being first into Paris. The 29th were behind them, marching thirty abreast down the streets, and behind them were Sudyk's artillerymen. He watched as soldiers in the 29th on the far ends of each line were accepting drinks from grateful Parisians standing curbside. It was a warm day, and soon the soldiers began passing out; they had to be picked up by the trucks following them. Unfortunately for Sudyk and his unit, it was their only look at Paris; they weren't allowed to linger and sample the local spirits themselves.

They were the first artillery unit to cross the feared defensive fortification, the Siegfried Line, into Germany. From there it was into the Hurtgen Forest, on the border of Belgium and Germany. The Germans were outnumbered during this five-month campaign, but they had the superior defensive position among the thick stands of trees. The battle became, according to Sudyk, "sort of a killing field for both sides. . . . We lost so many troops in there, we often wondered why we tried to advance in an area like that. The trees were so close together, big pine trees. The shells'd come in and hit the tops of these trees and explode, and big shrapnel would come down. You couldn't dig a hole because you dig a hole and the water'd run into it. So we chopped some trees down, put some logs about three logs high, maybe pile dirt on top, and dive under that to protect us from the shell bursts."

The 18th was in the Hurtgen Forest for about a month. Right after that, in December 1944, they were called in to support the 82nd Airborne and stem the German counteroffensive during the Battle of the Bulge. As for every GI involved, Sudyk's memories of that campaign were of the cold, as the temperatures plummeted to levels not seen in that part of Europe in forty years. They had only field jackets, no over-coats, and only two blankets each to sleep under, but the artillerymen invented a way to warm up their sleeping quarters. They took some unused powder charges, tossed them into their sleeping hole, lit a match, and WHOOSH! "We get a nice warm hole to sleep in."

They were at the northern end of the Allied advance lines with the First Army when the battle started. In January, Sudyk viewed the after-effects of the Malmédy Massacre, which had occurred in December on the second day of the battle, when German troops fired without provocation on Americans just taken prisoner, killing over seventy men. After the German offensive at the Bulge was spent, the Allies advanced to the Rhine. Just below the Remagen Bridge, he heard an unfamiliar sound from the sky—a swoosh. A new kind of plane streaked past, and he realized he had seen his first jet. They were unable to cross at Remagen because the famed bridge was out of commission. Repeated shellings by the retreating Germans had weakened it, and although the Allies had finally captured it, too much traffic caused it to collapse on March 17, killing twenty-eight American troops.

Once they were in Germany, they began to see a lot of horse-drawn outfits. They came upon a small concentration camp, and the American troops watched as the newly liberated prisoners came out and cut up horses for food. Near Munich, he saw a camp with hundreds of bodies piled by the road. "The smell is what lingers with you,"

Sudyk said. He couldn't believe the German citizens when they said they didn't know what was going on.

The 18th pushed south, and at the end of the war they were in Czechoslovakia. On May 7, he saw a Flying Fortress come over Pilsen and bomb the Skoda Works, a former auto plant converted to making munitions. Locals asked why the Americans were still bombing so close to the end of hostilities. Sudyk figured it was a political maneuver; the U.S. knew that the Soviets were taking over the area and didn't want them to have all the equipment from that plant.

George S. Patton and his Third Army arrived in the area. Sudyk got to spend three days with the general's entourage, serving as an interpreter, since he spoke German. Sudyk noticed Patton checking him out; he was a spit-and-polish guy who likely noticed Sudyk's helmet. Because of Sudyk's facility with the language, he was able to instruct a local citizen to put about ten coats of lacquer on it.

He was sent sixty miles behind the lines to serve as an interpreter in a meeting with a German officer, and he witnessed some tense moments between the victorious Russians and vanquished Germans. At a checkpoint along the road, a trio of German nurses came forward to surrender and fell on their knees, begging not to go back. He wasn't sure what to do, so the women waited under a nearby tree until he eventually let them go through. "If it had been soldiers," Sudyk said, "I wouldn't have let them through." But he had a sense of the fate that awaited these women at the hands of the Russian army.

During their eleven months in Europe, the 18th Field Artillery Battalion would support three Armies (the Ninth, the First, and the Seventh), seventeen different infantry and six armored divisions. They traveled 1,150 miles and fired 50,000 rounds from the time they landed in Normandy to the end of the war in Czechoslovakia; Sudyk estimated his own gun fired 10,000 of those rounds.

Throughout his time away from home, he was buoyed by his fiancée, Helen, who was living in Cleveland and working at Chase Brass, making steel mortar shells. She wrote two or three letters a day to John. He wrote to her frequently, more often than to his mother. But Helen didn't tell his mother that; after all, she had three sons in the military to worry about. [John Sudyk's audio interview includes a short session with Helen Sudyk.]

While Helen was making shells for the American army, someone on

Sudyk and a downed German aircraft.
At night, the enemy dropped flares,
trying to locate his gun; he would fire back,
hoping to preempt bombs.

the other side of the Atlantic was doing similar work—though not as well. One morning in France, John Sudyk got up and was busy at the slit trench when he saw some dirt kick up a foot from his hole. He looked over and noticed the rear end of a shell sticking up from the ground. "It never went off," he recalled. "It was a dud." Earlier that morning, another shell came in among eight GIs and splattered them with mud but never went off. Given how much ammunition was in the vicinity of that hit, a working shell could have done major damage.

This happened for about a week or two, and Sudyk attributed it to slave labor factory-workers sabotaging the fuses, as would later be documented in the book and movie *Schindler's List*. As John Sudyk noted nearly sixty years later, "Some Jewish factory worker probably saved my life."

RAFFI BAHADARIAN:
ADDRESSING SPIRITUALITY

"There was not a minute when I was afraid.
I revert back to training.
And I know that everything is in God's hands."

H IS PARENTS BROUGHT HIM FROM LEBANON TO AMERICA
to escape the horrors of war, but young Raffi
Bahadarian grew to love his new country so much he
was willing to serve in its armed forces and return to
the Middle East to fight in another war.

Bahadarian's mother and father were of Armenian ancestry, their
families having fled their native country during World War I, in the
wake of systematic Turkish attacks on Armenian citizens. They wound
up in Beirut, Lebanon. Raffi, the couple's son, was born there in 1977,
in the midst of another horrible conflict, this time a civil war involving Christians and Muslims. Not long afterward, the Bahadarian family, who are Christians, immigrated to the United States, settling in
Pasadena, California. Young Raffi attended private school until the
sixth grade, then public school, graduating from Pasadena High in
1995. He thought about joining the armed forces but instead attended a local university, California Lutheran.

In his sophomore year of college, the impulse to serve in the military returned, and he considered the reserves. But he was attracted
to the Marines, because "I was afraid and wanted a challenge." He
had also grown up hearing stories of the Marines coming into
Lebanon in 1958 and in the early 1980s, not as invaders but as

*Raffi Bahadarian (left) a reservist called up to serve in Iraq, had joined
the Marines "because I was afraid and wanted a challenge."*

peacekeepers. When a Marine recruiter told him, "It's not what we
can give you; it's what you can give us," that sealed the deal.

In boot camp, which he found identical to its depiction in the film
Full Metal Jacket, "except for the physical abuse," he agreed to be
Protestant lay leader of his platoon. Three days into camp, he was
counseling some of his fellow recruits who thought their drill instructors were devils. He recalls with a laugh that one of the DIs was indeed
a pretty scary-looking guy, with tattoos all over his arms. Bahadarian
did a two-year hitch with the Marines and decided to sign up for their
reserves, alternating reserve duties with his job in the Los Angeles
County Sheriff's Department. After Sept. 11, Bahadarian was notified
that his reserve unit would be activated for homeland security duty,
which they were, in late 2001. After one year at Camp Pendleton, he
learned that his unit would ship out to the Middle East for Operation
Iraqi Freedom.

In Kuwait, Bahadarian and his reservists were attached to the First
Marine Division, which was also going to be the first Marine unit over
the border into Iraq. Their objective was to punch through to Baghdad,

*Bahadarian in Iraq, spring 2003. "There were days when
we were short on food and water but it worked out,
because it was more important to get to Baghdad."*

and as their convoy drove north, through An Nasiriyah and Al Kut, what
slowed them down was not the Iraqi Army but fierce sandstorms.

While in Kuwait, Bahadarian had written his fiancée frequently and
received packages of goodies from his church back in California. But once
his unit crossed the border, for about a month he was out of touch with
anyone back home. The Marines actually outran their supply lines in an
effort to arrive in Iraq's capital as quickly as possible. "There were days
when we were short on food and water," he told an interviewer in 2004,
"but it worked out, because it was more important to get to Baghdad."

His impressions of the Iraqi people were not what he saw depicted in
the news media. "The only contact we had with Iraqi men, women, and
children, young and old, was incredibly supportive," he recalls. In particular, the children were enthusiastic, yelling, "Yay, Bush! Yay, Marines!"

Not that his tour of duty wasn't stressful. He lost about forty
pounds, "mostly my choice," frequently sharing his MREs with his
men. He found that the foundations of his religious faith were invaluable, not just for his own peace of mind but also in keeping up the
morale of his men. In the Marines, he points out, "spirituality is not
addressed. The focus is more on training and getting things taken care
of." He sensed a need among his troops. "When you're in a life-and-

Bahadarian in the desert. His unit was in country for three months.

death situation, it was a prime opportunity for them to hear about things that I knew they wouldn't give an ear to back in the States, where you have the luxuries of family, home, and friends." Bahadarian recalls that "it took from my stress and fears" to be able to share his thoughts on faith with his men.

"There was not a minute when I was afraid," he says, and what got him through were two factors: "I revert back to training. And I know that everything is in God's hands." His attitude boiled down to this: I could be here today and gone tomorrow—and not just in war.

He and his men were focused on their mission in support of the First Marines, and they knew very little about anything more than that during much of their time in Iraq. (They went into the country in March 2003 and left three months later.) Rick Leventhal, a reporter with Fox News Channel, was imbedded with them and passed on to them some news of the larger conflict, but for the most part they knew only what was in their sight every day.

As a way of reinforcing that vision, he would tell his men, "This isn't about politics or about the people back home. It's not about the flag. This is about the person next to me, on my left and right. In the end, it is just making sure that the person to my left and right stayed alive."

Readjustment to life back in the States was relatively easy. Bahadarian had a newfound appreciation for simple things like a warm shower and the taste of favorite foods. Conversely, he was less tolerant when he heard someone complain that "my cheeseburger isn't melted enough," given the living conditions he saw Iraqi citizens enduring.

Coming from a country that experienced civil war for fifteen years—even if he did leave it as an infant—Bahadarian has a perspective that few American servicemen who served in Iraq share, an appreciation for a stable society with great material wealth. Beyond that, his Christian faith dovetailed well with his attitude as a Marine: "As a Christian, my mission was to do the right thing, that being to carry out the orders."

HILLIE JOHN FRANZ:
THE SPIRIT IF NOT THE LETTER

*"The screeming of the shells was so loud it all most
would run any one crazy."*

A TEXAS FARM LAD OF GERMAN DESCENT, HILLIE FRANZ fought real Germans in World War I. While serving in France, he found a nearly unused German ledger book and, in spite of his lack of formal education (Franz's spelling was often phonetic at best), he decided to record his experiences in the book. A few years before his death, he gave his daughter the original bound journal, in which he made some attempts to edit and clarify his narrative. What Franz's account lacks in literacy it more than makes up for in capturing the chaos of the infantryman's life in wartime.

Franz divided his youth in Texas between working on a series of family farms and attending school, though farm work usually won out over education when it came to a conflict over time. He left home about 1916 at the age of 22 and spent time breaking wild horses on a ranch owned by his uncle Fritz and repairing cars for a local garage. In May 1918, a year after the U.S. entered World War I, he was drafted and reported to Marlin, Texas, for induction.

He was in training for three weeks at Camp Travis in San Antonio when an officer walked into the mess hall one day and asked for several hundred volunteers to join the Army's Seventh Division in Europe. "So you may know," Franz wrote, "I for one held my hand high. Off corse I didn't relice what I was litting myself in for."

In August, he boarded a troopship in Hoboken, New Jersey, as a member of Company L in the 34th Infantry of the Seventh Division, along with 8,000 other men. The soldiers were warned that their ship, a converted German liner, might be attacked by enemy submarines on the voyage and that they were to go to their bunks in case of an emergency. Several days out, they heard guns firing and the order went out to "get in the hole." Instead, everyone rushed up on deck to watch the action. "We seen some real subs," Fanz wrote, "trying to get to us and our destroyers were out there like rabbits chasing a round & a round."

When things calmed down, the ship's captain called in the unit's major, asking what kind of soldiers were on this ship who wouldn't follow orders to "get in the hole." "Our major replied to him he had regular army soldiers and they were ready to fight & not run for holes."

After ten days at sea, they landed in Brest, France. They were about to pitch tents when they were ordered to march seven miles farther east. They reached that location at dusk, in the rain, and set up their tents in ankle-deep mud. For weeks they continued marching east and drilling on the days when they weren't on the move. By mid-September, they were in a rail center he called "Reniers." They were loaded onto boxcars, the famed "40 and 8s," which could hold forty men or eight horses.

After two days and nights on the train, they stopped near a town where they could get some wine, beer, fruit, and nuts. They were warned to rest in preparation for another hike, but some of the men couldn't resist the chance for something more than Army rations. The hike to the next town was to be sixteen miles, but after several hours on the road, word came down the line, "Does anyone have a map?" It seemed they were lost.

They got pointed in the right direction and fell only one mile short of their destination, "Aranville." A week or so of drilling followed, and on September 29, 1918, they set off for Gricourt, where they found some empty barns to sleep in. They remained there one day and then set out at night for the front. Franz wrote, "Again we got lost. And we were in range of big guns. Shells were fall all around us. We could here big guns every where and how it made us feel. And it was raining real hard & as dark & black as ace of spaid. We were wet, cold, and hungry."

They were looking for dugouts in which to set up camp, but they finally decided to stay in a forest for cover. About three o'clock the next day, a squadron of German planes came roaring overhead, and soon a squadron of American planes showed up to divert their attention. "We were very much excited watching the air battles," Franz recalled, though no one was shot down.

It was a short, three-mile hike to the frontline trenches. Here they suffered their first casualty, Captain Allen, "who was looking out for his company, called Snappy Co. L," telling the men to be careful. A shell burst nearby and he was hit by shrapnel in the shoulder and foot. Bleeding badly, he was taken to a field hospital, and Franz later heard he had recovered and returned to the U.S.

There was much work to be done on the dugouts and trenches, but the soldiers were as much concerned with ducking bombs and shells as improving their accommodations. In three days, they completed their work and had barbed wire strung up for protection. Two privates suffered from gas attacks. There were gas alarms set up, and a guard was posted at each one. "With a keen nose," Franz wrote, "you could smell the gass." The guards were instructed not to take any chances and sound the alarm at the least suspicion of an attack, at which point the men would don their gas masks.

On their eighth night in the trenches, a private from Company I sounded an alarm to attack, and Company L responded by charging through some woods, only to find that the Germans had retreated. The private had panicked and sounded a false alarm, but while Company L was out on attack, several other companies lost men to the shelling of the trenches.

In mid-October, they heard rumors they were going to be sent away from the front, but like the frightened private's alarm, those reports turned out false, and they moved out on October 18 for the bridge into Metz, about twenty meters away. At two in the morning, they came upon dugouts the French had used earlier in the war. "We named this the French under ground town," Franz wrote, "and here the rats were plenty full and they bothered us some the first night or 2, when they would run over our face."

"But at this time," he wrote, "there was some talk of peace among the soldiers. The Co. commander put a stop to it."

German planes began dropping leaflets telling the Americans that they were cowards and, according to Franz, "you had better go home and put in this war eny further." In a couple of days, they got good news: "'boys get your towels & soap and be ready to go to take a bath.' They didn't tell us how far we would have to go, but we found out it was about 9 miles to Gricourt. The lads all were glad to get to take a bath, but gee, 9 miles to take a bath; gee what a hike it was."

They each got two gallons in which to bathe, and it was more like a shower; "we were rushed in & out," he wrote. "We received new underweir on our way out. It was just like we dip cattle at home, but it was worth it."

On November 7, they received orders for a hike and were told to make sure they had their reserve rations along. But some of the soldiers had already eaten those rations. Franz wrote, "food was aful slim at times." Two days before their hike, all they got were six prunes, one slice of bread, and a half cup of coffee.

They wound up back in the series of trenches they had come to the month before, where they did receive some food, although "with strick orders not to eat eny of them until orders was received to do so," as they "may get orders to go over the top at any time." All this time, they were under heavy shelling. "The screeming of the shells was so loud it all most would run any one crazy," he wrote. They did go over the top and advanced up a hill, even though few of them could hear their commanding officer over the roaring of the shells.

At the top of the hill, they found that the Germans had retreated to another stronghold 500 yards in the distance. It took an entire day to get to the next hill. Fresh troops were arriving, and ambulances were busy taking away the dead and wounded. E Company lost 242 men in the fight, though the rest of the divisions fared much better.

"As we were busy digging in again to keep from being located by the Germans," Franz wrote, "we layed quiet all day as this was Nov. 10—and it seemed as if the Germans were slowing down on their gun fire." Their orders were to lie low until further orders. That night they actually slept a little, as there was no shelling. The morning of the 11th all was quiet from the German side, though the American big guns kept on firing. "After a while we received word that the Germans had surrendered and the armest was to be signed at 11 o'clock Nov. 11."

They moved back to their trenches. "We couldn't hardly believe it," Franz wrote. The morning had turned sunny, and they sat outside with no fear of being ordered to get into the trenches or get their heads down. The American big guns kept firing, but at 11 o'clock all sound ceased, and it was so still and calm "we didn't know what to do."

Cook wagons moved in, and the men were able to enjoy some real food. Some of the soldiers were saying, "Do we have to stop now; we had them on the run; why caint we go & get them." Some of the men were laughing, others crying, and everyone was enjoying the most food they'd had in a long, long time.

Orders came down to fix up the dugouts with the suggestion that they might be spending the winter there. But a week after Armistice Day, they headed out to the German lines and began clearing up the equipment the enemy left behind. On November 28, Thanksgiving Day, they arrived in the bombed-out town of "Theacourt," and although there was no turkey dinner, "every one was thankfull for everything was at peace again."

Some of the men began gathering souvenirs, which could be a risky business. One man from the company, Private Balott, picked up a one-pound shell and it exploded and "blowed him all to pieces."

Hillie Franz stayed in France until June 1919 as part of the Army of Occupation. As an enlisted man, he didn't get as much leave as the officers, who used that time to tour the country, though he did get to see the French Alps on one pass in May. His troopship arrived in New York on June 18, and what struck him when they landed was the abundance of food and drinks and cigarettes. He wrote with great satisfaction, "[we] got more in 30 minutes then we got in all the time we were over sea."

KENNETH RAY RODGERS: THE SECOND TIME AROUND

*"Any man who went over there and says he wasn't scared
is a damn liar, and I'll tell him that to his face."*

S ERVING IN TWO WARS OVER TWENTY YEARS APART GAVE
Kenneth Rodgers a unique perspective on the many ways the
American military had changed between Vietnam and the
Persian Gulf War.

Rodgers was a native of Mayfield, Kentucky, who was seventeen
years old and living in Burlington, New Jersey, when he enlisted in the
Army. It was 1968, and he was following the lead of his older classmates, many of whom were drafted, rather than the wishes of his family. His parents and two uncles, one a military recruiter and the other
already in the Army, advised him to go to college, but he was too hard-
headed to listen. He didn't even wait to graduate from high school,
quitting in his senior year to enlist. In a 2002 interview, he recalled that
his mother was "all torn up about it because eventually she knew I'd
wind up in Nam."

Rodgers was sent to Fort Campbell, Kentucky, for basic training. "I
can laugh at it now," he recalled, "because it's a thing in the past, but
[basic was] a lot harder than what it is right now." He knew that
because at the time of the interview, he had a son in the Army stationed in Japan. He recalled crawling on his elbows under live machine
gun fire. At the time it felt like punishment, but later he realized it was
to teach him how to keep his butt down in a firefight. The drill

instructors at Campbell made it clear to him that he should get his GED, that he wouldn't get anywhere without a high school diploma, even in the Army.

He did his Advanced Individual Training at Fort Dix, New Jersey, and was assigned to man 81mm mortars. He went on to Korea, where he worked for about six months as a loader. One day, a recruiter from the 82nd Airborne came through his barracks seeking volunteers for a tour in Vietnam. Rodgers raised his hand.

His first impression of Vietnam was the same as he had had of Korea: "What have I got myself into?" He was nearly overwhelmed by the heat, the mosquitoes, and "the stench." He was in country for only a week before he saw his first combat, and he didn't feel at all prepared. He characterized the military leadership he saw there as "weak." The messages the enlisted men got were mixed and contradictory. Some leaders were more gung-ho than others; they demanded a spit-and-polish approach that Rodgers thought didn't make sense in the jungle. There was little camaraderie among officers; they never really got close to each other because they knew the other man was going to get killed or go home. "Either way," Rodgers noted, "he was going."

"Any man who went over there," Rodgers recalled, "and says he wasn't scared is a damn liar, and I'll tell him that to his face. There was not a time when you didn't think about it." He never got a good night's sleep while he was in country, and since then has been diagnosed with sleep apnea. He coped with the stress by relying on mail and goodie boxes from home. Before he arrived in Vietnam, he had no idea what marijuana was, but he got turned on to it. Rodgers had been brought up in a very religious family that frowned on smoking and drinking; so with his marijuana use, "You might say I lost my Christianity."

It was a war in which it was hard to measure progress; you took over the same village seven or eight times. He never got into hand-to-hand combat, but he was close enough several times to see the man he was shooting at. Getting wounded was sometimes the least of his worries. There were also malaria, heatstroke, and leeches; he still has scars on his legs from them. He lost part of his hearing from all the weapons fire; though he was issued earplugs, he was afraid to use them because he felt the need to hear what was going on to stay alert for an ambush.

He recalled that some of the South Vietnamese villagers he met were supportive of American troops, sharing what meager food supplies they had with them. Others were less friendly, standing by as people and animals were slaughtered. "We treated everybody over there as the enemy," he recalled, "and not everybody was. I've had a lot of time to think about this. Those poor farmers who were caught up in the middle, they didn't want any trouble from either side. I kind of feel sorry for some of the things I had to do now, but as a soldier I had to do it: burn your house, tie them up, destroy their crops. It still bothers me some today."

Rodgers was wounded and sent to Japan to recuperate. There he was given a choice of either going back to Vietnam and finishing his hitch or being reassigned to Korea. He took the latter, which he admitted was a big mistake, because he was sent up in the middle of winter to the Demilitarized Zone, where it was 50 below zero.

Nineteen sixty-eight was a tense year to be in Korea. In January, the crew of the *Pueblo,* an American surveillance vessel, was overwhelmed by North Korean forces, who claimed the ship had strayed within their country's territorial waters. The crew spent almost the entire calendar year in captivity in North Korea, while American diplomats tried to get them freed.

After his experiences in Vietnam and Korea, Rodgers felt "an emptiness" inside and decided he wanted out of the military. He came home to New Jersey, intending to attend college and get a job. All his high school friends had graduated and "were doing the same old thing they did in high school. And I couldn't click with them because, more or less, I had grown out of their stages," though he was only nineteen, still too young to vote. "Here I was, supposed to be old enough to go kill, and when I get home I'm still just a kid," he recalled. "They didn't recognize me as a veteran, they didn't recognize me as nothing."

He got a job working in construction. When some people found out he had served in Vietnam, they harassed him about killing babies, and he wound up in fights. "I had a lot of people turn their backs on me," he recalled. Although his parents and friends who knew him well treated him with respect, nothing else was going well. He was in a bad marriage, he was developing a serious sleep disorder, and he sometimes woke up in the night crying.

He talked to counselors, saw doctors at a VA hospital, and was even hospitalized for a short time, but nothing clicked. After his wife left him, he recalled, "I decided it's time to do something different, so I went back in the military." This was 1977. He talked to a recruiter and found that things had changed in the military. His first impression was that it was total chaos, officers were performing enlisted men's work, and enlisted men were doing officers' jobs. The Army offered him a chance to go into the reserves, and he agreed to that, with a specialty in small weapons and radio repair.

In 1990, he was living in Fort Knox, Kentucky, a captain in the reserves with an armored division, when preparations began for Desert Storm. He was called into active duty, and his unit loaded weapons onto boxcars and went through simulators to get trained for fighting in the desert. Everything seemed well organized and thought out. Rodgers recalled, "It was a piece of cake from what I had seen in the past," adding, "I'm not saying there wasn't hardships over there." He also saw a big change in the leadership. "They told us what to do when we went, and we knew what we had to do when we got over there, and that's the way it was played."

When he arrived in Saudi Arabia, he had a sense of deja vu from his first trips to Korea and Vietnam: "What the hell am I doing over here? I'm forty years old!" The worst part of the experience for him was the heat and having to drink so much water. He did his real training in country, but the fighting was one-sided. If they were ever in a skirmish, it lasted less than three minutes. For example, he saw a stand-off between two tanks. The Iraqi one was a 1948 Russian model, and when the tanks fired at each other the U.S. tank blew the turret off the Iraqi tank, and the Iraqi soldiers all poured out and surrendered.

He was a company commander, and for the first time he found himself having to discipline troops. He preferred a butt-chewing approach to taking away money for minor offenses. He could frequently put himself in his soldiers' role, remembering his own days as a young and inexperienced soldier in Vietnam and Korea.

On this second go-round, Rodgers recalled, "I considered the military more my family." After he reenlisted in 1977, it took him a while to adjust to the new order in the Army. With computers being introduced, he had to train hard to keep up, and then he was expected to

KENNETH RAY ROGERS: *The Second Time Around* | 49

turn around and teach his own men. Rodgers noted that, had someone told him in 1968 when he first enlisted that he would make a
career out of the military, he would have said, "You're lying to me."

But in 1977 things clicked for him, where in 1968 they didn't. Part
of that was his Vietnam experience. Though he thinks America should
have been more supportive of returning veterans from that war, "as far
as the war itself, I wish a thousand times I had listened to my parents
and never went. I could never ever tell anybody to do some of
the things we had to do to survive over there, because we were the
Americans. We were the aggressors."

CHAPTER TWO

THE BROTHERHOOD

"EVERY SOLDIER LEARNS IN TIME THAT WAR IS A LONELY BUSINESS," wrote Matthew Ridgway, one of America's great generals, who served in World War II and Korea. In the face of Ridgway's accurate observation is any soldier's sense that in battle, the man on your right or the man on your left could be the man who saves your life. Here are the stories of veterans who came to understand that, as lonely a business as war can be, the camaraderie planted in basic training and nurtured through the hardships of the battlefield is a powerful weapon against fear.

Asa Ball was a friend to many fellow G. I.s serving with him in Korea, and that friendship extended well beyond the end of that war. After Richard DeLeon served his comrades in Vietnam as a medic, he came home to a reception that reinforced his bonds with his men. Robert Franklin Dunning learned a valuable lesson from his father, who served in the military, about the ephemeral nature of the brotherhood, while Philip Thomas Randazzo saw in Vietnam another brand of camaraderie that operated outside of the mainstream Army. And Charles Remsburg's World War II experience was colored by a melancholy realization at war's end of all the buddies he'd lost.

*Asa "Bud" Ball in California, March 1951, about to ship out for
Korea, a place (and a war) he admitted he knew very little about.*

ASA BALL:
EVERYBODY'S BUD

"It's kind of a family deal, but they're closer than family."

ORN AND RAISED IN RURAL HAMILTON COUNTY IN EASTERN Tennessee, Asa Charles Ball—"Bud" to just about everyone who knew him—was a twenty-two-year-old garage mechanic in 1950 when he was drafted into the Army. Recalling his experiences in the Korean War could still bring tears to his eyes over fifty years later. Though he returned to his Tennessee home after serving his country, Bud Ball wouldn't put his time in the military behind him. A freewheeling personality, he didn't always play by the rules when he was in the Army, but he kept an eye out for his buddies and never forgot them.

Bud Ball's father owned a garage, where his young son worked part-time while he went to high school, and then full-time after he graduated in 1947. Ball recalls registering as a conscientious objector as an eighteen-year-old, but four years later, when his draft notice came, in October 1950, he had changed his mind about serving. Knowing he would likely be sent to fight in Korea, Ball told an interviewer in 2002, "I felt like I owed my dues."

At twenty-two, he was considered "the old man" by the largely teenaged recruits at Camp Pickett, Virginia, where he underwent basic training. "I wasn't used to the Army; I wasn't used to their rules," he recalled. He especially didn't like training with a unit of National Guardsmen from Waterbury, Connecticut. "I didn't like Yankees," he recalled with a laugh.

Ball got shuffled around a lot in his early days in the service; he remembers being in five different platoons in five weeks, and he wound up in an outfit of what he jokingly calls misfits. He claims he was assigned KP duty as punishment so many times that "they thought I was a cook."

He wound up in the First Cavalry, and after a long sea voyage to Korea, marked by constant seasickness, he arrived in Pusan early in 1951. In retrospect, he admits that he was totally unprepared for what he was about to see; "we didn't know what we were up against," he recalls. His first impression of Korea was to wonder why he saw in the streets "thousands of men younger than us who weren't fighting for their own country."

Assigned to a service company, Ball witnessed plenty of action during the ensuing calendar year, as opposing forces pushed one another up and down the Korean peninsula. In his interview, he's less focused on the details of battles than on the friendships those battles forged. "You're fighting for your country the first day over there," he said. "You get a buddy killed, you're not fighting for your country, you're mad. You just keep getting madder all the time because you're losing more all along the line."

Ball was appalled by their primitive living conditions. "I've had dogs that had a whole lot better life than we did." Ball and his buddies lived in ditches and were warned not to drink the local water, though some of them did and wound up at sick call with dysentery. What Ball remembers most clearly is the constant state of fear he was in. "You slept with your eyes open," he recalls. He remembers putting a stick in his mouth to keep his teeth from chattering, and not just from the cold of the Korean winter.

For Bud Ball and many other infantry soldiers in Korea, the war was a series of battles to take a series of desolate hills, punctuated by long nights dug into foxholes. "You get in God's hands real quick" when you're in combat, he recalled. He found comfort in a chaplain's advice to concentrate on reciting the Twenty-third Psalm while trying to advance up a hill under fire. That soldier was passing on the advice he had received from another chaplain while they were serving in World War II.

During Bud Ball's tour, he had one R&R break, six days in Osaka, Japan. He remembered the joy of sleeping in a bed for the first time

Ball posed at the 38th Parallel,
the dividing line between North and South Korea, in May 1951,
when there was heavy fighting in the area.

in six months. At a restaurant, he asked for five cheeseburgers; the order "liked to kill me," he was so unused to that much rich food after months and months of K rations. Though he didn't drink, he was hanging out with a buddy who did, a 6-foot 6-inch bruiser who liked to fight when he'd had a few. They stole a police car and crashed it into a swimming pool, somehow eluding the local police and the MPs as well.

Back in country that fall, his unit was part of a ferocious assault on Hill 347. He spent part of the battle in a foxhole with a guy from Pennsylvania he'd become pals with. After they were separated, he couldn't find out what happened to his pal and assumed he'd been killed. In 1999, Ball's son happened to be in Pittsburgh on business, and on a hunch Bud gave him the name of his pal. Sure enough, he was still alive, and Bud got in touch with him. They spent an hour and a half on the phone catching up on almost fifty years of their respective lives.

That kind of thing happened to Bud Ball frequently. Charlie, a six-teen-year-old Korean who spoke English and Japanese, was an inter-

Ball and a buddy, Bernie Grosse, summer of 1951,
near the Injin River in South Korea.
Ball kept in touch with many of the men he served with.

preter for Ball's company. Ball recalled not only Charlie's facility with languages but his bravery. Charlie, he claimed, once captured twenty-five North Korean troops by brandishing a gun that only he knew was unloaded. At a reunion of Ball's outfit, held in Pigeon Forge, Tennessee, in the 1990s, Charlie showed up. He had moved to California and become a Presbyterian minister. At the reunion, he handed Ball a medal that the Korean government had belatedly awarded Ball for his service. He asked Bud to go with him on his next trip back to Korea, but Ball couldn't bring himself to see that country again.

Jim Hagen was another pal. As a nineteen-year-old, he arrived in Korea well after Bud Ball had seen some of the worst fighting. He was supposed to go on the line, but Ball sensed that this kid just didn't have the training and field smarts to make it, and he volunteered to go in Hagen's place. The two kept in touch sporadically over the years, but it wasn't until 2001 that Ball received a special communication from Hagen: a letter in which Hagen belatedly thanked him for his generosity. Enclosed was a photocopy of a dollar bill signed by every guy in their platoon.

A few days before he was interviewed in 2002, Bud Ball went to visit an old friend with whom he had grown up in Tennessee who was still living in the area. Barney Lawson had also served in Korea, but he and Ball had never talked about their experiences. Lawson had just undergone heart bypass surgery, and Ball was able to commiserate with him, having had a similar operation a few years earlier. The two men, facing their mortality for the first time in half a century, began talking about Korea, and for four hours they compared notes on their experiences, realizing they had fought on the same hills at different times during the war.

Forging and maintaining relationships like that was important to Ball, in part because he never felt the country cared about his service. He saw his last action on November 17, 1951, and on December 7 he shipped out to Japan and then on to Seattle. He literally kissed the ground when he got off the boat in Washington. Though he was assigned to Fort Devens, Massachusetts, he headed straight home for Tennessee, knowing that his mother had recently suffered a heart attack. She was recovering nicely, and Ball remained AWOL just long enough to avoid serious trouble. "You never stayed more than twenty-nine days," he recalled with a laugh, "because that was desertion."

After his year of constant fear and primitive living conditions, Bud Ball found that "people here didn't care" about the war, that many Americans he talked to barely knew that he and his buddies were risking their lives in Korea. For that reason, he felt a special bond with Vietnam veterans, whose homecomings were often met with something worse than indifference.

Speaking about the friendships from his days in Korea, Bud Ball said, "It's a bond you don't understand....It's kind of a family deal, but they're closer than family."

RICHARD DELEON:
JOINING THE BROTHERHOOD

*"I realized that if I don't just respect
and remember and honor the boys who were there
with me, nobody's going to."*

I WASN'T ABOUT TO GO TO VIETNAM AND NOT KNOW WHAT IT WAS
about," Richard DeLeon said, many years after serving as a combat medic in 1969. In a brief but vividly recounted interview
conducted in 2002, DeLeon was unsparing in his descriptions of
"what it was about."

Drafted in 1968, this New Yorker did his basic training in San
Antonio at Fort Sam Houston. He was assigned to be a medic and
underwent an eight-week training course in life-saving techniques.
The recruits were shown graphic films of injured soldiers; "some guys
would pass out," in which case they were out of the program. There
were four classes of medics in training; three of them went to
Germany, and the fourth to Vietnam, a ratio that surprised DeLeon,
given the escalation of the war in Southeast Asia. DeLeon was in that
fourth class, and when asked if he wanted to be a hospital or combat
medic, he opted for the latter. "I wasn't going to spend [my time] in a
hospital doing bedpans, wiping down the guys who had been in the
jungle and had been shot up."

He was assigned to the First Cavalry Division, about to leave for a
mission in Vietnam's Central Highlands along the Ho Chi Minh Trail,
which actually was a series of trails used by the enemy. Some of the
trails were "carpeted" with a woven material that would allow bicycles

*Richard DeLeon and a Vietnamese civilian he describes
on the back of a photo as "a friend." As a medic,
DeLeon saw the worst consequences of combat.*

to pass easily; overhead, flexible trees along the side were tied together across the trail to limit aerial reconnaissance. "You knew," recalled DeLeon, "when you found a trail with carpeting, it was a major supply route."

His unit was flown in by helicopter, but the vegetation was so thick they had to jump out from about five feet above the ground. When they hit the ground, they could see that they'd landed in a patch of marijuana plants. "There were guys ripping up plants and shoving them into their knapsacks," DeLeon recalled. That night they set up camp. As the sun was going down, he was eating his freeze-dried food when he heard a thudding sound. It was a Chinese Communist grenade landing nearby. Everybody hit the dirt, and when it exploded, one piece of shrapnel wounded him in the ankle. Then "everything opened up," and they were assaulted with machine gun fire and rocket-propelled grenades. His unit was supposed to be setting up an ambush, but the enemy had turned the tables on them.

The soldier covering the unit's .50-caliber machine gun panicked, defecated in his pants, and was shaking so badly he couldn't operate the gun. DeLeon tried to crawl to a foxhole he'd dug for himself and was almost shot by the radio operator, who mistook him for an enemy soldier. He did make it to his foxhole, and a B-40 rocket went off near them. He was wounded again, this time in the leg. He grabbed a radio from the captain, who was incapacitated, and called for backup.

DeLeon spent the rest of the night using up all the bandages he was carrying. Amazingly, no one was killed, but thirty-five of the forty men in his unit were wounded, all by shrapnel, none by bullets. "Generally speaking," DeLeon noted, "you don't get shot unless you're standing up," and everyone had hit the ground when the first grenade came in. With that casualty rate, his company was pulled off the mission, because of a rule that did not permit any unit to continue if they suffered more than 30 percent casualties. He radioed for a helicopter to come in for the most severely injured and added that the evacuation could wait until dawn. He was afraid that if the chopper came in too soon after the attack, it would get shot down, and he knew that the men's wounds weren't so serious that they couldn't last the night. "One of the medevac helicopter pilots thanked me," he recalled, "because he didn't want to come in, either."

DeLeon spent three weeks in the rear convalescing. He noted a new technique, which left a wound open so that it wouldn't get sewn up with a possible infection already inside. After a couple of days, if there were no signs of infection, the wound was closed.

While he was healing, his company had been reassigned. Their next mission was to make contact with the North Vietnamese Army in a bunker complex deep inside a jungle area packed with bamboo so hard a machete couldn't break it. Although the company took the bunker complex, they had problems opening a clearing for choppers to land, even after they burned some of the bamboo. A recovered DeLeon was to fly in on a chopper, along with a chaplain and supplies. The chopper was then to return to base to pick up some replacements for his unit.

Waiting for the chopper to take off, he spotted the replacements, a group of "FNGs," an Army acronym for Fucking New Guys. Veterans said they didn't like FNGs, DeLeon noted, because their inexperience could get both them and you killed.

His company set off a colored smoke grenade to mark their position, and the chopper dropped down to about eight feet off the ground. "The padre," DeLeon recalled, "was, to say the least, frightened." DeLeon was happy to be reunited with his old guys. "It was like being home. Not the home you want to be in, but home." He noticed the company's new lieutenant was sporting a baseball cap.

The chopper crew dropped crates of ammunition and grenades, and when one crate of grenades hit the ground it opened up, spilling its contents all over the jungle floor. The men tried frantically to find the grenades, and managed to account for all but one. They were worried because the bamboo fires were still smoldering and might set off the missing grenade. "The problem with bamboo is once you get it lit, it doesn't go out. It's a slow burner." And that one grenade did blow up, hitting the lieutenant and putting a big hole in his head. He died, and they had to call for a chopper to pick up his body, as well as the padre, who was by now shaking with fear.

About 4 o'clock that afternoon, the chopper came back with the FNGs DeLeon had seen earlier. "They didn't even look like they were shaving," he noted. "They had these clean uniforms on. Such boys. They looked so scared." As the chopper moved into position to unload, the sound of 30mm machine gun fire broke out, and the chopper went down. One gunner jumped off and broke his leg. DeLeon hurried to the crash site and looked inside the chopper. Only one man was still alive, and he had suffered a compound arm fracture. Fuel was pouring all over everyone. He couldn't get the injured soldier out, because his leg was pinned in the wreckage. DeLeon was working with a buddy, Dave Nava, "one of the bravest men I ever met." "I said to Dave, 'We're under fire, there's fuel all over us, we're going to go up in a second.' Nava said to me, 'You can go, but I'm not leaving until this guy is out.' I don't think I ever admired anyone more in my whole life. I said, 'All right, let's try to get him out.'" DeLeon told Nava he would have to amputate the man's leg to get him out, but Nava managed to extricate him. Nava put the wounded man on his back and carried him away from the wreckage.

They called in a medevac to evacuate the survivor; "I knew the war was over for him," DeLeon said.

Then he was told that the medevac would be expected to carry out the bodies of the dead men from the chopper, that the Army did not want to leave any of them behind. "Funny thing was," he recalled, "none of the guys would come with me. It's like they didn't want to look."

There were no body bags for the dead soldiers, so he tied together two poncho liners as a makeshift shroud. DeLeon admitted that he blacked out after recovering the first body and didn't recall anything more about getting the other soldiers out of the downed chopper. "The next thing I remember was they were all lying there wrapped up

Dave Nava, DeLeon's pal and "one of the bravest men I ever met," helped him rescue a survivor of the helicopter crash.

in the shrouds, the poncho liners put together, waiting for a helicopter to come and take them out, send them back home. These boys never even saw a stick of combat."

After his tour of duty concluded, DeLeon came back to the States through San Francisco, where he spent one night before returning to New York. He wanted to go out and have a few beers with Glenn, a buddy from North Carolina, but Glenn wasn't interested. So DeLeon went to the airport to wait for his flight. He walked into a bar and sat there in his uniform, with his medals on, and no one came to serve him. "I finally got up, stood there, and I spit. [I said,] 'You people are not worth one ounce, one drop, of those men's blood.'" He walked out.

His mother wanted to put up a big banner on 74th Street, his home block in New York, to welcome him, but he insisted that he wanted to come home incognito. "I took off the uniform and said I'll never put that on again. I hated America. I hated Americans. I hated everything. I was ready for someone to spit at me. I was going to tear their head off. They must have seen it in my eyes: 'Go ahead; say something, do something, give me an excuse.' They probably looked at my eyes and walked away."

After he came home, he got a job on Wall Street and went to a psychiatrist for a year; his boss paid for it. He then joined a government-funded outreach program for vets, "and they took the violence out of me."

"We resented America when we came home," DeLeon recalled. "I think that's why I was so violent. I would fight at the drop of a hat, anywhere, at any time. I could have hurt people. That's why I put myself in the outreach program." Working on Wall Street, he met "so many spoiled rich kids." He recalled, "They had no idea there had been this kind of war, and if they did, they thought that they had been smart by being able to get out of it and go to college. And even when they would find out that I was there, they would say, 'Oh yeah, hmmm.' And then they would just go on with something else. I realized that if I don't just respect and remember and honor the boys who were there with me, nobody's going to. They live in my heart; they live in my memory. Not in anybody else's."

He had spent eighteen months in the service, but he spent a lifetime trying to come to terms with what he saw in Vietnam. He kept in touch with some of his buddies. For a while he attended Vietnam Veterans Association meetings, and one day, he looked through a directory and recognized the name of someone in his company. He called him up, and the guy recognized his voice right away on the phone. "I'll never forget you, Doc," he told DeLeon.

"It's a brotherhood," DeLeon said. "Sometimes I think they mean more than wives. You can change your wife, but you can't change these brothers."

He has a home in North Carolina, where ten years ago he planted a weeping willow in his yard. He said he was going to put up a bronze plaque on it with the names of two medics he trained with who were killed in Vietnam, "so that somebody remembers them." When he did, he would get in touch with their parents and let them know he hadn't forgotten their sons.

"In a way, [serving in Vietnam] made my life," DeLeon said. "I would never be the same again. It made me a man. A tortured man, a wounded man, but a man nonetheless. And when I finally got over it, I was a better man for it. It's a shame that a man has to become a man through something like that."

ROBERT DUNNING :
THE ILLUSION OF BROTHERHOOD

"We all had our fears but seldom talked about it."

"I DON'T REALLY KNOW WHY I AM WRITING THIS ACCOUNT OF MY experiences in World War II," Army veteran Robert Dunning confessed in 1991. His 313-page memoir, written from extensive notes kept over the years, is an attempt to reach some understanding of his impulse to record those long-ago events. Dunning's father had himself written an account of his service in World War I, and Robert admitted, "perhaps the same feelings that led to his endeavors are present in me."

Robert Dunning grew up in Lynn, Massachusetts, during the Depression. Times were tough in his working-class neighborhood, and though "nobody starved, some might have been hungrier than others." After serving in WWI, his father had become a member of the National Guard's 102nd Field Artillery, quartered in the Salem Armory. In 1936, the summer after Robert turned fifteen, his father asked him if he would like to drill with the 102nd's Headquarters Battery. As Dunning recalled, the Guard was called the "Mudguards," a nickname that could be "affectionate or derogatory, depending on whether you belonged."

For the next four years, Robert trained on communications equipment, including radios, signal flags, and ground panels. In 1939 he transferred to the instrument section, which became the "basis of all my assignments for the rest of my involvement in the Army." He learned how to use instruments to read maps and draw them on plotting tables to calculate the relationship between guns and their targets. Both Dunnings participated every year in Memorial and Armistice Day parades, and for two weeks every summer, Robert was off to Guard camp, drilling and practicing with real artillery.

Even as a boy, Robert was aware of the possibility that events in Europe and Asia might "eventually engulf the good old U.S. of A." So he wasn't surprised when, "as the clouds of war darkened and war erupted in Europe, we began to receive a little more, and newer, equipment, and our training intensified and took on new importance." In 1939, he got an appointment to the Massachusetts Military Academy, where he could expect to spend the next four years and graduate as a second lieutenant. He was there for only one year; at the end of 1940 the Academy suspended activities pending the federalization of the National Guard.

Dunning had been hoping for a commission and took a screening exam for a West Point congressional appointment, but that didn't pan out, so he took a correspondence course from the Field Artillery School at Fort Sill in Oklahoma. He had been told the best way to get a commission was to apply for Officer Candidate School at Fort Sill.

He took a job at Champion Lamp Works in Lynn, awaiting his call to duty. It came in January 1941, when Robert Dunning reported to the Salem Armory for active duty. "For me," he wrote, "this was the day I left home for World War II, never returning, except for leave and furlough, until September 1945." He was officially inducted into federal service on January 16, 1941, and reported to Camp Edwards, the site of his former Guard camp, now bustling with newly constructed barracks that would eventually house 30,000 troops.

The largest unit was his, the Yankee Division; there was also an all-black unit and another that "consisted of rednecks from the South." Somebody had the good sense to put a third outfit between the blacks and the Southerners, who were a continual source of trouble to both the blacks and the Yankee Division. "They seemed to hate both of us with an equal passion, and there were numerous brawls on the post and in town, particularly New Bedford, where there are lots of local Portuguese blacks from the Azores."

By this time, Dunning had made sergeant, taking on various assignments, including instructing the regimental band in matters of first aid and hygiene. With his background in the Guard, Dunning eventually found his way into the Instrument and Survey Section.

Soldiers from the camp spent their weekends in Boston, taking one of many scheduled trains to get there. The last train back on Sunday night was famously known as the "drunk train," full of soldiers the MPs had cleared out of the bars and tossed onto the cars.

In July, Dunning's outfit moved to nearby Fort Devens for maneuvers. Late that summer, rumors began floating around that the Guard units that had been activated in October 1940 would have their time extended for another year. Some of the married men in the units expressed concern about being away from their families that long. The watchword became "OHIO" (Over the Hill in October)," Dunning wrote. "We could hear the howls of "OHIOOOO" ring out about midnight, and the reply from the officers' tents, 'Shut your Goddam mouths or you'll all be courts-martialed.'"

His father was serving alongside him. The elder Dunning would spend much of the war working coastal defenses along the New England shores. His unit was sent overseas in 1944, attached to various artillery groups in France, Holland, and Germany. But except for a couple of times during leave, father and son did not see each other again until the end of the war.

In the fall, Dunning's unit went on maneuvers in North Carolina. In late November, they joined a convoy of vehicles driving back to the Boston area, through Washington, Philadelphia, and New York. On the night of December 6, 1941, they were in New London, Connecticut, sleeping on the floor of an armory, about to make the last leg of their trip back to Camp Edwards. They left early the next morning in a steady rain. Shortly after lunch, back at the camp, he heard a radio from another room and the words "Japs" and "Pearl Harbor."

Dunning wrote: "The feeling of shock, despair, and disbelief was to continue for several weeks. We kept waiting for news that we were hitting back somewhere. It never came. Only bad news piled up, one event after another. I cannot speak for the whole country, but from what I saw, we as a nation were pretty mad and pretty discouraged. Roosevelt took the air that first night to try to reassure the country that we would win in the end. It may have helped some, but not much. We of the wooden guns and political generals knew it would be a long, long time." He wrote, "Perhaps the major effect of Pearl Harbor on my life was the removal of any doubts about the near future. 'OHIO' was now obsolete. The length of our service period was extended to two years even before Pearl Harbor, and afterwards our tour of duty was for the 'duration.'"

In the wake of December 7th, he applied to the OCS at Fort Sill and was accepted in April 1942. "If Pearl Harbor had never occurred," he noted, "and I had been released from the service after two years, I don't know what direction my life would have taken." He believed that America's involvement in the war was inevitable, but the way he was able to enter war service, not as an enlisted man but with the promise of an officer's commission, "pretty well established the course of my life from that day on."

At Fort Sill, Dunning was on his way to becoming one of the Army's ninety-day wonders when his career was nearly sidetracked. One of his tent mates went AWOL and was picked up in town by the MPs. Dunning and the other four men in his tent were called in to explain why they hadn't reported the missing man. The recruits never suspected that there was some kind of honor code to be observed, but they were let off the hook, and their tent mate was dismissed from the program.

When he was asked for his preference in duty stations for field training, Dunning narrowed his choices to two, both in Oregon: Camp White, near Medford, with the 91st Division, or Camp Adair, near Corvallis, with the 96th. A buddy who hailed from near Medford urged him to choose the 91st, and that was his assignment. As it turned out, the 96th eventually wound up going to the Philippines and Okinawa, arguably more dangerous duty than what Dunning drew in Europe.

The commander of the 91st Division was General Charles Gerhardt, whom Dunning described as "a real character of the Patton mold, lean and wiry, an old horse soldier. He knew nothing about artillery. On the firing range one day, he inquired how to aim a howitzer using the gunsight. He looked into the wrong end and exclaimed, 'Chrissakes! All I see is myself!' They let him pull the lanyard, and he rode off happy.

Gerhardt had a ten-year-old son who was an honorary sergeant; he wore sergeant's stripes and a pith helmet and brandished a riding crop. He always rode his horse ten paces behind his father."

After about a year with the 91st, Gerhardt was transferred to the 29th Division, which landed at Normandy on D-Day. The last Dunning heard of him, Gerhardt was in charge of military missions in South America. "Considering the tact required for such a job," Dunning remarked, "it seemed sort of like quartering the bull in the china shop."

The summer of 1942, Dunning helped the locals fight forest fires, visited Crater Lake, and helped to train "fillers," the nickname for new recruits. He spent nearly all of 1943 in Oregon and Washington. In January, he was promoted to first lieutenant, and in March he was sent to the Artillery Firing Center near Yakima, Washington. Shortly before that, he got a temporary transfer to the Division Artillery staff as survey officer in Yakima. In July he was in the high desert of central Oregon for more training, and in October he was made captain.

Dunning was part of the 346th Field Artillery Battalion. In September, he had been made an S-2, whose duties were various. He was in charge of the survey section, he kept the situation map, and he was responsible for all intelligence matters, among other jobs.

Late in 1943, the 346th moved into Camp Adair, and Dunning found the area around Corvallis prettier country than Medford, plus they had both Portland and Salem as places to spend their leave. On March 19, 1944, the 346th took a train cross-country to Camp Patrick Henry, Virginia, to embark for Europe. They sailed on April 1, hit a four-day storm, had one submarine alert that put everyone in life jackets, and spotted Tangiers on April 16. After a stop in Oran, where Dunning noted the extreme stench from sewage running into the harbor, they set up camp near the Algerian village of Port aux Poules.

On June 16, they sailed for Sicily. From there, it was off to Naples, which already had been secured by the Allies. Dunning wrote that "the only opposition to our landing would be the beggars and vendors of the Naples waterfront. The weather was warm and sunny and we stayed on deck most of the time."

They set up a bivouac area in the middle of an extinct volcano, "once owned and managed by the King of Italy as a private hunting preserve." Shortly after arriving, there were several incidents of enlisted men "accidentally" shooting themselves in the foot with their carbines. "This was a common occurrence with all outfits just before first combat," Dunning wrote. "A few men would get so worked up and nervous that self-mutilation seemed the only way out. We all had our fears but seldom talked about it. If we in the artillery were scared, imagine how the infantry must have felt just before being fed into the well-publicized Italian Front meat-grinder."

What Dunning took note of once his unit landed in Italy was the polyglot composition of the Allied forces, which included soldiers from the U.S., Brazil, Britain, Canada, South Africa, New Zealand, Australia, India, Africa, Poland, France, Greece, and Palestine, as well as Italian partisans and defectors.

The Germans had retreated well north of Rome, and the 346th found themselves attached to the 34th Division. At that point, in the summer of 1944, the 34th was a battle-scarred unit, having been involved in combat operations for two solid years with little let-up. They had nearly taken the impregnable abbey at Monte Cassino in some of the fiercest fighting of the war. Dunning wrote: "The Division could still do its job and fight but would not willingly accept the casualty rate that it once could. When things got too tough or hopeless, there were ways, learned from bitter experience, to slow things down and reduce casualties. The cycle was typical of just about every division that fought in Europe in World War II and was a result of the American practice of keeping a division in the line and on the attack continuously even though it no longer had enough riflemen left to do any effective fighting."

Dunning's convoy followed the Italian coastal road north, where lovely scenery alternated with scenes of destruction. Signs left by the retreating Germans warned in German and English of hidden land mines.

As an aside, Dunning wrote of the various terms he used in his memoir. "Krauts" was the most popular American nickname for Germans, followed by "Jerries." The British often called the Germans "Boche," as they did in WWI. For the Americans, the Italians were "Eyeties" and the British were all "Limeys." To the British all Americans were "Yanks." To the Germans they were "Amis," and the

Italians either called them "Inglisi" or "Americanos." To American artillerymen, the infantry were called "Doughboys," "Doughfeet," "Doughs," and sometimes, with affection, "Dogfaces." But, as Dunning reported, "They were not called GIs, an insulting term to a combat soldier. There were GI cans and uniforms, but the only GI soldiers were those in the states that hung around service clubs, appeared in Hollywood movies, or had cushy rear area jobs. Bill Mauldin's 'Joe,' of Joe and Willie fame, was and is not, I repeat, not GI Joe, and Bill has apoplexy if he is referred to as such."

The 346th saw its first real action, working with the 151st Field Artillery, south of Cecina, where "the Germans apparently were going to make a stand." For twenty minutes Dunning and two other officers crouched behind a wall while German shells landed nearby. "We were now a sober bunch that night, with the realization having dawned on us that 'A man could get killed around here.'" Someone broke out some white wine, and Dunning drank up. That night he suffered a case of "the runs," getting up several times to relieve himself. "It happened to be the same night that the Lufwaffe came out in force for the first time in months [he wrote]. From my squatting position, it was like a big fireworks show, the green Kraut tracers and the red and orange Allied tracers creating all kinds of intricate patterns across the night sky. The scary part were the bombs. Even though they seemed to be landing a mile or more away, the earth under me trembled."

The next day, he saw how the Germans were going to fight—and surrender. "They fight like hell, inflicting heavy casualties on our attacking doughboys even when surrounded. When their main body reaches safety at the next obstacle or when they run out of ammunition, the survivors cheerfully surrender, cite the Geneva Convention, tell us anything we want to know and brag how Germany would still win the war. This procedure would infuriate the doughfoots who had lost buddies in the preceding action, and it would require a great control effort by the officers to prevent the wholesale shooting of prisoners."

Another incident involving the shooting of prisoners soon arose, but this involved two Polish teenagers whom Dunning believed had been conscripted or volunteered to fight with the Germans. Dunning's colonel had him interrogate them through an interpreter, himself a Polish deserter. The Poles claimed they had been drafted against their will. When the colonel asked them if they would fight on the Allies' side with the Polish Corps, then part of the British 8th Army, the young men declined, saying they had had enough of war. "At that, the colonel exploded. 'You sons of bitches, you fight for the Krauts that raped your country, and now you get a chance to fight against them with your own countrymen and you turn it down!' Then to the guards he ordered, 'Take the bastards out and shoot them!' Well, that really shook up us newcomers. We understood the colonel's viewpoint and agreed with him, but shoot them? They looked like a couple of young kids, white with fright and uncomprehension as they were led out the door. The colonel's driver later assured me that they were sent to a POW cage, but one can never be sure."

After the Allies took the town of Cercola, Dunning saw his first instance of dive-bombing. The attacker turned out to be an Australian in a Spitfire, obviously confused about the positions of the two sides. Every antiaircraft gun in the valley opened up and shot him down. The pilot actually parachuted to safety and was picked up, apologizing before he was shipped back to Division HQ. "As to which outfit shot him down," Dunning wrote, "that is always difficult to determine. Usually every AA gunner in the area takes credit, one reason why you should never believe everything you read in the newspapers about damage to the enemy."

In July, with Pisa captured, the 346th found themselves in the same position for a couple of weeks. They used the time to fire their propaganda shells, regular shells "with a light charge and stuffed with one-page pamphlets," copies of which Dunning saved. The pamphlets stressed the hopelessness of the Nazi position and suggested an honorable surrender. "I never really knew whether our pamphlets did any good," he wrote, adding that if a German soldier picked one up, he was subject to severe punishment. He heard stories of some deserters coming in to the Allied lines waving the pamphlets, but the only confirmation of a surrender involved a buddy, Bill Robinson, who picked up a pamphlet when a wind blew them back over the Allied lines and called the Command Post offering to surrender to his own side.

As the pace of the war slowed down, the amenities improved: there was better food, real showers, and Red Cross girls showed up with doughnuts and coffee. The men liberated a radio and listened to

German stations. The music was good American pop, but "we had to sit through the nauseating, sweet voice of Axis Sally and the stiff upper lip of Lord Haw Haw. [Sally] would tell us in each division where we were, where we were going, and warn us that they would be waiting. The little bitch was usually right on the button every time."

Dunning had more mail to censor, a duty he had begun in Africa and thoroughly disliked. "I finally got so I could pretty well skim through a letter and skip the private talk completely and concentrate on 'where I am' and 'where I am going.'" He actually got some leave, visited some hill towns, and even rotated to Rome for a three-day visit.

Late in the summer of 1944, the 346th was assigned to assist in the attack on the so-called Gothic Line, a recently constructed defense line in the Apennines. By late September, despite stiff resistance—"the Krauts never retreated in disorder in this Italian war, not until the very end," Dunning remarked—the mission was accomplished. Dunning noted that the 346th had taken few casualties to that point—a half dozen wounded, none of them critically. He credits his colonel's wise selection of positions that "were always close enough to do our job but never too close to take foolish and unnecessary casualties." He also noted that they "spared no effort to dig in and camouflage."

By early October, the Po River Valley was in sight of the Allies, but the accumulation of days under fire was starting to tell on the men. That fall, the intense fighting had left little time for rest and relaxation. Dunning reported that "beer and PX came a couple of times," and Red Cross girls showed up with their coffee and doughnuts, braving German artillery shellings. One Sunday, a chaplain held a church service in a barn, and that night a trio of USO entertainers took over the barn for a show. These weren't well-publicized celebrities, but Dunning was sorry to have missed the show (he was on reconnaissance) because two of them, a duo who called themselves "Hum and Strum," were from Lynn, Massachusetts, and had served in his father's outfit during World War I.

Dunning's closest shave of the war came around this time, in the Sillaro Valley, south of Bologna:

"I had just stepped out of the CP [Command Post] when there was a dull thud, and the ground about ten feet in front of me erupted into the air, showering me and the CP with dirt clods. At my feet was a new shell hole, about six feet in diameter and five feet deep still reeking with smoke and fumes, which I jumped into immediately in case there were any brother or sister shells coming along. I was too shocked to be scared, it happened so fast. By all rights I should have been blown apart. What saved me was the soft ground and the probability that the shell had a delayed fuse. The shell easily tore into the ground and exploded five feet or so below the surface. The thick layer of dirt kept the shell fragments from flying through the air. I know it wasn't a dud because I found a fragment that proved it had exploded. I still have the fragment, and if I was superstitious, I would carry it around my neck like a rabbit's foot."

The Germans were in retreat, but they still had some fight left in them. On December 26, ten days after the Battle of the Bulge began with a huge counteroffensive in France and Belgium, Italian Fascist and German troops came out of the mountains and attacked the U.S. IV Corps on the western part of the Italian front.

Christmas Day, however, had been peaceful for Dunning and his men. They enjoyed a feast prepared by the locals in Valle, where they were quartered. Dunning was amazed at how hospitable the Italians were, given that "it was their land, that many friends and relatives had died from shells, bombs, and sickness, that many of their homes were destroyed, that they were cold and in rags, and that their land was occupied by foreigners, first by Krauts and then by well-fed Americans."

Dunning spent his first and last winter in Roncobertolo, "a typical little Italian mountain hamlet" hidden in a ravine in the Savena River Valley. The American soldiers took over all the buildings, but Italian families lived alongside them.

On March 29, 1945, Dunning and his men were finally relieved for a true break from fighting after 197 days on the line. They went to a rest area at Gagliano, near Mount Calvi, and enjoyed real showers, clean uniforms, visits by the donuts girls, games of horseshoes, softball, and volleyball, and outdoor movies—not to mention passes and leaves. He checked out the town of Montecatini, which he described as "a poor man's Venice," because at certain times of the year the streets were filled with water to simulate canals. He also visited Florence.

In April they were back in the Po Valley, and on the 24th of that month, two weeks before the end of the war, they lost two men in one day to a German bomb. In all, the 346th lost only four men killed in action during the war. Dunning's unit now began to see a steady stream of captured prisoners, whom they considered "a nuisance. We usually turned them over to the nearest infantry." For some, taking prisoners was a serious business. "At the time, it looked like they were working for browny points. Little did we artillerymen realize the money to be made on POWs. Every Kraut had a very good Swiss or German watch, which was usually grabbed by the first Ami on the scene. Thousands and thousands of dollars were made by POW guards selling watches, cameras, and rings to Air Corps and rear area soldiers."

On April 30, they reached the town of Paese, just west of Treviso. On May 2, they learned that General Heinrich von Vietinghoff, commander of the German Army Group in Italy, had on April 29 agreed to the terms of unconditional surrender. One of Dunning's buddies, Charlie Brown, went to the local church and asked the sexton to ring the bells in celebration, but neither he nor the parish priest "had any interest in celebrating the end of the most devastating war in history." So Brown and a couple of men climbed the steeple and rang the bells for five minutes.

"Except for the jockeying for position by the partisans," wrote Dunning, "the local population of the Treviso countryside seemed apathetic about the end of this bloody six-year war," in sharp contrast to the outpouring of emotion in many other parts of Europe that month. "Apparently," he concluded, "the war had not hurt these people that badly."

Dunning stayed in Italy until August, dividing his time between duties connected with the Occupation and sightseeing. He made a point of visiting Venice and was stunned by it: "It was sort of like, 'Gee, I never could really believe that this place even existed, and here I am right in the middle of it.'"

By the time his unit reached their point of embarkation, at Casserta near Naples, the atomic bombs had been dropped on Hiroshima and Nagasaki, and there was no question that they were headed back to the States and not to the Pacific Theater.

"On the morning of September 10," he wrote, "the day we were scheduled to reach port, I think I was the first one at the rail, peering into the dense fog for the sight of land." The fog lifted midmorning, and Dunning began to spot familiar landmarks, and then the skyline of Boston.

They were taken in trains to Camp Miles Standish in Taunton, from where everyone would get their connections to the four corners of the U.S.

Dunning didn't have far to go, just up the road to Fort Devens. The next day at Devens, he was leaving the mess hall, about to catch a bus into Boston, when a buddy from his old National Guard unit appeared and grabbed his arm. "[He] steered me back into the mess hall. There at the other end was my father. By great coincidence, he had returned from Europe for redeployment ...landed at New York, and arrived at Devens the same day that I had. We were tickled to see each other, and he looked great."

About an hour later, Dunning's mother arrived in the family car, a 1939 Pontiac, and they were on their way home. Dunning wrote, "This was not quite the way I had pictured my return. I had planned to be real nonchalant, take the bus to Boston, the train to Central Square, Lynn, saunter into Hovey's Bar and Grill for a couple of beers, and then hail a taxi for 24 Bailey Street. But then again, who can argue with the way it really happened."

Dunning began his memoir with a description of how different combat units were from other units in wartime. "The advantage of being in a combat outfit was that the very purpose of your existence, the observed results, and the inherent danger resulted in closely knit activities with comrades you could stake your life on and life-long friendships that can seldom be duplicated in the same way in civilian life." When he first got home from Europe in 1945, he wrote of "an empty feeling in the pit of my stomach." He had been "cut loose from the ties and a feeling of security one gets from a very close association with good friends that lasted over three years, often under difficult conditions."

Although he stayed in touch with his buddies, mainly by attending reunions, Dunning wrote in 1991 that "I have to admit that I find it hard to regenerate completely the old feelings of 1945, even at reunions. I wonder at times if we really know each other, or want to know, as we are now, or whether we are searching for each other as we were in 1945."

His father had warned him about these feelings. Shortly before his father's death in 1974, Dunning was telling him about a trip he planned to Camp White in Oregon to get together with some of the guys from the 346th. "I was a little disappointed he didn't share my excitement. He sort of looked at me wistfully and advised me not to expect too much, and that I might come away disappointed. Dad was right as usual."

PHILIP RANDAZZO:
A SELF-CONTAINED SOLDIER

"Then after a while you become one of them.
That is when your body, your mind changes....
You are out there all the time; you get separate from the Army.
You don't belong to the real Army."

I N A WAR LIKE VIETNAM, WITHOUT DISCERNIBLE FRONT LINES, engaging the enemy often meant going on patrols, looking for trouble. The mechanized cavalry, self-contained in the bush for weeks and months at a time, formed its own subculture, vividly described by soldier Philip Randazzo in a 2004 interview for the Veterans History Project.

Randazzo was born in Gross Pointe, a suburb of Detroit, and grew up in the nearby towns of Center Line and Shelby Township. He was contacted by his draft board before he completed his senior year in high school, because he'd turned eighteen. His counselor got him a deferment, in part because he was attending a barber college part-time. After his 1965 graduation he went to barber college full-time and was able to get another deferment when the draft board sent him a second notice.

His third notice came when he was twenty years old and no longer in school. He was inducted on May 8, 1967, and took a train from Detroit to Fort Knox, Kentucky, for what he recalled as "very, very intense" basic training. "They knew where we were going," he said. "They allocate so many men to Vietnam and so many men to Germany and so many somewhere else. Apparently they knew where our group was going to go." The recruits had no weekend or even three-hour passes, and once he graduated from basic, he went into

Advanced Intermediate Training (AIT), staying at Fort Knox. That's where he learned how to be a reconnaissance scout.

"The main purpose of a scout," Randazzo explained, "is to locate the enemy, make contract with the enemy, hold contact with the enemy until help arrives." Scouts traveled in small units, working day and night, mindful that the Vietcong operated mostly under cover of darkness. "You look for trouble," he said. "When you are out there, you just have to cross their camps. When we cross their camps, they would attack us. We have to fight it out. That was the only way to do it."

"The recon scout does everything," he said. "Ambush, LPs, which is listening posts, OPs, which is observation posts, S&Ds, which is search & destroy, tunnel work, which they call tunnel rats. Whatever there is to do to kill the enemy, or to locate the enemy, or to disrupt him, that's what our job was."

Randazzo and a South Vietnamese who served with the U.S. Army as a scout and interpreter, late 1967.

They lived at Fort Knox in the General Disney Barracks, of which "everybody used to make fun, calling them Disneyland. But it was far from being Disneyland. It was worse than boot camp." AIT went on for ten weeks; then they spent a week or two on mountain training, working in three-man teams. In all that time, they still hadn't enjoyed even a one-day pass. Randazzo recalled, "They don't want you to get softened. You can't have any visitors from home either. If they do come and see you, that means you do a lot of KP duty or physical training. They keep your mind pretty well occupied. They keep you terrified, really. We were terrified of our own DIs [Drill Instructors]. But you got to thank them, too. They trained us in what to do if we were faced with the enemy. The enemy really didn't mean that much to us. I feared the DIs more than I did the North Vietnamese."

Finally, at the end of AIT he was allowed twelve days' leave and went home, only to find out "everything was different. I couldn't take it in the house. My sister was already messed up, and I couldn't eat the food, and I had to leave." He left early for Oakland, California, which was his point of embarkation. From there, he got on a plane headed west. "I never heard the word Vietnam all this time," he recalled. "I didn't know what any of it meant. I had all this training about killing this or killing that, but I never heard the word 'Vietnam.'" The flight was a quiet one; "the other GIs knew where we were going."

When they disembarked in country, they were told to go beneath a pavilion and remain there. Although "the heat was devastating," they were not allowed to take off their shirts or to drink anything; they were to wait for their sergeant to give them their instructions. They spent the next three days in a barracks, living on C rations and water, awaiting further orders. When his number was called, he got onto a C130, "a really crappy plane" with cracks in the floor, where they were all seated. "You could look down and see jungles," he recalled. "We didn't know that we were on our way to hell."

They landed at Cu Chi, one of three base camps for the Army's 25th Division; he was directed to a tent that was the orderly room for his camp and greeted by a man who told him, "I'm going to enroll you in the jungle bunny school." Randazzo was mystified. He was shown the tent, or hooch, he would bunk in, and he was the only person sleeping there for the next five days. In the morning he was directed to the far side of the camp to start jungle bunny school.

The instructors taught him about booby traps, how to deal with the heat (don't take off your shirt for three days after you land "or otherwise you'll fry"), about the kinds of weapons the enemy used, about their own weapons, about recognizing enemy uniforms. That went on for five days. On the sixth day, he could hear the rumble of tanks and he saw dust kicking up. "I wasn't used to that at Fort Knox. Everything there was shiny." Then he saw the men on their mechanized vehicles. "I am standing there looking at these animals. These are animals coming, the guys, you couldn't recognize them. There was so much dirt lined on their faces, into their ears, their noses. They were just crusted in filth. I never seen nothing like that. When they came in, I was inside the tent. These animals came in and they took off their pants, they took off their shirts, and they laid naked on their air mattresses. Then the cook came with mail for them. I was scareder than hell. They put a lot of fear into you—where the enemy, he can't instill that kind of fear that the military can." Randazzo asked one of them what day it was. "October 4th" was the reply. Randazzo said it was his birthday and that he was now twenty-one. "That's what I am," one soldier replied. "I'm twenty-one. I go home tomorrow."

That night he was issued his M16. "No hand guards on that," he recalled. "The butts were cracked up. Nothing pretty, nothing pretty at all." The next morning, the word went out: "Mount up." All of the men in his tent got back into their armored personnel carriers. A sergeant yelled at Randazzo to get up on his "track." There were three .60-caliber machine guns mounted on it, and he was ordered to man one of them. The sergeant asked Randazzo what was the worst thing that ever happened to him, and Randazzo told him he had once hit a windshield at sixty miles per hour. The sergeant said, "Okay, then you'll be able to take a mine. You'll be all right then."

The scene reminded him of a movie or TV Western. "We were the same thing as you see walking out of the forts: the cavalry," he recalled. "Back then, the cavalry leaves the fort, they don't come back until weeks later. We stayed out. That's what we were, the cavalry."

He learned quickly about his comrades. Their battle experience varied from three months to nearly a year. He recalled:

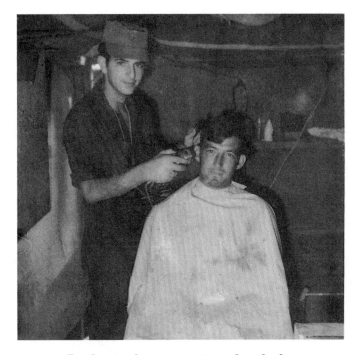

*Randazzo, who was training to be a barber
before he was drafted to serve in Vietnam,
kept practicing his trade overseas.*

"You've got guys who will kill you in a minute if you screw up. They are mean guys. They are draftees. Mostly they don't want the seventeen-, eighteen-, nineteen-year-old kids on the field. They get the older ones that are married and have children. They have people back home. That's who they want on those vehicles. I was twenty-one and was called a kid. Then after a while you become one of them. That is when your body, your mind changes. You are filthy. You got rot all over your feet and rot in your crotch. You are out there all the time; you get separate from the Army. You don't belong to the real Army. You never get food; you get C rations. If you run across sugar cane, you chop so much of it up, two-foot lengths, and kind of pile it up on the side of the tracks. Then you can chew on that. C rations, we kind of stretched them out, because you don't know when they are going to bring them out again. They don't like coming out to us. The choppers give our position away. We were a self-contained unit. Nobody was self-contained but the cavalry."

He learned, too, about his weapons and ammunition, how there were three layers of sand bags beneath their vehicles to absorb the effects of hitting a land mine. He found that he couldn't depend on his M16 because it would jam on him, but that his machine gun was another matter: "Those guns could really do a lot of talking." The problem with sitting on top of an armored personnel carrier was that it offered the enemy an easy target. Between the noise of the engine, the noise of the three guns, it was hard to hear the enemy bullets coming toward you. "You try to pick up flashes or green tracers, or the muzzle flash. Once you have been out there so long, you get good."

They weren't sure when they could return to Cu Chi. Once, a chopper came out with a couple of nurses on it, and they were told that if they each donated a pint of blood, they could go back in to base camp for a day. "So we all gave blood. They took off in the chopper and we wanted to turn around and go back in, but they never did [let us]. So now, we are traveling all night long, patrolling in the dark, a pint short. What does that do to a person?"

Even when they got back to camp, they were confined to a certain area. "They didn't want us to mingle with the rear echelon because they got nice Hawaiian shirts on, they got packages from home, CARE packages, and they have food, they have mess halls. So they kept us away from them. We could not leave our area." They were given their mail, but they were told to destroy the letters. "They didn't want us to smell the spray you smell on your letters in the field. You look at the pictures, you look at the envelopes and think, This is coming from civilization." They were told that if the enemy found any mail on them they would contact the soldier's people back home. When they did get to go back to base on what he called a three-day stand, the scouts spent much of their time cleaning and maintaining their weapons.

This "cavalry," Randazzo later realized, constituted the nighttime warriors for the American forces in Vietnam. During the day, the bombers would make their runs, but by night, it was "our job to run Highway One, which is the goal line. Now, the enemy knows we are out there with them. When they are moving, we are moving. We're trying to cut them off."

They returned to Cu Chi on January 30, 1968; that night, the Tet Offensive began. Rockets and mortars hit Cu Chi, but "we weren't scared of that stuff. It's nothing personal, and you know we're not the target. You are not really concerned about rockets and mortars because you are way above that. You have graduated."

About 2 o'clock in the morning, they got the order to mount up. They left the base, not through a gate but through a section of barbed wire. After three hours of making their way through the jungle, they hit Highway One. For the first segment of the trip, Randazzo was wearing a flak jacket and had one in his lap in case he was hit with an RPG (rocket-propelled grenade); he also had a "pot" (helmet) on. "Now, I never wear stuff like this," he admitted. "I did on this [mission] because that jungle, that was a rough three hours." Once they hit the highway and the sun came up, he took off the jackets and the pot and began to relax, but only a little.

They came to a section of barbed wire barrier that marked the perimeter for another base. Randazzo's track was in the lead. Several officers converged around his track, and Randazzo covered them with his machine gun. One vehicle from behind them tried to maneuver to pass them on the narrow road, and he noticed there was a village to the right.

"Next thing I knew, Sergeant Strayer jumps on top of the tracks, pulled himself up on the left side and was yelling at me. We had been together for four and a half months. He's yelling at me to open fire, destroy everything, destroy that village. I started opening my .60, but Strayer's face is all bloody and I started opening up with the .60, destroying the village. You could start seeing the NVA [North Vietnamese Army]. They were all laying down in berms. Just then, I got hit with an RPG. My track got hit square on. I got blown off of that one into the ditch. Sgt. Dolan was in the ditch with me and Sgt. Strayer. They both had .45s, and I had nothing because I was blown off with nothing. Strayer is telling me that everybody is dead in the tank, and everybody is dead in Captain Moran's track. The North Vietnamese jumped on the tank and jumped on the track and shot everybody in the head. Sgt. Strayer had his .45 and is shooting at the enemy coming over between our tracks and he's killing them as they are coming over. Sgt. Dolan was doing the same thing. They [the enemy] didn't think any of us were alive. They thought they killed everyone in our vehicles. Before I know it, Sgt. Strayer's head fell right next to me. I picked his head up, and he had a bullet hole right in his forehead. I took his .45 and pointed it. I had no ammo. I put my head down and tried to get underneath Sgt. Strayer's body.

Randazzo was pinned down for a time by enemy fire, but a buddy, Steve Porter, came to his rescue with a .60-caliber machine gun and killed the four North Vietnamese soldiers who were closest to Randazzo's track. A lieutenant showed up with a case of grenades, and the Americans began tossing them toward the advancing soldiers.

When it was safe, they began to load their wounded onto the tracks to get them to the base's medical facility. The battle for that area lasted another two days before the NVA withdrew.

Then Randazzo drew an assignment in Saigon. "We came to this building that was called the U.S. Embassy," he recalled. "I don't know what it was. All I knew was that we had to secure this building that was under attack." Next door was President Thieu's palace, surrounded by South Vietnamese soldiers in bunkers. The gates to the embassy opened, and they backed their track inside the compound, right up to the front steps, blocking them. He could see that the building was full of holes from RPGs.

A Marine colonel came outside and asked for two volunteers. Randazzo's commanding officer, a lieutenant colonel, ordered him and a buddy named Longabardi to volunteer. Randazzo was still covered with blood from the NVA ambush on Highway One; he had lost many of his teeth in that fight, and had had nothing to eat for three days except for juice from the canned fruit in his C rations.

"He wanted us to salute him, this guy [the Marine]. Me and Longabardi looked at this officer—he was looking kind of pretty—and told him he had the wrong guys, and we walked back out the door. The lieutenant said that this guy wanted us to do it. He said he wanted two volunteers, and the lieutenant said they are under my command, not your command. He said [the Marines] could ask [us] to do something, but [we] didn't have to do anything for him. So we understood the situation."

They were ordered to guard a door at the end of a hallway: nothing goes in, nothing comes out, and if either happened, everyone is going to die. "We understood orders like that," Randazzo recalled.

Randazzo and Longabardi noticed two American women in the hallway. They started down the hall, and the soldiers told them, "You better stop right there, ladies."

"They asked, 'You guys want some food?' We said, 'Yeah, if you got some C's we'll take them.' So they came back and they had cafeteria trays with food on them. We couldn't leave that door. They put the trays down and they backed up. We couldn't leave that door. Then Longabardi walked and got the tray full of food."

He looked at the food but couldn't eat it. Later, the doctors told him his stomach had shrunk at that time, and he wasn't able to enjoy food. The ladies came back and asked them if they wanted cots. The soldiers didn't understand what they were trying to say, so the women soon returned with mattresses. He recalled, "We checked the mattresses in case they were booby trapped, you know. You can't trust nobody." The women backed away, and "we sat on the goddamn mattresses all night long, and it was pretty comfortable. We never seen nothing like this."

In the morning, a colonel came down the hall and told them, "I'm going to open up the door. There is going to be a man come out. When the man comes out, I want you to walk shoulder to shoulder against the guy, one on each shoulder. Then I want you to follow me."

The man was a U.S. military officer. Randazzo got on his right shoulder. They walked down the hallway to a big foyer and a large pair of glass doors. They were told to walk through the doors and place the man inside a vehicle waiting outside. The colonel told them there were trees all around the garden area where the car was parked and that if a hand grenade came down from any of those trees, Randazzo or Longabardi was to jump on it. "He was telling us kid stuff," Randazzo recalled. "I would know if there was anybody in the trees. I wasn't going to be jumping on no hand grenade. I just might be able to throw it away myself. They underestimated us. They didn't know how good we are."

The interviewer asked Randazzo if he ever found out who the man he escorted was. "It was General Westmoreland. He was stuck in the Embassy when Tet hit."

Randazzo was wounded a few days later when his track was ambushed by RPGs. He was blown off his turret into a ditch, then shot again when he came up, suffering shrapnel wounds in his arm, hands, knee, and leg. After he was treated at an aid station, he was having difficulty walking, but his lieutenant insisted he go back out on patrol, because there were too many new guys now in the unit, and he wanted someone with experience out there in the bush.

After Tet, he recalled "it slowed down until we were just in normal fights." He left Vietnam on September 28, 1968, just short of a year in country.

Randazzo boiled down his service to one simple mission: "We protected the village people, the children and the women, and the older men, the people who were sick. I've seen villages after the Vietcong got done with them. It was very, very bad what they did. Our job was to secure the villages, day and night. We have a purpose, not to defeat the North Vietnamese, not to defeat the Vietcong. That was part of it. What ours was, deep down inside, was to protect the people over there. The kids loved us." His collection from Vietnam includes 8mm film, transferred to a VHS tape, of some of those kids and those villages.

He has contributed stories to the Web site of his unit, the 3rd Squadron of the 4th Cavalry, or the 3/4 Cav. The widow of Sergeant Strayer, the man who was killed in that Highway One ambush, called him after she read the story of her husband's death. She sent him a letter with a picture of her grown daughter in a wedding dress. The widow also sent Randazzo the sergeant's dog tag. She was grateful to him because she hadn't known how her husband had died; she was told there had to be a closed casket for the funeral because he had been blown up. "She was mad at me because he died next to me and not next to her," Philip Randazzo recalled, then added, "The lady's not mad at me, but she's mad."

CHARLES REMSBURG:
THE CAREFUL SOLDIER

*"Where a month earlier we had been afraid of the unknown,
now we knew something of what war was like and that
almost no one was immune to fear."*

L IKE MANY GIs SERVING IN WORLD WAR II, CHARLES REMSBURG wrote home frequently to his family about his experiences in the infantry and later in a unit public relations office. And once the war was won, he got on with his life, putting all his war experiences behind him. After forty years, a belated discovery of nearly 200 of his wartime letters spurred him to reconstruct those experiences in a detailed and often moving memoir.

On December 7, 1941, Remsburg was a sixteen-year-old high school student whose family lived in a northwest Detroit subdivision called South Rosedale Park. He was attending Redford High School and working a paper route to save money for college. The draft was a distant possibility for him, but a possibility nonetheless.

One year after Pearl Harbor, four Redford seniors, including Charles Remsburg, were selected for a special program at the University of Michigan called "The Division for Emergency Training." They would absorb one year's worth of college education concentrated into twenty weeks, followed by service in the military. Remsburg was an honor student, but he found the academic workload daunting at the University of Michigan in Ann Arbor. In June, he almost dropped out of the program, but he was persuaded to stay in and completed it in July.

Charles Remsburg, Jr., at Fort Benning, Georgia, November 1943. On his first trip to the South, he was shocked by racial segregation.

In March he had passed a written exam for entry into the V–12 program for naval officer training, but he failed the physical, mainly due to his poor eyesight. He tried his luck with the Marines and Air Corps but came up short there, too. "As a last resort, he wrote, "I applied for entry into the Army Enlisted Reserve Corps." Although he was unofficially found to be "blind as a bat without glasses," he was still found fit for service, and after processing at Fort Custer, Michigan, shipped off to Fort Benning, Georgia, for his basic training.

For ten weeks he and his fellow recruits were restricted to the post. Then brief passes were issued, and Remsburg got his first look at life in the Deep South when he went on leave in Columbus, Georgia. What struck him most about that town was that he rarely saw any of its "sizable Negro population." Although housing in Detroit was segregated, employment opportunities in the auto industry and other plants allowed for some mingling of whites and blacks at work. "In the South," he noted, "there was an almost total separation in every phase of life. Whites held all positions of authority, both in government and in business. It struck many of us that something was radically wrong." He knew that in Nazi Germany so-called "inferior" people were being confined to concentration camps. "Here in America," he wrote, "the land of the free, colored people were being treated little better. This wouldn't be the last time that we would see a wide discrepancy between the dream and the reality."

In January 1944, Remsburg and 150 other graduates of basic at Benning were assigned to an engineering program in Ohio at the University of Dayton. On their left sleeves they wore a patch for the ASTP (Army Specialized Training Program) with the yellow lamp of learning. "Secretly," he wrote, "we were slightly ashamed of this patch. It marked us as something less than soldiers. We couldn't hide the truth. We were college boys in uniform."

Before long, the ASTP was terminated, and the War Department announced that, as Remsburg wrote, "due to the exigencies of the service—whatever that meant," he and his fellow student soldiers were eligible for reassignment. In March 1944, he reported to Camp Swift in Texas for training with the 102nd Infantry Division. Charles Remsburg was about to become a combat soldier.

In Company C he found himself "under the supervision of a new type of NCO, one I never knew existed." Sergeant Lisman was, of all things, a friend to the recruits. He was interested in them as individuals and came across as "a leader rather than an authority figure." Remsburg wrote, "I decided that, if I should ever become a sergeant—a most unlikely prospect—I would try to pattern myself after Sgt. Lisman."

After several weeks of training, Remsburg went against conventional Army wisdom and volunteered for something: the mortar platoon in D Company. He had no idea what a mortar was, but "I figured anything had to be an improvement over lugging a rifle." He and a buddy, Art Soddeck, were among those chosen for the unit. He wrote in his memoir, "This move, we later discovered, would probably significantly increase our chance of surviving the war." In mid-June, the 102nd Infantry passed in review in honor of Texas governor Coke Stevenson. D-Day had come and gone, and the news from Europe was mostly encouraging. For many soldiers like Charles Remsburg, eager to get in on the action, shipping out seemed an exciting prospect.

They sailed for England in September and finally arrived in Cherbourg, France, late that month. He was surprised to see how little the German Occupation had affected the people of Normandy. Their lives as farmers scratching out a living were not easy, but their occupiers had not harassed them, either.

Remsburg was in the regimental reserve and not on the front lines of the advance through France and Belgium, but that didn't lessen the tension. "Even the troops we relieved had the shakes," he wrote, "and they were veterans." In particular, the sound of artillery, even if it was your own, put everyone on edge. "The general feeling in regard to the sounds of war became: 'You can never be too careful!' Although we soon learned to distinguish between incoming and outgoing shells, very often subconsciously—all of our senses became fine-tuned. After all, even our own rounds had been known to fall short."

By October 25, they had crossed into Germany. He described the town of Baesweiler, just over the border from Holland: "Every home, no matter how humble, contained at least three items that seemed to be of great value to the occupants. One was a framed photograph of Hitler, looking austere and statesmanlike. Prominently displayed on a table in the parlor was a copy of *Mein Kampf*, full of the Führer's dream for a resurgent Germany. As far as we could tell, most of these books had never been opened. Apparently they were there to make an impression. Also present was a large Nazi flag to be hung outside the house on ceremonial occasions."

Once a town was captured, Remsburg, reported, "liberation" began. "Some might say 'looting,' but usually nothing was destroyed for the sake of destruction." He was amazed at what the occupants had left behind—a curious measure of trash and treasure—and what the GIs considered items worth appropriating. One of his men disassembled an "ancient" sewing machine powered by a foot treadle and actually had it shipped home piece by piece. On the other hand, anything of real value that could easily be carried off by the fleeing citizens was gone. "Liberating anything we really wanted," Remsburg wrote, "was usually a rare occurrence."

What was of immediate value was found in the basements of many homes: row after row of canned vegetables, fruits, and even meat. And they would "really hit the jackpot" when a bottle of wine or schnapps was uncovered. "At first some of the guys said, 'I'm not touching that stuff! It's probably poisoned—or maybe even booby-trapped.' This hesitation lasted about ten minutes." He reported they never ran into poison or booby traps in any private home. In pillboxes, that was another story.

In a letter dated November 1, 1944 from "somewhere in Germany," Remsburg remarked on how relatively unscathed were the portions of Holland and Belgium he had seen when compared to France. He then offered this pointed analysis: "After seeing so much of France and observing its people of all walks of life, I can readily see why she fell. The nation itself is rotten to the core, and it may take centuries to again rise to the position it once held. The only large city or town that we didn't see was Paris, but they are giving frontline troops passes there, so I might see it yet."

He admitted to a close shave, something many GIs would not tell their families, for fear of worrying them. "I was out on a mission and caught in the open when a bunch of 88's [88mm, the Germans' most devastating artillery shell] started laying them down. It's a funny thing about artillery—when you can hear the air rushing thru and around the shell you are pretty safe, but when she starts whistling, it's time to hug that good old earth! When I heard that thing whistle I took one flying leap into a gutter—one round landed about fifty yards from me and smacked into a wooden post about two feet away, but that was about as close as they came. I dug the thing out after the shelling stopped and am carrying it as a lucky piece. Since that first day none have come that close, but we don't take any chances either."

Remsburg's memoir contains a little deconstruction of that letter. "Although generally true in its overall outline," he wrote, he also admits to some inaccuracies and omissions. "It is obvious now to recognize how desperately I wanted to be considered a combat soldier and how I twisted events toward that end." In a reserve position, it was very rare to see shells landing close by; "our share of combat" was puffing things up, since he had been in the vicinity of the front lines for only a week at that point; "out on a mission" was code for "out exploring the town."

In November, the 102nd ran into opposition from the German Army at Beeck. On the second night of the battle, Remsburg was part of a carrying party, assigned to return to the rear and bring more ammunition up to their mortar positions. About 500 yards into his trek, he was ducking a sudden German artillery barrage when he decided to dive feet first into a hole. It took a while to notice the odor of something soft beneath his feet, but when he did and lit his Zippo to check it out, he was appalled to see that he was standing on a partially decomposed face crawling with maggots. "Nothing in my previous experiences had prepared me for this," he wrote, "yet in the months ahead I would become very familiar with the smell of death." Despite his revulsion, he stayed in that hole for perhaps ten minutes, "a lifetime" in exchange for safety from the German shells.

After Beeck, which the Americans took on November 30, Remsburg wouldn't have to exaggerate stories of combat to his parents. "Anxiety became our constant companion," he wrote. "Although we didn't talk about it, we knew it was there. Where a month earlier we had been afraid of the unknown, now we knew something of what war was like and that almost no one was immune to fear." He described how individuals found ways to deal with their fears. "Most of us practiced self-deception. 'Sure, some guys are going to get it, but not me.'" He did point out that experience "was a plus for a longer life in combat. The longer you lived, the longer you could expect to live. You stopped doing dumb things like standing there, watching shells exploding around you. And, you became very careful. All of your senses were concentrated on identifying potentially dangerous sights and sounds."

Experience did help, but "in the final analysis the fact that you were careful, had combat experience, and/or were a hell of a nice guy didn't really matter." What did was your luck. "Were you in the wrong place at the wrong time? Tough shit! That's all she wrote."

On December 7, 1944, Remsburg wrote home to say that he had been shifted to another squad by request and was now a gunner in the 6th squad under S/Sgt. Clifford Wilson, "who is tops." He was also reunited with two buddies, "and we think we make a damn good team."

In January, he had a new assignment: forward observer. He was part of a three-man team, and his responsibility was to string telephone communication wire "from the forward observation post back to the mortar platoon when we were in a stationary situation." Wire was more reliable than radio, though it could be cut in a number of ways. His next job, then, was to find the break in the wire and splice it. "Repairing a break in the wire could be quite exciting," he reported.

At that point, Remsburg, wrote, Americans and Germans were literally staring at one another across the Siegfried Line, the German bulwark of defenses that stymied Americans on their final push into the Fatherland. Remsburg described conditions in his pillbox, a former German defensive structure now housing fifteen American GIs. There was no electricity, so the interior was lit by a bottle of gasoline with a rag for a wick. It threw off a pungent black smoke. After a while "we looked like we belonged in a minstrel show," he wrote. And they coughed up sooty phlegm for weeks afterwards.

The war at this point seemed to be at a stalemate, and the men in the pillbox passed their time playing cards, pulling guard duty, preparing "exotic meals by mixing the contents of our K rations in new ways," and sleeping.

In a letter dated January 16, 1945, Remsburg wrote with admiration of a unit that had recently joined their Army, the 2nd Armored Division, "a bunch of hair-raising hell-for-leather guys who have more guts than a dissected whale!" He cited their résumé of combat experience in North Africa, Sicily, and Normandy. "There was a good deal of truth," Remsburg wrote years later in his memoir, "in the theory that if you survived a month in combat your chances of making it through the war were vastly improved." He then cited some basic rules for survival: "Always dig in, the deeper the better. Keep moving. Don't bunch up. If possible keep away from your own tanks and artillery. They draw enemy fire. Try to avoid wooded areas. Tree bursts can be deadly [A tree burst occurs when a shell hits the tops of tall, densely packed trees, raining shrapnel and large tree limbs down on soldiers below]. Don't get too concerned with small arms fire—it inflicts only a small percentage of all casualties. Trust your instincts. Don't just stand there with your finger up, do something. Keep firing your rifle. Even if you don't hit anything, it tends to keep Jerry's head down. And above all, be lucky!'"

After the Americans had crossed the Roer on February 23, and until March 3, with the capture of the town of Krefeld, they covered thirty-three miles, captured eighty-three towns and villages and three cities. They took 4,187 prisoners and lost 1,748 men, 178 of them killed in action and the rest either wounded or injured in non-battle incidents. Remsburg would write, "Not many when compared to the battles of the Somme or Verdun in the First World War, or to Tarawa, Anzio, and D-Day in the present conflict. Yet far too many when some of those names on the casualty list were your friends."

On March 16, he wrote to his family of his new duties—now away from the battlefield and in the Public Relations Office of the 405th Infantry Regiment. He had been offered the position on March 10, and he took it with some reluctance, mainly because of the friendships he had made as an infantry soldier. His new duties were to contact men in the First Battalion, "pump them for interesting anecdotes and experiences," and then write up stories for the men's hometown newspapers. He knew how tight-lipped most soldiers were about what they had done and seen in battle. But he had no trouble getting GIs to open up, in part because he knew so many people already. He was in effect, one of them, now wearing a different helmet, so to speak.

And he made new buddies at Headquarters, including Foster Porter, a onetime rifleman just returned from the hospital after being wounded at Beeck and now assigned to limited duties. He was, as Remsburg wrote, "a typical 'all-American' boy. Originally from Idaho, he was very intelligent, personable, conscientious. Everyone liked Porter."

His office also distributed a daily newssheet, *Up Front News*, which offered a brief summary of world news, sports results, an editorial cartoon, and a commentary. They would write up the stories after listening to the BBC every night. "I went," he later wrote, "from being almost totally ignorant about what was going on in the world to reasonably well informed."

In April, the war was winding down, though there were still

Remsburg in Arnstadt, Germany, August 1945,
around the time he wrote a poignant letter
about the buddies he lost in the war.

dangers from night raiders, German planes that buzzed their positions. In a letter dated April 22, he wrote, in an indication of how calm things were, especially in the daylight hours, "If the sun comes out, Port and I are going to take some pictures. We have a lot of film for his camera.

We have collected some stuff we captured—helmets, officers' caps, dress swords and daggers, Nazi armbands and flags, etc. We are going to use these as 'props' for our photos."

Midmorning, May 7 the telephone rang in Remsburg's office. "Someone up at the river in Tangermunde thought we might want to watch the last battle of the European war, which was about to begin there." Soviet troops had arrived near the east bank of the Elbe to seal off a bridgehead there. It was a rare chance to see the Russians in action, and it would be safe; the vantage points were rooftops of houses on the American side. Port wanted to go. Remsburg hesitated, then decided, "I didn't need to experience any more war, even vicariously." Port went on alone, saying he wanted to get some pictures with his new camera.

About 2 P.M., Conrad, one of Remsburg's pals, came in. "After a very long time, with a look of anguish and in a voice barely above a whisper, he said, 'They just called from B Company. Porter was killed about a half hour ago.' I heard his words, but they didn't seem to make much sense. He cleared his throat with difficulty. 'They want us to go over to Tangermunde and pick up his body.' All of a sudden, I got very cold, almost numb. I couldn't seem to think, or even move. Conrad waited for a few moments, then came over and put his arm around my shoulder. 'Come on, let's go.'"

A Russian artillery shell had exploded almost on top of Porter and several other Americans observing the action from what they assumed was a safe vantage point on a rooftop. Porter was the only one killed; several other observers were injured. At the site, Remsburg and Conrad watched as several men picked up the body wrapped in a shroud and carried it to a waiting trailer. They gently placed Porter in the bottom of the trailer.

Remsburg and Conrad drove to Graves Registration in a town about twenty miles away. They rode in silence, but Remsburg's mind was racing with thoughts of his dead friend and unanswerable questions: "'Why Porter? He was one of the best.' And most difficult of all: 'Why just hours before the war ended?' These questions would be my close companions in the months ahead. As we drove, I tried not to hear Porter's body thumping around in the trailer behind us. I felt tears streaking my face. Of course, soldiers weren't supposed to cry."

After they dropped off Porter's body, Conrad spoke up on the way back to HQ:

"'You know, Chuckie, I've experienced a good many things in life that I didn't understand. Like today. Perhaps there is no answer, or the answer is there but we don't see it.' He paused to clear his throat. I began to understand that this had affected him deeply also. He continued: 'It seems to me that the best we can do is simply to go on, accepting that we don't always understand why these things happen.' Maybe he was right. I just didn't know. I had never hurt this much before."

That night, they gathered around the radio and listened to Winston Churchill's victory speech from London. The next day, May 8, would be observed as Victory in Europe day throughout the Allied world.

Later, Remsburg sat down to write a letter to Port's parents in Idaho, trying to relate what happened the day he was killed and to express the "goodness and courage of their son" as well as "the sense of loss which we all felt." A month later he received a reply from Port's mother. He wrote, "The thread which seemed to be woven throughout the letter was, again and again, why? To this I could offer no answer." Port was buried with thousands of other American soldiers in the U.S. Military Cemetery at Margraten, Holland. Foster Porter was nineteen years old.

Very late in the evening of V-E Day, Remsburg's captain came into his bedroom/office. Remsburg was still awake; he wouldn't sleep that night. After small talk, the captain told Remsburg that he wanted him to be part of a four-man detail going to Brussels the next day to pick up the officers' liquor rations.

Remsburg tried to decline the request, but the captain insisted, and he finally gave in. "It wasn't until long after the war," Remsburg wrote, "that I finally understood Capt. Schwabacher's depth of compassion. He saw an opportunity to get me away from the surroundings that would only prolong my depression."

Charles Remsburg was still in Germany, serving with the occupation forces, on August 15, when the Japanese surrender marked a second day of celebration and solemn remembrance that year. In a letter he wrote that day, he said, "My thoughts turn to the men who were my buddies—the men who lie under the white crosses in France and Holland—the soldiers who are not able to enjoy the happiness of this moment. They were my friends. It was they and not I who gave the one thing in the world that all of us hold most precious: their lives. If it were only possible for them to know that the things for which they fought, suffered, and died were not in vain. I believe that in some way, somehow, they do know. We can only hope that now, after they have sacrificed their lives, we—the ones who are still alive to carry on their fight—will once again make this world free for all men, always."

CHAPTER THREE

THE HEALERS

THEY ARE CHARGED WITH THE MISSION OF UNDOING THE DAMAGE OF war. The process starts with the corpsmen, working along the front lines to treat the wounded, risking their own lives in the process. It continues in the field hospitals and then farther away from the battle-field, in the convalescent facilities, staffed by tireless and resilient doc-tors and nurses. No job in any hospital is preparation enough for the relentless task of dealing with the wounded and dying of war.

Ruth Deloris Buckley worked in World War II about as close to the fighting as any nurse would get, and she paid the price. In Vietnam Julia Grabner Haskell and Carolyn Hisako Tanaka worked grueling, long shifts on wounded G.I.s, as did Wendy Wamsley Taines in the Persian Gulf, where she also had to tend to Kuwaiti and Iraqi casualties as well. Frances Liberty served abroad in three wars, main-taining a straight arrow professionalism while never forgetting her sense of humor. Eugene Curtin was in Europe as early as any American serving in World War I as a much-needed doctor attached to the British Expeditionary Force, while Dodson Curry came in on the tail end of Korea, witness to the exhausting effects of three years of fighting to a stalemate.

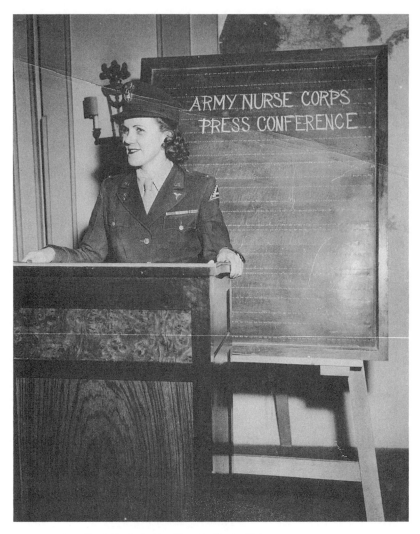

Ruth Deloris Buckley in Paris, February 2, 1945,
at a press conference marking the 44th anniversary
of the Army Nurse Corps.

RUTH DELORIS BUCKLEY:
INTO ACTION WITH THE BOYS

*"I always wondered what kind of a feeling it would be to think
you are a goner; but I found I wasn't excited,
or afraid, or felt any unusual emotion."*

T WO NURSES ON THE DECK OF A HOSPITAL SHIP IN THE
Mediterranean strike up a conversation. It is 1943, and they
are about to leave Tunisia for Italy, where Allied troops have
established a beachhead at Salerno, their destination.
Deloris, the nurse from Minnesota, worries about their ship attracting
torpedoes. Fern, the nurse from Nebraska, looks around the ship,
which is painted white with red crosses on its deck and sides and
assures Deloris that there's nothing to worry about, that they're clearly marked as a hospital ship and off-limits to enemy fire.

Born in 1918 in a small town in western Wisconsin and raised
across the border in Minnesota, Deloris Buckley graduated from the
University of Minnesota Nursing School at a time when, even in the
Midwest, it was hard to ignore the war being fought in far-off Europe.
Buckley signed up for the Army Nurse Corps right out of school and
insisted on overseas duty, "hoping that it wouldn't be too long before
I moved into action with the boys," as she would report in her mem-
oir, *Front Line Nurse*, written by war correspondent Michael Stern.

Front Line Nurse opens in September 1943 with Buckley sailing to
Italy from North Africa, which was her first duty assignment overseas

as part of the 95th Evacuation Hospital. "I realized that the war was, to me, no more than a far-off, impersonal conflict; that actually I knew very little about it," she admitted. She had been nursing battle casualties at a hospital on the beach at Ain el Turk, Algeria. There she treated wounded from the 82nd Airborne Division, which had participated in the Allied invasion of Sicily. "I heard countless stories from the wounded about the terrors of war," she said. "I could see it only as some awful, unknown experience that a number of my carefree, happy-go-lucky paratrooper boyfriends went into; some to come back broken in body, some in spirit."

Off duty she "had a lovely time," swimming in the Mediterranean, frequenting snack bars that were open all hours, going out on dates. "We had enough of them to become spoiled," she said. "It was a far cry from the little girl who was brought up in Spring Valley, Wisconsin, and who, just a few years ago, was playing the clarinet in the high school orchestra."

The *Newfoundland,* the British hospital ship Buckley boarded to take her and her fellow nurses to Salerno, Italy, was painted white, with large red crosses on its sides and deck. While it was still anchored in the Tunisian port of El Bizerte, Buckley spent time in her room updating her seven-year diary. Up on deck, she expressed her fears of a torpedo attack to Lt. Fern Wingerd of Omaha, Nebraska, and Wingerd reassured her.

On September 13, the ship moved into the Bay of Salerno. The Allies hadn't yet totally secured the port, and, Buckley reported, "I could see the pinpoints of colorless flame flash from the muzzles of the German 88's that dotted the semicircle of hills around the harbor. German shells exploded in the water around us. Some of the projectiles straddled the ship and it was a miracle that they missed."

The skipper of the *Newfoundland* was wary of mines in the harbor, so he turned the ship around and sailed to a point 30 miles offshore, out of range of the batteries. Just after dusk, Buckley heard the sound of an airplane motor. She assumed it was a friendly plane, then watched in horror as the pilot lowered the plane's nose and went into a power dive. 'It wasn't until then that I recognized it as a Nazi dive-bomber," she recalled. "I saw him release a stick of three bombs and I hit the deck." The first bomb landed off the port side, and the explosion almost lifted the ship out of the water. The second bomb landed squarely in the middle of the red cross that was painted on the deck.

"I don't remember hearing the third bomb go off," Buckley said. "I don't imagine I would have heard it even if it did explode because the roar of the flames was far too loud."

The ship's water hoses were destroyed, and fires spread out of control. Buckley scrambled into a lifeboat with Fern Wingerd and 70 other people. They tried to row toward Salerno, but when they got within range of enemy guns, they realized they would have to turn back. A British destroyer picked them up and returned them to Bizerte.

She had lost her seven-year diary, as well as a set of parachute wings her boyfriend had given her, a number of souvenirs of Africa, and all the clothes she had packed for the trip. A story from a Minnesota newspaper included in her collection was headlined:

Lt. Deloris Buckley of Waverly
Loses Clothing but Saves Life in
Sinking in Mediterranean

The article reported that Buckley wrote home two days after the sinking to let her parents know she was in need of some personal items, discreetly omitting the reason why. (The paper obtained details of the bombing and rescue from an Associated Press reporter.) In a follow-up story a few weeks later, the paper quoted from an October 3rd letter Buckley wrote to her sister: "We have been debating whether we should write home about our experience, but now that it is over and we are safe I guess there is no cause to worry. I wrote you once that I had been in everything except a lifeboat, but now I've been in that too." After revealing the fact that her ship had been bombed and sunk, Buckley went on:

"I always wondered what kind of a feeling it would be to think you are a goner; but I found I wasn't excited, or afraid, or felt any unusual emotion. I had two sane thoughts—one when the bomb struck when I thought of my mom and hoped she wouldn't take it too hard, the other when I was up on deck. I rolled my pants up in case we had to jump into the water. I went down in the lifeboat when they lowered it, although some of the kids climbed down the ladders and ropes.

"The kids tell me I was a picture they will never forget. They were worried and were sitting on the ship that picked us up when I came aboard. They all went into hysterics. I was barefooted—my pants legs rolled up—my life jacket on upside down (and I had it on just as tight as I could), my helmet was on at an angle—and on my face was an expression of don't-give-a-heck bewilderment. I think I aged 10 years in that hour."

Buckley was frustrated that she hadn't made it to Salerno, especially because some officers in her unit had gone ahead on a separate ship and had made landfall successfully. A week later, Buckley boarded an LCI (Landing Craft Infantry) for what she remembered as a "bouncy three days' journey" to Italy. This time they landed at Paestum, a resort town between Salerno and Naples. She got a ride in a truck to the mess hall, where she was reunited with the officers in her company. The nurses' quarters were staked out in a "muddy bleak wilderness" area of the beach. Buckley recalled,

"We got to work at once, turning an ordinary army pyramidal tent into home. Ration boxes made a dressing table. We covered it with scatter scarfs, which were held down by feminine nick-nacks. Pictures lent a touch of color. We put a shade over the light and grass rugs over the floor. A long ammunition box made an attractive pantry. We managed to pretty up the potbellied stove. Outside one of the girls collected rocks and made a path to the door."

She was assigned to the pre-op tent, but she wasn't very busy because there were so few casualties. Then one night the camp was hit by a tornado. During the storm, Buckley and her fellow nurses made sure the patients were okay, and once the storm subsided they headed back to their tent. "What had been a touch of home was now an absolute shambles," she said. A bag containing her good clothes—those she had left back in Africa when she tried to cross on the *Newfoundland* "now looked as though it had been swallowed by a mud mixing machine. I felt so helpless, I burst into tears."

On October 5, four days after Allied tanks rolled into Naples, Buckley's unit was loaded onto trucks and driven there. "We must have been the first American women seen by the Italians," she recalled, "because the sight of us made them gasp. A few ran after our trucks yelling, 'Oh, Signorina.'" Much of the city was in ruins, either destroyed by the retreating Germans or blasted by Allied artillery. As a parting gesture, the Germans had wrecked many vessels in the bay. The

95th Evac set up shop at a large German hospital. Buckley's strongest memory of the building was the profusion of bedbugs. "It was so filthy," she recalled, "it took us days of hard labor to clean it up."

And the Germans hadn't totally given up. Artillery still pounded the city, and planes swooped in for bombardments. "I stood on the balcony of the hospital," Buckley recalled, "and watched the Nazi planes zoom in under the flares. Long shadows of the ships skimmed over the city. I could see streaks of flames shoot upwards as the ack-ack batteries fired away at the target." One night, she was standing near a glass door when a patient, who had heard the familiar sound of a nearby bomb coming in, yelled at her to move to the center of the room. The resulting concussion of the bomb blast shattered the door she had been standing next to.

Buckley was impressed with the fortitude of the men whose wounds she was treating. As she told Michael Stern of her patients:

"They have the real guts. I have seen them wheeled in suffering from every conceivable wound. There were boys who knew they were going to lose a leg—or maybe both—and not making any fuss at all. There was the soldier who knew he had but an hour to live, calmly asking me for a cigarette. My hand trembled more than his when I handed it over to him. It was all I could do to keep from crying. Yet you couldn't feel sorry for them. It went much deeper than that. My heart was filled with a feeling of pride and admiration that was so strong that sometimes tears came to my eyes. I'd like to make a point of that. They were not tears of pity."

After long days working at the hospital, she was ready for a break and asked permission for some leave time to tour the city. But the Germans had left behind booby traps, which were being discovered— sometimes with fatal consequences—all the time. A typhus epidemic swept Naples, restricting movement and contact even further. Finally, at Thanksgiving, she and several nurse pals were allowed some leave. They played tourist, taking a boat to the Isle of Capri and then a flat-bottomed boat into the island's Blue Grotto.

Back in Naples, she learned the 95th was moving again. Their new location was a field north of Capua, a site she recalled as one of "utter desolation," with knee-deep mud. "It was here, too, that I got my first real taste of the bloody business of war," she recalled. They were receiving heavy casualties from fighting at the Volturno River, where the

Germans had established a strong defensive line. Buckley was assigned to night duty, from 8 P.M. to 8 A.M.. Working alongside her were three good pals: Gert Morrow, whom Buckley recalled as a sweet girl devoted to her family; the Assistant Charge Nurse, Lieutenant Carrie Sheet, a vivacious lady who was "always fixing parties for us" and was married to a Naval officer on duty in the Pacific; and Blanche Sigman, the Charge Nurse. Sigman, Buckley remembered, fought hard for her girls, always investigating a complaint before meting out punishment to her staff. She recalled that Sigman once read the riot act to a colonel who tried to impose a curfew on her nurses.

As the calendar turned into 1944, plans for a New Year's Day party had to be scrapped when their hospital was hit by another tornado. The storm destroyed many of the special rations they had accumulated for the festivities, and they had to eat their holiday meals out of cans.

A few days later, the 95th was ordered to pack up for a trip by boat. No destination was given, but from what they were told to pack, it sounded like they were going to make another amphibious landing. They drove back to Naples, and in spite of reports of the continued threat of typhus they had a last-night party. "We were seasoned veterans," Buckley said. "We had been through the thick of it at Capua, and there just wasn't anything worse. At least that's what most of us thought."

Their destination was Anzio, 32 miles south of Rome. Five days after the beachhead there was established in late January, Buckley and her colleagues landed, and furious unloading ensued, as they tried to forestall an expected counterattack. Soon the German planes came in. "I dug away furiously in the sand," she recalled, "and only had a shallow pit when the Jerry bombers came over. I threw myself into the hole and buried my face in the damp sand." After the raid was over, she climbed aboard an amphibious vehicle waiting to take nurses to the staging ground for the hospital across the harbor.

Now she was on day duty. Air bombardments continued both day and night, and the shelling seemed to be indiscriminate. After three days the hospital was moved three miles inland to avoid getting hit. Buckley could only recall that she was too busy taking care of wounded soldiers to think about the shelling.

"The American girl is a very adaptive creature," she noted. "I was amazed to discover that I could get used to this life. All fear drained out of me except at the odd moments when I appeared to be the target of a bombardment."

On February 7, at about 3 in the afternoon, she was putting a post-op dressing on an abdominal case when she heard a plane flying very low. Buckley turned to Sergeant Smith, saying, "Smitty, will you hand me…"

"I never finished the sentence. There was a mighty roar that sounded as though the heavens had fallen down around my head. My whole body went numb. I remember thinking in a somewhat detached way that it was strange for me to be lying on the floor. I somehow managed to get to my feet. My arms and fingers felt stiff. It seemed strange that I couldn't move and my eyes moved downwards. They noted without any surprise that my clothing was drenched with blood. I thought then that I was hit in the abdomen and that an artery had been severed."

She had actually been wounded in the thigh; a piece of shrapnel had gone all the way through. She clamped off her own bleeding. She soon learned that in her friend Fern's tent, the damage was much worse. A healthy soldier visiting his wounded brother was killed. Gert Morrow lay on the floor, bleeding to death, and Blanche Sigman had been killed outright. One major lost his arm. All told, the blast had killed 26 people—doctors, nurses, and patients.

She recalled,

"I lay in an ambulance alongside Smitty. His face had a white, drawn look. He twisted his head so that he faced me. 'What about a cigarette?' he asked. I got one out, lit it and handed it over to him. He drew two deep puffs and then it fell from his fingers. Smitty was dead."

The German pilot who had dropped the bombs was shot down a minute later by a Spitfire. After the pilot parachuted to the ground and was captured, he explained that because the Spitfire was in pursuit of him, he had jettisoned his payload to elude the British aircraft, oblivious to where the bomb landed.

Three days later she and Fern, who was also severely wounded, were evacuated on an LST to Naples. "The British were in charge of the ship," Buckley told an Armed Forces Radio reporter in May. "They certainly were good to us. They couldn't do enough for their 'sisters,' as they called us." They learned that the pilot of the German plane who had bombed them was also on the ship. Fern Wingerd told the reporter that "he was cared for just like everybody else."

They spent 11 weeks in the hospital in Naples, then were moved to a nurses' rest home in a beautiful villa near Oran, Algeria, run by a countess. A newspaper clipping dated May 17 described them as eager to return to the front. "This place is really heavenly," Buckley told the reporter, "but we feel we have no right to be resting here when there is so much to be done and so few nurses to do it." They were asked one day by a colonel if they wanted to go back to the front, and they both said yes. *Front Line Nurse* concludes with Deloris Buckley back in Italy at work. She mentions that she just read a newspaper item about a new hospital ship launched in the U.S., christened the U.S. Hospital Ship *Blanche F. Sigman*.

DODSON CURRY:
THE RELUCTANT PHYSICIAN

"I was in a state of denial....
To my surprise I learned that several of the passengers
had the same emotional dilemma."

NEWLY WED PHYSICIAN, WHO WAS JUST BEGINNING TO
expand his practice and had started planning his first house,
had to put his plans on hold in 1952 when he got the call
to serve in Korea. Even after he got on a plane for the Far
East, Dodson Curry couldn't believe that he was going off to war.
Though he was stationed for a time in a field hospital near the front
lines, perhaps his most memorable experience in the service was a
two-tiered party in Japan.

The twenty-nine-year-old Curry had just celebrated Christmas of
1951 with his new wife when he received a letter from his draft board,
instructing him to report to the Alabama Military District Office, in
his hometown of Birmingham, for the purpose of induction into the
inactive reserves. "I then recalled reading something in the local paper
about some disturbance in a faraway place named Korea," he later
wrote, "but this news was usually relegated to the back pages of the
paper and caused me no concern."

Curry took his physical and waited. And waited. "Several months
passed, and I heard nothing," he wrote in a memoir. When he called
the Military District Office, he was told that he was in fact a patient in
a military hospital. Assuring them that was not the case, Curry was
then told to report for another physical at Fort McPherson in Georgia.

On April 25, 1952, Curry received notice that he had been found acceptable for induction into the armed services. More waiting ensued, and after a few more months, "I was sure that the whole episode was just a formality and nothing else would be forthcoming."

The second week in November, Curry answered a knock on his door to find a man with a telegram that ordered him to report for military training in Texas—in three days. Since Texas was a two-day drive from his home, he had one day to secure his files, clear his desk, and pack his furniture.

Curry reported for duty at Fort Sam Houston in San Antonio on November 19. "I found that I was in the class with about thirty-five other disgruntled physicians whose circumstances were just the same or worse than mine," he wrote in his memoir. "The first instructor entered the room and said, 'Most of you would give one million dollars not to be here; however, when you have finished your tour of duty you will not take ten million for the experience.' At this time I had no idea of how true this statement was."

The doctors were given more than a dozen books and manuals to read and were put through physical training exercises, including having to crawl on their bellies while a machine-gunner fired live rounds over their heads. As Curry recalled, "The military expertise of this group of physicians was summed up by two small children who happened to pass while we were trying to learn to march in step and not hurt anyone in the process. One kid said to the other, 'Gee, what a sloppy bunch of soldiers.'"

Although he was allowed to request a duty area, Curry said, "We knew that nearly 80 percent or more of the class would be going to the Far East, Japan, or Korea, due to the war in the region." In January he was ordered to proceed to Camp Stoneman in Pittsburg, California. He saw few of his classmates from Fort Sam Houston there. On the morning of January 19, 1953, he and about thirty-five officers boarded a Pan American plane to Korea. On board were two civilians: June Christie, a singer with the Stan Kenton Band, and Herb Jeffries, who once sang with Duke Ellington's orchestra. Both were going to Korea to perform in USO shows.

"All during this boring flight," Curry recalled, "I was in a state of denial. I was sure that when the plane landed in Japan that someone

*Dodson Curry served in the Korean War and later,
when this picture was taken, with a rescue unit in Japan.*

would tell me that a mistake was made, and I would be sent back to
the states. To my surprise I learned that several of the passengers had
the same emotional dilemma."

The plane landed near Tokyo, and after a couple of days at a replacement depot, Curry was taken by train to Beppu, where he was assigned
to a BOQ (Bachelor Officers Quarters), his home for the next six
months. It was not exactly stressful duty; he worked every sixth day in
sick call and every sixth weekend, as well as supervising athletic events.

As an officer, Curry was also assigned to certain social events. On
one occasion, the senior officer told him that it was his turn to supervise the company party. When Curry asked what was involved, he was
assured that it was an easy job and that another officer would tell him
all he needed to know. The second officer confirmed that the assignment was not a difficult one, "but it would be an experience that
would be long remembered." He assured Curry that he would accompany him to the event.

On the Saturday of the party, the officer told Curry his driver would pick him up at six o'clock. This seemed a bit early, since the party was not scheduled to begin until seven, but Curry was told he would need time to check out the vehicles and arrange ambulances near the door. They drove up a mountain road to the Kokusai Hotel, which was hosting the party.

His first surprise came when he saw a huge quantity of alcohol stacked in cases on the floor in the middle of the hotel lobby. When he asked his companion how many people were expected, the officer assured him that "all questions would be answered shortly." At about 6:45, Curry heard the rumblings of several 2½ ton Army trucks. The vehicles stopped outside the front entrance to the hotel, next to the ambulances, and about fifty soldiers poured out. The entrance doors to the hotel lobby were locked, and the men pressed themselves up against the glass, waiting to be let in.

As Curry recalled, "At exactly the hour of seven the doors were unlocked and everyone on the inside at this moment stood aside to prevent being trampled by the enthusiastic partygoers as they rushed through the front doors of the lobby. This sight I was totally unprepared for. All four members of the supervisory group coolly and calmly took seats near the wall and asked me to join them and enjoy the show. The sight that ensued proved to be an interesting spectacle. The first men to enter went immediately to the cases of whiskey and with one sweeping motion tore open the cases and each one extracted a bottle of whiskey, which was opened and drunk with great gulps while standing in the middle of the floor. At the same time cases of beer were similarly being attacked. Within a time frame of ten minutes the entire floor was filled with soldiers drinking with reckless abandon. Some had a can of beer in each hand, others with a quart whisky bottle in hand, all were drinking like sharks in a feeding frenzy. I looked at the other supervisors, and I was told that in just a few minutes the party would settle down.

"About five minutes later another occurrence transpired that was not totally unexpected, so it came as no big surprise; it was the suddenness of the sequence that made it amusing. These men started to fall to the floor as if by command. It seemed that they fell to the floor as if hit by snipers. Some just seemed to melt to the floor as if pressed down by the weight of the alcohol, others just toppled over with a thud. In a short time the floor of the lobby looked like most of the company had been mowed down by withering machine-gun fire."

One of the supervisors pointed out to Curry that a soldier in the middle of the room was wearing a shoulder patch from another out-fit. "Before I could ask what difference did it make, it was said that he would not last another five minutes. Just as this statement was made, this soldier was hit by a vicious left hook to the jaw." The soldier fell to the floor, and a medical aid man went to check on him. Now Curry realized why the ambulances were parked outside.

Curry ordered the unconscious man loaded into the ambulance, and when he started to tell the driver to take the soldier to the hospital, he was stopped by one of the supervisors, who informed him the ambulance couldn't leave yet because it wasn't full. At that moment there was a huge crash, and Curry turned to see two soldiers come fly-ing through the glass front of the lobby, taking four panels of glass with them and landing facefirst in a fish pond. The medical aide turned the men over to keep them from drowning, and then with some assistance loaded them into the ambulance. Curry was then told that the ambu-lance was full and he could send it along.

By now the party was about thirty minutes old. Curry noticed sev-eral groups of "more mature" soldiers standing along the wall. Some had been watching the activities, others were just chatting among themselves. But once the glass front of the hotel was destroyed, that seemed to be the signal for cleaning up. The upright soldiers began hauling the incapacitated ones to the trucks and loading them. "These men were stacked like logs of wood until the truck was full, then were driven back to the barracks, where another crew unloaded them. How they survived the journey is a mystery, but they all did."

In the hotel, the debris had been swept away, the floor cleaned, and tables re-arranged. Curry's companion told him the party had now settled down, and he was leaving because there was nothing else to supervise. Curry walked him to his jeep, saying he had never seen such a large quantity of alcohol consumed in such a short time. "Yes, I know," said the officer, getting into his jeep.

When Curry re-entered the lobby, "it seemed like I was in the wrong place." Every table was now covered with a tablecloth, there were cou-ples sipping drinks and talking quietly. "Apparently the older and wiser soldiers had their female companions secreted away in the hotel rooms," he wrote, "to wait until the debauchery ran its course, then bringing them to the tables only after the drunken revelry had met its own end." The party proceeded quietly and without further incident.

The next day Curry happened to see one of the "rowdy revelers." The man saluted him, and when Curry noticed a couple of bumps and bruises on his face, he inquired about the man's health. "His reply was that he was fine. As he left he added that he sure had a good time at the party."

A day or two later Curry saw his officer companion from the party. He asked the man about the damages to the hotel. Did the hotel host these parties all the time? The officer assured him that the hotel's owner was well aware of the nature of these parties, and he charged a break-age fee, which was collected before each party started. "As a matter of fact," Curry was told, "this fee was more than adequate, thereby making him a profit with each outing." Curry asked his driver to take him to the Kokusai, where he saw that the lobby was perfectly restored.

Late in June 1953, Curry and a group of medical officers and med-ical service officers got orders to move out to Korea. They were to be attached to the 187th Airborne Regimental Team. They left their camp at 1 A.M. and were flown to an airstrip in Korea, landing while it was still dark. The troops were then served a breakfast of hot coffee and a can of corned beef hash. "For some reason," Curry recalled, "still a mystery to me, this would rank as one of the all-time best meals I have ever had."

For several days, they stayed in a holding area behind the lines. His first casualty was a Korean civilian. There had been a rash of robberies by civilians sneaking into squad tents at night while soldiers were sleeping, slitting open their duffel bags with razors and stealing the contents. This man had been caught by a guard, who ordered him, in both Korean and English, to halt, and when the thief advanced on him, the guard shot him. There was nothing to do for the thief; he was dead.

The next morning, the Medical Company commander, Captain Miller, asked Curry if he'd like to go for a ride. Curry recalled, "I knew the question meant, Get in the jeep; we're going somewhere." In misty and foggy weather they drove over a bumpy road until they came to a bunker. Miller made a phone call there, and then assured his driver it was safe to go on. He told Curry that they were on a reconnaissance mission to determine where the 2nd Battalion medical aid station would be set up. The call was to see if there was any action on the front lines. Curry saw plenty of evidence that they were close to the front lines, but he also realized that his commander knew it was safe to venture out that far; they wouldn't take any enemy fire because of the poor visibility.

That night, Curry and his unit moved out to set up their aid station. After they erected two-man hex tents, Curry and his tentmate, a sergeant, lay down on their cots to put their feet up. Within five seconds, shooting began. "Having not been in combat before," he wrote, "the horrendous sound of the mortar round being fired nearby was a sound I had never heard before." He wrote, "After a few of these explosions, the battle-wise sergeant heard a different sound and shouted in a very loud voice, 'Incoming.' He left the tent at the same instant, and I followed. An enemy mortar round had just exploded a few yards from the tent, leaving a large crater. I dove headfirst in the crater."

An eerie stillness ensued. In the distance, Curry heard a trooper calling out the names of the men in his squad. One by one each answered. When there was no answer, a search was made of the area. Casualties were treated and evacuated to the local MASH unit by whatever vehicles remained undamaged by the attack. Curry was advised not to sleep in a vehicle because when they were hit, the secondary shrapnel was as dangerous as the shell fragments. The doctors were also advised to paint over the red crosses on all their ambulances, because they gave the enemy an aiming point. "This was strictly against the rules of the Geneva Convention," Curry wrote, "but this was a vicious war."

Soon, Curry's unit moved into a small bunker formerly occupied by the ROK (Republic of Korea) army. Living in a bunker offered more security than a tent, but their quarters were rather cramped, the ceilings so low they had to learn to walk in a stooped position at all times. Living with the imminent threat of enemy fire, "emotions were a constant state of fear mixed with alertness, which in turn led to constant fatigue." It was mid-summer, and they were all dressed in full battle gear. The only place to bathe was a stream in a clearing, but it was within sight of enemy guns. "Under these conditions," Curry recalled, "one cannot imagine the odor that was generated."

After that first night's attack, they settled into a rather predictable routine. He recalled, "The CCF (Chinese Communist Force) would routinely fire five mortar rounds at daybreak, five more rounds at noon, and end the day with another five rounds at dusk. It was noticed that the enemy would not fire unless there were three or more soldiers gathered at the stream in the clearing, where the brave troopers ventured out to bathe. The enemy would fire if they saw an officer in this clearing; as a result, all officers were told to remove any insignia that would designate their rank."

The fact was, the war was winding down. Curry's unit wasn't very busy, tending to soldiers with minor wounds. No one, at least in his area, seemed to want to risk his life in any further action.

On the night of July 26, Curry heard "a lot of activity by both the enemy and the American forces." There was more than usual chatter on the phone lines, and big guns down the hill from their position were firing constantly, "unusual for them."

In the early dawn, he was surprised to see the company commander standing in front of his bunker. The commander told Curry he was concerned about their position because the enemy had broken through the line the night before, and he thought their position might be overrun. Curry assured him that all was okay, and the commander drove away.

The next day, the war ended with the announcement of the signing of an armistice. "There are no words in any language that could express our feelings at this turn of events," Curry wrote. "Utter joy and delight would be an understatement."

EUGENE CURTIN:
HOLDING BACK NOTHING

*"It's all gigantic, the scale this business is run on,
and the only pity is that it's not directed
to another purpose than destruction."*

MONG THE FIRST AMERICANS TO SERVE ON THE GROUND IN the first World War were physicians attached to the British Expeditionary Force. Britain had lost so many medical personnel in the initial three years of the war that by April 1917, when the U.S. entered the conflict, little time was wasted in contacting America for medical support. Among those doctors who served in England and France was Eugene Curtin, whose frequent letters to his family painted a bleak picture of the war.

In July 1917, Curtin was in Washington, D.C., for Army training, suffering through a typical capital summer. His discomfort was made worse by an adverse reaction to several inoculations; he complained of a "splitting headache and a temperature of 104," adding that "I'll be happy but lonesome wherever I am."

In the fall Curtin was stationed in Stourbridge, England, at the Southern General Hospital. He was in charge of a ward of 150 patients. About twice a week, they received a trainload of 200 patients from France, thirty-six to forty-eight hours after they were wounded, with, he wrote, "the mud of the front still on them." The work they did was "all kinds except abdominal and brain." He went on to note that "the Tommies are a most intelligent class to work with and when it comes to nerve you got to hand it to those boys.

After what they have been through operations and pain are pie to them, and as long as they have a 'cig' they don't care what happens. It is different from a civil hospital where you hear moaning from the least little thing; you can tear these boys apart and they won't make a sound but will thank you when you are through."

Despite his lofty opinion of the British soldier, when Curtin got to France in October—he was stationed at Rouen late that month—he expressed a preference for his new hosts. "From what I have seen of France I am inclined to like it much better than England," he wrote his mother on October 30. "The French people are of a more friendly disposition, more interesting and attractive. The poorest of them look neat and clean, which cannot be said for the poor English classes. As for the belles of the towns they sure know to wear the clothes, and I think even the swells of the small villages get their clothes in 'gay Paree.'"

He was now working with an ambulance company consisting of nine officers (three of them Americans) and 250 men. They were the first medical company in back of the lines, taking immediate casualties and then moving them on to the rear.

"It is quite exciting here," he wrote to his brother Vince on November 17, adding,

"All the time you can hear the artillery, which keeps you up day and night. In the air are planes, numerous ones, all the time, while over the roads, which are thick with mud, moves as much traffic as you can see on Fifth Avenue on a busy day. It's all gigantic, the scale this business is run on, and the only pity is that it's not directed to another purpose than destruction." Curtin was optimistic that once America entered the war with a serious force of fighting men, the tide would turn in the Allies' favor.

After a battle around Thanksgiving Day, he wrote on December 6 to his mother, "The real details of the battle and the sights one sees are things I for one want to forget as soon as possible. It's not sport or game any more but just a terrible bloody slaughter."

Later that month, he began a letter to his cousin Clare with the same feelings about the "slaughter" of war, but a couple of pages later, he admits to being fascinated when watching the planes in combat. "The most thrilling thing one can see is a fight between planes thousands of feet in the air, and I [do not] know of, nor can I think of, any sadder sight than to see one of those graceful and gallant birds, be it friend or enemy, come crashing to earth in flames. It's a heart-stabbing thing to see, and over here one sees it often." He spoke of the thrill of watching a plane attack one of the observation balloons and seeing two black specks leap from beneath the burning balloon to parachute safely to earth.

On December 28, the Scranton *Times* reprinted a letter Curtin wrote to his sister Kate, in which he described the steady procession of casualties from the front: "Then the wounded began to come back. Some wrecked forever, others soon to be no more, all flushed with excitement, but glad to be at last out of that awful hell. We were in the line five days, and it was five days of horror. They speak of the grandeur of war. There is no such thing; it's just a deadly, sickening, bloody slaughter."

Unlike some soldiers, who tried to spare their families, and especially their parents, the gruesome details of war, Curtin was forthright in his correspondence. In April 1918, he wrote to his mother with a vivid description of a battle. "The Boche made it rather unpleasant for us by distributing some of his perfume, in the shape of gas bombs, about, and as a result I have picked up a lovely pair of eyes and a voice that was only a whisper."

Two days before "the show started," his unit was awakened at 4:40 A.M. by a barrage of high-velocity shells. Curtin complained, "The one thing I don't like about these battles is that they start out so early." The old-timers called this opening bombardment the worst they had seen. It continued until 10 A.M., at which point the infantry tried to attack under a smoke barrage. As Curtin saw it, the Germans accomplished nothing except to lose "a terrible lot of men."

At two the next morning, his division did the attacking; had they kept their line straight, Curtin thought, they would have advanced much farther and done more damage. A couple of days later, it was down to small arms and machine-gun fire. "It was out in the open and much more exciting than the old trench stuff, for you could see a lot more," he wrote. "In the daytime the whole countryside was smoking, and as far as the eye could see there were huge fires where our dumps were being blown up before we left them. The nights were fairly quiet, but we were out in the blue and without any accommodations so we did not sleep very much."

In May, when he wrote to his aunt Mary, he was more optimistic than in months, with the arrival of American troops. "All through the winter we few American medical officers with the British have been reading the papers about what the United States was doing. We knew there were many troops being sent over but hard as we looked we never could see any. During the trying days of March, when the Hun had us two to one, we wished so hard some of them could be up with us and give us a little help. They didn't come. Now all is changed and that's why we feel good. As I look out on the quiet, dusty road a few yards away I see a group of tanned, finely built, businesslike-looking young chaps who speak the good old U.S.A. as it is spoken around Harlem or on 42nd Street. You may depend we are glad to see them." With the arrival of the Americans, Curtin's letters also seem to lighten in tone as well as content. He was more amused than dismayed when on July 16 he finally received his Christmas package from home—minus a box of matches, which had been removed by the military censor.

On November 14, he wrote to his mother about the Armistice. "It's certainly a great relief to have it over, for you may say what you want to, it's rather a strain to be at war, and it sure is an unnatural existence. While one doesn't worry an awful lot, yet someplace way back in your mind is the thought that the next minute you might get it. To have it all quiet and without the continual roar of artillery alone seems to add a few years to one's life."

Curtin stayed in France at least until the spring of 1919. The last letter in his collection, to his mother, is dated April 18. In it, he did not express regret about having to stay with the Army of the Occupation: "Rather than being down-hearted I personally feel more determined than ever to see the Boche get his just due, and it certainly can and will be done if everyone sticks it out."

In an undated letter to his mother, likely written in October 1918, as the war was winding down, Curtin wrote eloquently of a rare day of undiluted joy:

"The other day we had what I think was the best experience of the war, for we took a small-sized town, and after it was out of range of Huns' guns many French civilians who had been ruled by the Hun for over four years emerged from their cellars and dugouts into a land that was France. To see their beaming faces and hear their expression of joy and happiness was enough to repay anyone for coming to this war! The first days we were there everyone from the very old and bent women to the small kids saluted an officer when he passed, and when they were asked about it they said if they did not salute the German officers they were beaten or otherwise punished. They were only allowed to leave their homes at certain hours on certain days; all they had to eat was a very small quantity of terrible bread, a good part of which they said was sawdust, and some few vegetables, which they raised themselves. The Germans took everything of the slightest value from them, made them work for a few pennies a day and in general went out of their way to make the four years as horrible a hell as they possibly could.

"And then after we got there, to see the change. The main occupation of the Tommies was to see how much food they—the French—could take without bursting, and after four years without a real good meal some of them sure did hang up records. They called our bread cake, and from the way they put away bully beef I guess they thought it was turkey. To see the soldiers chumming about with them and talking Tommie French, patting the old ladies on the back, making a fuss about the kids and stuffing them with chocolate, swapping stories with the ancient men and feeding them cigarettes by the boxful; to see the old tattered flags of France that had been hidden away all the time, waving again in free air from the windows of the houses and from the Hotel de Ville—the flags of France and England, our own stars and stripes—and then in the afternoon toward sunset in the pretty little church to see them all attending Benediction with the old bent priest, who perhaps was their main guidance all through their martyrdom; to hear them all singing the "O Salutaris" with the organ played by a British officer—Yes, it certainly was the very best day that I have had since I came over here."

JULIA GRABNER HASKELL: THE LITTLE SISTER

"They were the best patients I have ever taken care of."

T HE DESIRE TO SERVE ONE'S COUNTRY IN TIMES OF WAR ISN'T limited to warriors. Doctors and nurses answer the call to duty as well, even when there are deeply held doubts about the justness of the cause. Julia Grabner, a twenty-two-year-old New York nurse, asked to serve in Vietnam at a time when many potential draftees were looking for ways to avoid serving at all. Her one year in country affected her in ways that took many decades to come to terms with.

Fresh out of New York's Bellevue Nursing School in 1965, Julia Grabner saw her career take off when she landed a staff job at the Elmhurst General Hospital in Queens, New York, where she grew up. Grabner was soon promoted to acting head nurse in the Psychiatric Department, but when the nurse whose place she was taking returned, she had to go back to being a staff nurse again. "With the experience I had, I didn't want to do that," she recalled forty years later, "so I thought I could be of help in Vietnam. I used to walk to work, and going one way I would pass the [military] recruiters' office. I would talk to them, asking which branch of the service would get me to Vietnam. The Army was the only one that would give me a guaranteed assignment, so I joined them."

It was 1967, with American involvement—and criticism of the war—escalating. There was also a growing need for medical personnel. She didn't tell anyone of her decision until she had signed the papers. "My

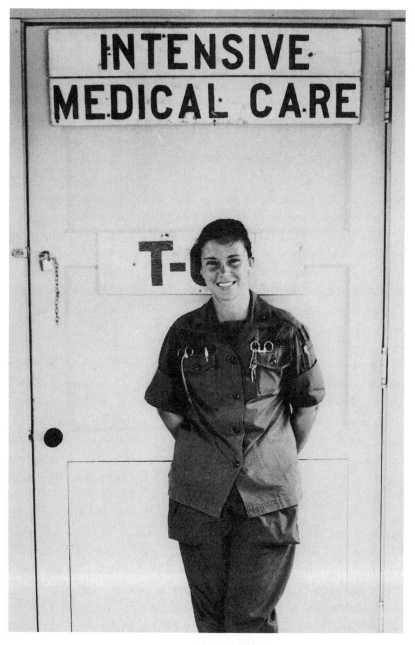

*Julia Grabner in 1969 in Tuy Hoa, Vietnam,
her second duty station, the 91st Evacuation Hospital.
She was the last woman working there before it closed.*

mother said it felt like I had hit her in the stomach with a sledgehammer when I told her I was going off to war. My friends thought I was crazy, but that didn't stop me. I guess I had to feel helpful. I also promised God two years of service if He helped me get through nursing school. He tapped me on the shoulder and said it was time to collect that promise."

Grabner was commissioned as a second lieutenant and shipped out for basic training on January 2, 1968. What she remembers from that experience is her serial number, because of one drill: she was placed in a gas chamber from which she could be released only after reciting that number. She recalled her daily routine: "We marched in formation in the morning, went to classes all day, and partied in the evenings. That was a new thing for me, to become a party animal."

After basic, Grabner recalled in a 2003 interview, "I did something that they said never to do in the service, and that was to volunteer." But she knew what she wanted: a posting at Fort Campbell, Kentucky, home of the 101st Airborne and a clear pathway to Vietnam. At Campbell, she trained in the base's emergency room to get a feel for working under stress and pressure, and in June she shipped out. Her port of embarkation was Travis Air Force Base in California, where "they ushered me into this hanger, which was just filled with the most gorgeous men our country has. I thought I had died and gone to heaven. An officer came over to me and said, 'You look like you could use some protection and help. I'll be your brother until we get to Nam.'" He sat with her on the plane, and at their first stop in Hawaii, "my brother got me something to drink as I wrote a postcard home telling my parents I was underway." She can't recall his name, but, she said in her interview, "I hope he made it home."

Grabner was one of two women on that Continental Airlines flight. Her legs were too short to reach the floor from her seat, and when the plane made its second stop, in the Philippines, she found that the sudden change in humidity made her legs swell up so badly that she could barely make it back up the stairs into the plane. Between the Philippines and Vietnam, the mood among the soldiers turned pensive. Grabner sensed that all around her men were wondering what they might experience in the next year, and whether they would return. "I had this inner peace knowing that I was coming back, and I looked around at the other faces and wondered how many of them would also."

The bus Grabner and her fellow recruits took from the airport to their first quarters was stifling hot, because the air conditioner was broken. When someone suggested opening the windows, the driver replied, "Sure, if you want a grenade to be lobbed into the bus and be blown up before you get to where you're going, go right ahead and do it."

Grabner got more attention that night on a visit with a couple of other nurses to the local officers club. No sooner had they sat down at the bar than a long line of beers appeared in front of them. The standard explanation for this generosity: "I gotta buy you a beer, cuz I'm leavin' and you're here."

Several plane rides and one helicopter hop later, Grabner arrived at her duty station, the Sixth Convalescent Hospital in Cam Ranh Bay. Her patients were soldiers who had sustained shrapnel wounds or were suffering from malaria or hepatitis. "While they were there," she recalled, "we did psychological care with them to psych them up to go out into the fields to get shot at again."

Grabner's roommate was Barb, a physical therapist who was also a very businesslike Army lifer. Once off duty, she came back to their room to work on her knitting. "After about a week of that," Grabner noted drily, "I had to get out of there and see what life was like." She found herself befriended by a series of men who became her surrogate big brothers; they were "always there to pull you apart, but then put you back together again."

Her schedule at the hospital was brutal: twelve-hour days (7 A.M. to 7 P.M.), six days a week. Nevertheless, the arrival of Friday night meant the beginning of a weekend of fun, prepped for by a beer run by one of the hospital's ambulances. "Growing up," she wrote in 2005, "I was always the obedient child. I went to an all-girls' school so had little experience with men. The service was an eye-opener. I never drank very much until I went to Vietnam, and I drank to fit in. And because I could dance, I wouldn't get drunk. I only got drunk once in Nam, and that was enough to convince me I didn't like it. I was the twinkletoes of Cam Ranh Bay."

At one time the Sixth CH officer's club had a band to fuel the parties, "but when the guys got transferred back home the club was dead, so we came up with alternative ways to entertain ourselves." The hospital was situated on a peninsula, with only one road leading in and out. None of the doctors or nurses had vehicles, and one Friday, when

*Grabner and an enlisted man taking part in MEDCAP
(Medical Civil Action Program), in which the Army sent personnel
to villages to treat specific ailments.*

"things were kind of boring," one of the doctors persuaded an ambulance driver to take a load of party animals up the road to an Air Force base, whose club did have a band. "We went up and danced till midnight when our ambulance—or our coach—picked us up. As we were coming back through the checkpoint, the MP would say, 'Whadya got?' 'Oh, wounded, sir!' And we passed right through." They all stumbled out of the ambulance and fell into bed—but were ready for work the next morning. The ambulance run then became a frequent Saturday night routine for Grabner and her pals. "I literally danced the night away." While many of the men treated her like a little sister, some required handholding. After one GI shared a letter from his pregnant wife, who had written that he should remarry if she died in childbirth, he was distraught for several days over why she would even raise that possibility. Then one day he showed up with a telegram announcing that his wife and new son were doing fine.

Her relationships with the patients were more complex. "Many times," she recalled, "the guys would wake up and say, 'Did I die, did I go to heaven? You're the first round-eyed woman I have seen in months.' Although you also got the other kind of remarks, like, 'Please ma'am, don't come near me. Your perfume is the kind my wife wears, and I don't wanna be reminded.' Most of the guys wouldn't let you do anything for them because their buddies needed the attention more than they did. They were the greatest." But, as Grabner admitted, "You had your difficulties as a woman because these were men who didn't know whether they were going to be alive the next day."

The only time she felt in danger was one night when the Viet Cong were "lobbing mortars down Main Street" of her camp. The nurses were instructed to report to the medical offices, but Grabner resisted, thinking, "Heck, I'm not gonna be with a bunch of women. We can't even have weapons. So I took off. I went with the guys and stayed there and had their protection for the night. I would rather be with the guys than the girls."

In March 1969, she was transferred to the 91st Evacuation Hospital at Tuy Hoa. The facility was being phased out as part of the Vietnamization of the war effort, and Grabner was the last woman on the hospital's roster. She worked with patients suffering from fevers of unknown origin, also caring for Vietnamese civilians with various ailments. She recalled working with a couple of young girls who had contracted the plague, teaching them how to brush their teeth, something they'd never learned.

At Tuy Hoa, her most memorable patient was an ailing GI whose main symptom was uncontrollable diarrhea. Grabner was assigned to check on and juggle his intravenous fluids, which had to be constantly maintained to keep him hydrated. One doctor even spent the night in a bed next to his patient, he was so worried about his progress, but the young man pulled through. Grabner had the pleasure of writing a note to the soldier's mother, telling her that her son would soon be transferred to a hospital in Japan.

In June, her tour of duty ended, and when she got on the plane back to the States, she ran into three or four people who had been on her flight on the way over. "There were a few doctors on board," she

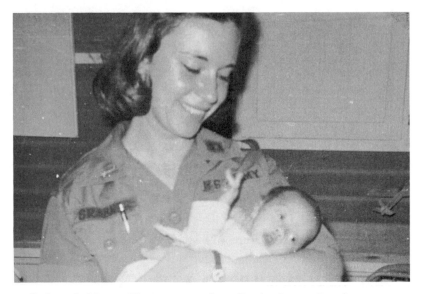

Grabner holding a Vietnamese orphan. Serving in wartime for a nurse wasn't always about treating wounded soldiers.

recalls, "but when the stewardess cut her hand, they yelled right away for the nurse to patch her up." Grabner noticed that it was very quiet on the plane, but when the wheels hit the runway in Seattle, "it was like a bomb [went off]"; people began screaming and cheering. "That probably was the last time we felt the camaraderie and support of those we were with, because on the way back through the airport we began to feel the anger, the hostility of the American people toward the soldiers. They didn't like the war, they didn't think we should be there, they were calling us baby killers." The first time she experienced outright hostility was at Chicago's O'Hare Airport, when she asked for directions from someone behind a desk. The employee said with a sneer, "Go find it yourself."

Grabner served out her time and got out of the Army in December 1969. "I only went into the service to go to Vietnam and see what it was like for our guys and to be of some kind of support for them. Not that I was pro-war or anything, but I was pro-helping and making sure that they had the support they needed." For many years she didn't talk about her experiences. "You didn't want to share, because nobody could understand what that year was like."

It wasn't until 1995, after she'd worked as a nurse on Indian reservations in New Mexico, been married and raised two children on an Indiana farm, got a master's degree in community health education, and cared for two elderly parents through the final years of their lives, that Grabner, now Julia Haskell, came to terms with her year in Vietnam. "When my ex-husband asked for a divorce in 1991," she recalled, "all the hurts returned. I started taking counseling in 1995 at the Vet Center in Indianapolis," an hour's drive from her home in Lafayette. "I was one of the first women to be seen at the center, since funds were just released to include women veterans of the Vietnam era in treatment. Women weren't supposed to have any post-traumatic stress because we never talked about the war or our experiences." Going to the center every week for six months, she met women like herself, who were still struggling with their memories. She decided to do something for them and founded the Women's Veterans Association in 1996. "We meet about once a month, about fifty of us," she said in her interview, "and they're the best women you could ever run into. When your spirits are down, they're there to pick you up."

Haskell also found professional fulfillment in working as an education coordinator at the Indiana Veterans Home, a state-run long-term-care facility in West Lafayette for veterans of all wars. She understood what those veterans had experienced, but especially those from Vietnam. "Just being there, just being in the trauma of a war zone took its toll on all of us. And when we came home, we tried to suppress it. I suppressed it for basically thirty years. And when you start experiencing losses in your family life, it starts bringing back all those memories."

"It was probably the best year of my life," she would recall of her tour of duty in Vietnam. "I grew up a lot, learned a lot of lessons that I continue to use in my everyday life. Nursing stateside could never compare to the feeling of satisfaction, dedication, love, and compassion we felt for our brothers. They were the best patients I have ever taken care of."

FRANCES LIBERTY:
THE STRAIGHT-ARROW NURSE

"My girl, you have a talent that the country needs right now."

WHEN TWENTY-YEAR-OLD FRANCES LIBERTY TOLD HER father, "I'm going to join the Army," his reply was blunt: "No, you're not." She went ahead and joined anyhow. It was 1943, and she had just been allowed to take her state nursing board exams early, because, as she would later recall, "they were desperate for nurses in the military—or anyplace." When she told her father what she'd done, his blunt comment was, "You made your bed; you're going to have to lie in it now."

Twenty-eight years later, Frances Liberty, known to all as "Lib," retired from the Army as a lieutenant colonel with a reputation for being blunt—no surprise there—and for being a straight arrow. Not a straight arrow as in teetotaler (she wasn't averse to a drink or two at the officers club) or as in humorless (she wasn't above a practical joke now and then). Lib was a straight arrow because she shared her opinions—solicited or not—with anyone, and because she could get the job done—whatever it was—with a minimum of fuss and bother. She tended to wounded soldiers in three wars, and she also cared for a dying secretary of state and a four-star general, as well as more than a few Washington dignitaries she won't name. Lib loved to tell a good story, but she was, like any good nurse, discreet about her patients.

Born in the upstate New York town of Plattsburgh, Lib had her eyes opened when she went off to join the Army. "It was very exciting for me. I came from a Catholic hospital and Catholic schools. So this was a big world to me—taking a shower with everybody else and all that stuff." Basic training was "very invigorating, very rewarding." As she recalled in a 2002 interview, when she got shot at while crawling through the mud, "that's when I learned to keep my fanny down."

She entered the service as a second lieutenant, but she learned that was a complimentary rank only. She wore the bars, earned the pay, but she wasn't officially made an officer until ten years later. Not that it mattered to her. She wasn't much interested in rank anyhow. She admired the conscientious objectors who volunteered to be ambulance drivers and work in hospitals, finding them "as brave if not braver than the boys with rifles. And once you taught them something, they didn't forget it."

From Fort Dix, where she worked in the wards of the base hospital, she was off to Camp Patrick Henry, Virginia, her point of embarkation for the European Theater. She recalled struggling up the gangplank to her ship: "You've got a duffel bag in your left hand, you have a helmet on your head—which is God's worst invention—and you have sixty pounds of medical supplies on your back." At the top of the gangplank, she gave her name and serial number, and the clerk said, "Oh my God, you're a woman." Lib's reply: "Last time I looked." Someone had misspelled her first name, and she had been billeted with the men. Another nurse named Marian soon appeared, and she had the same problem. So a couple of hammocks were rigged up for them between two bunk beds in a small stateroom with four other women.

It was October, a stormy season in the North Atlantic. Four women in the room got seasick, "and I wasn't one of them," noted Lib. She spent one night sitting in the hall outside her room, and the next night she and a pal from a neighboring room went up on deck and crawled behind a gun emplacement. Two seamen spotted them and told them they could stay there as long as they didn't make a sound or light a match. The next night the women went up to their temporary quarters and found two pillows and blankets.

In England, she was assigned to a Texas outfit, "where I learned that damn Yankee was all one word." They shipped out to Africa in preparation for the landing at Anzio in January 1944. Their unit was supposed to be in the third wave of troops to land, but they turned out to be among the first. As they gathered on the shore, she recalled, "This big, big colonel—God, he looked like a giant—he says to our chief nurse, 'My God, you're women; you're not supposed to be here yet!'" Her commanding officer was "all of five feet tall, and she had a long red braid that she wore down her back. And she looked up at him, put her hands on her hips, and said, 'We're here. Deal with it.'"

They lived for days in foxholes, where her training on keeping her fanny down came in handy, as they had to crawl along the beach to bring in the wounded. A rather large foxhole became their first-aid station. Was it terrifying? "We were not afraid. We were all young, twenty-one, twenty-two years old. We were not afraid. We were stupid." Their unit lost seven nurses during that awful battle that dragged on for almost five months.

Taking Anzio opened the door to advancing on Rome. Along the way, Lib saw her commanding officer in action again. At one camp where the nurses stopped to rest, they discovered the only toilet facility was a slit trench. When she complained and was told, in effect, to deal with it, she snapped, "My ladies are sitters, not pointers. Fix it." It was fixed.

Allied troops entered Rome on June 4, and soon Lib and her unit had taken over one of Mussolini's summer palaces for a hospital. She remained there through the end of the war, happy to be able to walk to St. Peter's every day for Mass. After Germany surrendered, everyone from the hospital who could be spared was allowed to go to the Vatican and see the Pope make his first postwar appearance in St. Peter's Square. Lib went with a dentist friend. "We were kneeling in the mud and crying," she recalled, "and the Italians were hollering, '*Viva la papa!*' This doctor looks at me and says, 'I don't know why I'm crying. I'm Jewish!'"

With the war's end, Lib thought her career in the military was over. She went back to New York and worked as a night supervisor in a hospital in Troy, her experience in Europe granting her a position that would usually go to an older nurse. But when the U.S. entered the Korean War, Lib discovered that she had been separated, not discharged from the Army, and she was called back to serve. She resisted at first, claiming that she had to take care of her father, who was hospitalized with heart trouble. But the government pointed out that she had several sisters who

Frances Liberty, in an undated photo.
She served in three wars, was forthright with her opinions,
but wasn't above playing practical jokes.

could cover for her. Then her father called her to his hospital bed. He said, "My girl, you have a talent that your country needs right now. I'm very proud of you." And, she added, "He was not a flag waver."

Lib was soon back at Fort Dix, then on to Fort Campbell, Kentucky, caring in the orthopedic ward for soldiers who had been shipped back home from Korea. She spent some time in Osaka, Japan, then was assigned to a hospital train in Korea that was shuttling patients from a MASH unit to a port where hospital ships were docked. "I liked the hospital ships," she remembered, "because they had hot water. And clean clothes." She would "borrow" a set of gray Navy coveralls each time she went onboard.

A Navy pilot gave her a flight jacket, which soon came in handy when Lib realized that her train wasn't very well stocked with supplies. "I didn't like filling out those papers when the patients died on me," she noted, so she used the bulky flight jacket like a shoplifter to conceal armloads of supplies from the MASH for her train.

She also had to deal with an unruly master sergeant assigned to the train. His drinking was giving her headaches, hobbling his ability to help her with the patients. One day, she offered him a deal: She would pass on her liquor rations to him if he promised to stay sober for the trip. It worked, and, as she admitted, "Someone would always buy me drinks at the officers club."

One night at the MASH unit she and the other medical personnel learned that the rest of the company had suddenly pulled out. They had to assume that North Korean soldiers were advancing on their position, and it was all they could do to keep from panicking and alarming the patients. "Don't worry, Captain," one corpsman told her. "I've got a gun." "Well, I hope you're a good shot," she replied, "because you're going to have to get me with the first one." Soon, a convoy of trucks appeared, a unit of Marines who had heard of their plight. They loaded patients on the trucks, stacking them in makeshift tiers.

Back home from the war, Lib decided to stay in the service. Her father had died while she was overseas, and she found inspiration in his blunt observation about her talent for military nursing. She taught corpsmen at Fort Sam Houston in Texas and pulled duty at the Presidio Army General Hospital in San Francisco. Along the way, she was developing a reputation. "I was as tactless as they come," she admitted. "Some of the other nurses were polite. I wasn't." She had also picked up a high security clearance, and when she was assigned to Walter Reed Medical Center in Washington, D.C., she drew night duty with former Secretary of State John Foster Dulles, then hospitalized with terminal cancer. Dulles liked to play pinochle with his Secret Service detail, and Lib sat in on the all-night games. One morning, as she was going off duty, she was confronted by the head nurse: "He sleeps all day. I want him awake during the daytime. What does he do all night?" She also cared for General George C. Marshall in his last days. He had a reputation for hating women. Once, she was assigned to change his IV; Marshall, who was blind by then, gruffly asked who was there, and Lib answered right back. A couple of days later, there was a problem with another nurse changing his IV, and Marshall put out the word that he wanted "that woman with the Taboo cologne," Lib's brand, back at his bedside.

Lib's days at Walter Reed weren't all spent caring for dying statesmen and generals. In front of the hospital was a big fountain. After a particularly rough week, a bunch of nurses coming home from the officers club walked by the splashing water, and someone said, "I wonder how that would look with bubbles in it." Drunk with inspiration, the women rushed over to the nurses' quarters and seized every box of bubble bath they could find. Lib recalled, "It was a beautiful sight in the moonlight," but when they realized what they had done, "they ran like hell." The next day, the Surgeon General, Leonard Heaton, turned up in a room where Lib was working. "Damndest thing," he said. "Someone poured bubble bath in the fountain out front and killed all my goldfish." With a straight face, Lib offered what a terrible thing that was but didn't fess up. After Heaton left, a doctor standing nearby told her he was glad he had a surgical mask on that disguised his grin.

Other duty stations followed: Tripler Army Medical Center in Hawaii; Florida during the Cuban Missile Crisis, when the Army took over a motel as a possible hospital, and the staff was on alert for three weeks; and Heidelberg, Germany, where she was stationed when President Kennedy was assassinated. After a stint at Fort Monmouth, New Jersey, she was off to her third war, in Vietnam.

She did three tours there. The first one was spent sorting out problems with portable MASH units that were supposed to fit on a pallet. She and a team investigated and made recommendations. The second tour called on her talents as a disciplinarian—bubble bath–laden fountains notwithstanding. The Army was having trouble with several nurses in some of the larger MASH units. "This was my least favorite job," Lib recalled. "I asked them why [they chose me to do the job] and they said, 'It's because you're a straight arrow.'"

Her third trip saw her stationed in Saigon and then in Cam Ranh Bay. That's where she came under fire from sappers, the highly trained

Viet Cong and North Vietnamese Army troops whose specialty was sudden attack on a supposedly secure area. Crawling away from the action, she remembered to keep her fanny down. "A kid covers me with his body and says, 'Colonel, if anything happens to you, they're gonna kill me.' I said, 'If anything happens to me, you're gonna be dead!'"

Of her patients in Vietnam, she recalled, "We got 'em right off the field. They still had their ammo on 'em; they were covered with mud and slime." The nurses would use a water hose to clean off the casualties. One day, a high-ranking woman officer from Washington paid a visit to Lib's unit. "She said, 'Oh my, do you have to use a hose?' 'Well, what would you suggest?' 'Well, there must be something.' 'Well now, you go back to Washington and sit behind your nice desk, and when you think of something you tell us.' 'I think you're being sarcastic,' she said. 'Yes, I am. Now don't get too close; you might get dirty.'"

Another day, Lib was riding on a helicopter with a half-dozen young nurses. Enemy fire forced them down, but the pilot was able to set the copter down without crashing. The co-pilot required first aid, but another soldier on board was hurt too badly to walk. Lib produced a litter and ordered the nurses to carry him to safety. One of them said, "I didn't join the Army to carry litters. I'm a nurse." Lib's reply: "You're either gonna carry that, or you're gonna share it with him." After a time they heard a noise that sounded like soldiers approaching. Lib hustled them into a ditch for cover, thinking, I can't let these young nurses get captured. It turned out to be a Marine patrol that had seen the chopper go down and came out looking for them. As Lib recalled with a smile, "They were delighted to see those young nurses."

She encouraged any young nurse who was pretty to use cologne and sit with the patients, "because I figured if they're going to die, at least let them see an American woman that smells good." One day she relieved a nurse who was tending to a patient whose condition was grave. Lib pulled out her rosary beads, which she always carried in her pocket. "Without opening his eyes, the patient asks, 'What's that noise?' When you're dying or when you're that close to death, your hearing is more acute. I said, 'I'm saying my rosary beads.' He said, 'You don't read, do you?' I said, 'I read very well, thank you.' He said, 'Well, I'm Jewish.' I said, 'You believe in God?' He said, 'Yes.' I said, 'Same guy.'"

She sat for a while, and just before he was taken into the operating room, he asked for the beads, muttering they might be lucky. The next day, she learned that his surgery had gone so well that he had been transferred to a hospital in Japan. This was near the end of her last tour in Vietnam. Her next assignment was Fort Belvoir, Virginia, which she described as "a little Walter Reed. You got all the senators' wives," though she refuses to name any names, even after forty years. She was at Belvoir a couple of months when a package arrived. "I don't know how this guy found me, but it was a pair of rosary beads. And a note that said, 'I'm keeping the others.'"

Lib retired from the Army in 1971. About twenty years later, she was at home one day and picked up a ringing telephone to hear a voice from her past. "I don't know how this guy finds me. He's in New York; he's the vice president of a bank. He said, 'I just want you to know that in an ashtray on my desk is your rosary beads. Nobody can figure that out. And another thing: I just had a granddaughter born in Israel, and she's Liberty Ann.' I said, 'How could you do that to a kid?' He said, 'I always talked about you, and my son wanted her named that.'" After telling this story to an interviewer, tough, straight-arrow Frances Liberty smiled and recalled, "I cried."

"I had a good life, I had a good education, I had good experiences," Lib recalled thirty years after her retirement. She admitted that on the day of her discharge in 1971, she was a bit nervous. She was not only the sole female in the ceremony but at lieutenant colonel the ranking officer, which meant she was to lead the parade. She found herself thinking, Oh my God, what if I step off wrong? The fact is, according to Lib, "Medical people aren't good at saluting. We didn't know how."

But something about the Army beyond rank and chain of command and rules and regulations did appeal to her. "It's the most satisfying career you can have," she summed up. "It's the most promising career you can have. It offers you untold benefits that you won't realize until you actually try it. And I think every nurse should take a stab at it for three years. You will use the best equipment in the world, you will work with some of the smartest, most dedicated men, along with the women. You meet the most fascinating people. It's a very satisfying career. I wouldn't change it for the world."

WENDY WAMSLEY TAINES:
HEALING HANDS

*"That was the first night that my own mortality really hit me.
That was the last and only night I cried."*

THE STORY OF THE TROUBLED TEENAGER WHOSE LIFE IS turned around by a hitch in the military is a reassuring one. But what happens when her tour of duty includes a wartime stint overseas, seeing the awful effects of combat firsthand? In 1989, Wendy Wamsley was a seventeen-year-old high school student in Tucson, Arizona, with bad grades and an attitude to match when her policeman father informed her she was joining the Army— or she was moving out of the house. "I didn't have any other options," she recalled. "I didn't want to be homeless." On her eighteenth birthday, August 20, she showed up at Fort Dix, New Jersey, more than ready for basic training "and very angry." She recalled in a 2005 interview, "My anger probably served in my favor at the time. That anger and resentment I had at my parents only made me—I'm very stubborn by nature—[say] 'Okay, I'm gonna show them. I'm gonna show everybody. I'm going to be the best they ever saw.' The drill sergeant came and was screaming in my face, and I loved every minute of it."

She admitted that it was quite an adjustment to go from wearing miniskirts and high heels in high school to getting out of bed at 3 A.M. when it was raining and putting on combat boots for a long hike. Wamsley recalled that "the M-16 and I didn't get along right away," but a compassionate drill sergeant cut her some slack until she learned

Wendy Wamsley (center) at Fort Dix, New Jersey, 1989,
an 18-year-old recruit with something to prove.

how to handle the weapon. She feared the gas chamber drill, an exercise that required recruits to take off their gas masks in a tear gas–filled room and recite their name, rank, and Social Security number to a noncom before they could exit the chamber. But she made it: "I did what I had to, and I didn't react until later." While women around her were crying, throwing up, or refusing to go into the chamber, she had what she called a "soldier moment": "You do what's required to do, and your training kicks in."

Wamsley then trained at the huge army hospital at Fort Sam Houston, Texas, to become a combat medic. The Army steered her in this direction, given the scores she made on her enlistment test and her education level. The six-month training program was "very, very stressful." They were in classes ten to twelve hours a day, though they had to keep up with their soldier requirements and duties. That meant getting up at 4 A.M. for physical training and being in class by 7 o'clock. She recalled that the hardest task for her was not to fall asleep in class.

When she came into the Army, she was asked to name three dream places she'd like for her PDS, or Permanent Duty Station. She put down Hawaii, California, and Germany. She got Fort Polk, Louisiana. She had never heard of Louisiana; "if you showed me a map of the United States, I could not tell you where Louisiana was." Her first impression of Polk: "Where the hell am I? It felt like a big swamp, something like out of Civil War photos I studied in high school." The nearest town was two miles off base, and she didn't have a driver's license. Stressing out, she decided to apply for a license. The instructor told her to drive around the block, and after she did, she was told she had passed the test. That eased her tension.

She spent a year learning how to be a medic in a MASH unit, working with the 15th Evacuation Hospital. It was a laid-back unit that knew how to have a good time in off-hours. No one ever talked about an impending war in the Middle East.

Around August 1990, about the time she noticed some big brass coming around the base—a sign that something was up—she saw an item about Kuwait and Iraq in *People* magazine. Still, it was "a real shock" that month when orders came down to deploy to Saudi Arabia. She returned to Fort Polk but didn't ship out until November 1990.

She saw many women in her unit with children and families "coming up with all sorts of ways to get out of going," and she resented them. "At the time it was really hard for me to watch that," she recalled. "The way I felt about the Army was so strong it just angered me that these women didn't want to go do what we were there to do." She saw their maneuvering affecting the morale of the unit. "They were generating fear, which is not allowed."

Wamsley didn't get to see her family before she left for the Middle East, but she did draw up a will and power of attorney. "I was so proud of that will," she said, even if she had only a car, a stereo, and some clothes to account for. She went to the PX with her credit card on a shopping spree. "I already had it in my mind that I was going to die," she recalled. "From the minute I knew I was going, I had this sense that I wasn't going to come home." In preparing for the trip, she stuffed much more than she was allowed to take into her duffel bag, and her sergeant kept coming by and telling her to repack her bag.

From Eglin Air Force Base in Florida, they flew to Germany, then to Italy, and finally on to Saudi Arabia. After a twenty-seven-hour "ordeal" in the air, they arrived in the middle of the night at King Faud Airport. As they disembarked, the stewardess of their 747 was offering a chirpy goodbye to them, as if they were embarking on a vacation. "I just remembered wanting to shoot her," Wamsley recalled. Their bus driver was the first Arab they'd seen. He seemed very odd, acted very tense, and he didn't speak English. He did have a tape recorder by the driver's seat, and once they were underway, he hit the Play button and out came a song by MC Hammer. "He was trying to say, 'Welcome to Saudi Arabia.' That was his way of welcome."

She recalled getting cultural training before they left for the field. Among the lessons: If you pull out a cigarette, you have to offer one to everyone present. Don't show the soles of your feet when you're eating. Don't read *Cosmopolitan* magazine in any kind of public setting. Women were to stay covered. (That was one rule she remembered not following, because it was so hot.)

Their first quarters were unfinished condominiums built for Saudi citizens; the Saudi government allowed American GIs to stay there. There was no running water. They were rationed two bottles of water every day for bathing, brushing their teeth, washing their hair, and drinking. After three or four days, she went with an advance party to the Evacuation Hospital's first base, Log Victor, in Saudi Arabia, about thirty miles from the Kuwait border. They began building tents for the rest of the unit, but had to wait for materials to come from Germany before they could finish. It was difficult working in the desert, she recalled; there was "sand in our lungs and in our mouths."

Once the rest of the unit arrived, they set up their next hospital at Log Base Charlie in about a week. Part of their preparations involved security drills. One of their colonels was a Vietnam veteran, and she noticed those soldiers really knew what to do in these situations. During one drill, he slipped something into her shirt when she was playing a patient, and she went through about ten assessments with this object, which was labeled BOOM to represent a bomb. The drills made them aware of how important security was during a war.

Their first casualty was an Iraqi prisoner, about sixteen years old. "His eyes were so big, he was so scared," she recalled. "Everyone in the compound knew we had an Iraqi and ran to look at him like he was some kind of lab animal." She recalled the moment the first helicopter came in with American casualties. The first patient they got off was a Marine co-pilot, who was screaming. They dropped him, because it was the middle of the night and not well lit around the chopper landing area. Once they got him into the light, they could see that one of his eyes was hanging out and that he had compound fractures all over. "He was a mess," she recalled, "but still alive. The fact that we dropped him in that condition still upsets me to this day, but I have to get over it."

Their second patient's arm kept flopping off the stretcher, and she kept putting it back on. Later she found out that he was dead on arrival. He was a captain and a pilot, "a really beautiful soldier, really handsome. That was the first night that my own mortality really hit me. That was the last and only night I cried. I was outside my tent asking God to please don't let me die. I must have needed to do that."

After that moment, her life kicked into high gear. They were taking care of everybody: Kuwaitis, Saudis, Americans, and Iraqi POWs, each group in a separate tent. She recalled treating a five-year-old Kuwaiti girl with multiple gunshot wounds, running back to another tent to take care of an Iraqi soldier who may have shot her. One night she snapped at the idea of treating anyone but Americans and began yelling: "This is crazy! I don't know why I have to take care of these animals who are shooting at these people. And I don't even care about these Saudi people, whoever they are." A colonel came over with a big book and threw it at her—the first thing in it was the Hippocratic Oath. "That," she recalled, "was an adult moment."

Her job was to work on the Intensive Care Unit in twelve-hour shifts, but she also pulled responsibilities like guard duty, burning latrine waste in the desert (commonly known as "shit detail"), and sandbagging. They all slept when they could: "Sleep was something you took advantage of when you could do it. By the time you hit your cot, you just slept." They kept their gas masks always close (she estimated she spent 70 percent of her time wearing one), and she slept with her M-16. In the middle of the night, rather than put on all her protective gear and stumble off in the dark to the latrine, she used a water bottle with the top cut off to urinate in. She braided her hair so she didn't have to wash it as often, went many days without hot food (she ate MREs three times a day), and developed cravings for chocolate, American cigarettes, and McDonald's. There was no access to alcohol. "We were pretty much Muslim while we were there."

It wasn't all work and stress. Wamsley spoke openly in her interview of the amount of sexual activity going on in her hospital. For some of the medical personnel pulling long shifts and caring for badly wounded people in a war zone, there was a sense that "this could be your last day, this could be your last night." In fact, she said, "That was a favorite line: 'This could be it. We could get hit.' We made the best of every moment." She had her own romance. She was an E-3 at the time, and the "love of my life" was an E-7, a master sergeant. During that time, "he was my protector. He made it bearable." The man was older and more experienced, and he promised her mother he would take care of her daughter. He proposed marriage to her over there. But when they came back to the States and she was transferred out of the unit, "I noticed the excitement died for me." She broke it off.

Her biggest frustration was not having the equipment to deal with the various injuries they saw, especially those afflicting burn victims. One GI came in with third-degree burns; in the States, he would have been placed in a whirlpool to soften the burned areas so that layers of tissue came off naturally. In Saudi Arabia, she had to scrub him through his screams and give him as much morphine as he could stand. That first Marine coming in with the multiple compound fractures could have used certain splints they didn't have. She did the best with what she could, but "there just could have been so many things done better."

Not every American they treated was suffering from wounds inflicted during combat. There was no speed limit in Saudi Arabia, so her hospital saw a lot of vehicle crash victims, including some of their own soldiers. With liquor impossible to find, some of the men started drinking gasoline from trucks for the alcohol content. What they didn't understand was that gasoline ingestion causes respiratory problems. The hospital also received patients who had shot themselves, some accidentally and some intentionally, to be excused from duty. It was important to be able to diagnose the difference; the latter could be court-martialed and discharged for abusing government property. "That was hard for me," she recalled. "I'm seeing a scared little boy who wants to go home. The other side of me is saying, 'No, you're a soldier. You're supposed to be out there doing your job.'"

Their chaplain was "the best." When the unit had to make sandbags to create bunkers in case they got hit by a Scud missile, a truly tedious job, the chaplain came up with a device that helped to fill bags quickly. He was always there with them doing the dirty work, cleaning latrines, filling sand bags.

When she came home, their plane landed in the U.S. at 3 or 4 o'clock in the morning. They had been on one plane or another for thirty hours. The pilot said they were stopping off in Bangor, Maine, and that there were some people who wanted to say hello. The soldiers got off the plane to find a long line of American Legionnaires there to shake their hands. A band was playing, and there were civilians, too, to congratulate them, and kids asking her for her autograph on their t-shirts and in their diaries. "I felt like a movie star that day," she recalled.

At the time of her interview, Wendy Wamsley Taines was being treated for post traumatic stress disorder. When she returned from the Gulf War, she said that she went back to life as usual. But what she had seen during those long shifts in the 15th Evac Hospital started to haunt her. Her delayed reaction to her wartime experiences in the Gulf was exacerbated by the events of 9/11. After that day, she spiraled down into drinking, pill-taking, and literally self-destructive behavior—she referred to several suicide attempts. When she did the interview, it was still difficult for her to read a newspaper or watch the news on TV, but she was in therapy. "I am one of the lucky ones," she admitted, "because I am determined to be healthy in spirit and mind."

She has come to understand the need for more immediate aftercare of vets returning from war service. "They need to talk about what they did," she said, "make sense of what they did, have an opinion about what they did." She wanted to work with the Veterans Administration to push for more psychological treatment when vets come home, before transitioning back. "I say that from my own experience."

What Wendy Wamsley Taines loved about working as a medic in the Gulf were her GI patients. "They just have this sense of humor that never stops," she recalled. "I love them to this day. My calling is to be back with my vets." She hoped to work with them in a VA hospital, a setting less frenzied but just as nurturing as her evacuation hospital in the Saudi desert in 1991.

CAROLYN HISAKO TANAKA: THE FORGIVING NURSE

"I have a skill that is needed in Vietnam, and I'm going there to do my duty for my country."

A LITTLE GIRL SEES HER FAMILY'S HOME AND POSSESSIONS taken away, and they are forced to live for three years in a relocation camp. It happened to Carolyn Hisako Tanaka, but when she became a nurse, she couldn't let bitterness toward the government that stained her childhood memories change her convictions about serving her country.

In her memoir, *Road Runner*, Carolyn Hisako Tanaka wrote eloquently of an idyllic childhood in southern California. Her paternal grandfather emigrated from Japan in the early 1900s, settling in Guadalupe, a farming community about fifty miles north of Santa Barbara. She described him as "one of the pioneer vegetable farmers in Guadalupe." He sent for a picture bride from Japan, and they married and had seven children. She and an infant son died in January 1919 during the flu epidemic.

Her father, George, was born in 1904 in Guadalupe, her mother, Helen, in 1907 in Fresno. They married in 1930, on the heels of a second romance. George's sister Aki was attracted to Helen's brother Harvey Iwata. But according to Japanese custom, George's father wanted his son to marry before his daughter. So Aki introduced George to Harvey's sister Helen, and a marriage. was arranged.

Hisako was their second child and only daughter, born in 1935. Her fondest memories of her early childhood were picnics on nearby

Pismo Beach, with extended families on both sides in attendance and plenty of homegrown vegetables and fruit to eat. The Tanakas lived in a large house with a fine front porch. A third child was born in 1940.

December 7, 1941, forever altered Tanaka family life. The picnics on the beach ceased. Six-year-old Carolyn remembered one good thing about those opening days of World War II. She had been attending Japanese language school every day after regular school. The instructor was a forbidding older gentleman who swatted any disobedient child with a willow switch. The school closed in the wake of Pearl Harbor, and a six-year-old couldn't be expected to miss it.

Hisako's grandfather was taken from his house with no notice at all. The family only heard from him when he alighted in Bismarck, North Dakota, and asked them to send him warm clothing. Her own family was given no time to sell their belongings or furnishings; most were given away to friends or neighbors. The children moved in the spring of 1942 to Dinuba, a town north of Guadalupe and farther inland, where Aki and Harvey were living. Their parents followed after their fourth child, named Arthur after General Douglas MacArthur, was born in April.

Hisako completed the first grade in Dinuba, and then the family was sent off to Poston, Arizona, where they would spend the next three years waiting out the war. They arrived in the middle of the night. She recalled in her memoir, "We saw barbed wire all around the camp, and MPs with rifles watching our every move. We were being told we were going to camp for our protection. Then why were their rifles pointed inward at us, instead of outward at our perimeter?"

Her father worked on a crew that constructed the camp's schools. Tanaka attended school taught by either residents or qualified local residents, and her fourth-grade teacher, Mrs. Koga, instilled in her a love for music. After the schools were finished, outdoor stages were built for plays and movies, and then wading and swimming pools, especially welcome for the hot Arizona days and nights. The young men played baseball; the field in her camp was called Yankee Stadium. The teams would travel to other relocation camps around the country. "Were it not for baseball," Tanaka wrote, "life in camp would have been unbearable."

She recalled many young men in the camp signing up to fight with the newly formed 442nd Regimental Combat Team. A cousin, Abraham Ohama, and his brothers enlisted. He was sent to Europe, where "he died a hero trying to save his buddy who was trapped behind enemy lines."

During the Tanaka family's last year in camp, Hisako's father traveled east from Arizona in search of work. He was dark-skinned and spoke fluent Spanish, so he passed himself off as a Mexican, but he had little luck. He invested his savings to rent a field on the Texas–New Mexico border and irrigated it with water diverted from the Rio Grande. He grew a lovely crop of lettuce, but on the day before harvest a hailstorm wiped him out.

After VJ Day, the Tanakas were allowed to return to Guadalupe. They found their home burned to the ground. George Tanaka moved his family to Fresno, and he and Helen decided to give their children American names. Hisako entered public school under the name Carolyn. She attended Edison High School, excelling in basketball, softball, and other sports. After she graduated in 1953, the family borrowed money for her to start college at Fresno State. She wanted to become a physical education teacher and sports coach, but her mother saw little future for her in those fields and steered her toward nursing.

Carolyn Tanaka applied for and got a three-year scholarship to Fresno General Hospital School of Nursing, entering in September 1955. Her first job was in the emergency room of the hospital, and she fell in love with the work. She wrote, "I soon learned why there is a saying among ER nurses, 'Once an ER nurse, always an ER nurse.' That held true with me because I didn't find a specialty I liked better." She worked her way up to supervisor, earning a reputation for professionalism and for high energy—which led to her nickname, "The White Tornado."

In 1965, she received an offer from the Agency for International Development, which was asking for volunteer nurses to serve in Vietnam. Tanaka had seen a number of doctors at her hospital receive orders for duty in Vietnam, and although she was tempted to join the armed forces to go, she thought it would upset her mother too much, so she compromised, applying to go as a civilian with AID.

After an interview with AID, she was informed that they wanted her to get a master's degree and a midwifery certificate before she could be part of their program. That didn't interest Tanaka at all, and after a failed attempt to enlist in the Air Force (they wanted a four-year commitment during which she would not be guaranteed duty in Southeast Asia), she

Carolyn Hisako Tanaka at Fort Sam Houston, in the fall of 1966,
upon graduating from basic training.

settled on the Army. She wrote: "My nursing classmates were angered at me for joining the Army to serve in Vietnam. They asked, 'How could you, who were treated so badly by your government during WWII, go off to this senseless war in support of that government?' My answer to them was, 'I have a skill that is needed in Vietnam, and I'm going there to do my duty for my country.'"

She threw herself a going-away party and invited all her skeptical friends. "After much good food and even more booze," she wrote, "they decided that this was a noble thing for me to do."

October 3, 1966, was the starting date for her orientation to Army nursing, at Fort Sam Houston in San Antonio, Texas. She arrived in Bien Hoa, Vietnam, on Valentine's Day 1967. She and a Red Cross worker were the only women on a plane with 180 GIs. If she wasn't scared already, the pilot announced they would be making a "nosedive landing" because the airbase had suffered a mortar attack the night before.

At the processing center, she asked a sergeant how to tell the enemy from friendly Vietnamese. He said the Vietcong wore black pajamas. "As we crossed Bien Hoa," she wrote, "all I could see were Vietnamese wearing black pajamas. So you can be right next to the enemy and not even know it!"

She wanted to be assigned to a MUST (Medical unit, self-contained, transportable), because that was "where all the action is," but she received orders to report to the 24th Evacuation Hospital in Long Binh. At least she was assigned to the ER. The hospital had opened a month before she arrived, and business was "pretty slow." Nevertheless, after two weeks, she was made hospital supervisor on her shift—"what we Army refer to as the ramp tramp."

She found out the best way to get around in Vietnam was to hitchhike. At first she had trouble getting someone to stop. "I looked like one of the guys with my short hair and flat chest," she wrote, but then she learned to wear a dress, and rides came easy. One time she and a male buddy were off to play tennis and go swimming; they stood along Highway 1, and a truck going the other way did a U-turn and offered them a ride.

She brought a manual typewriter to Vietnam, and she was cranking out up to twenty letters a day on it. She used onion skin and carbon paper to, in effect, write six of them at a time. "My friends in Quarters #1," she wrote in her memoir, "thought I was writing a manuscript the way the typewriter clicked most every day." She wrote to her colleagues back at the ER in Fresno about the patients she took care of, but no one saved those letters, so most of what she drew on for her memoir were letters to family and friends about "the fun times I had on my days off." And she was bad about dating her letters, but for the memoir she reassembled them in what she thought was chronological order.

In May 1967, she spent a day out in the field under a program she called Medical Education in Defense of Civilian Allied Personnel. It was a means of bringing medical knowledge to the underserved people of rural Vietnam. They visited two villages "in our eagerness to save the world" and were late getting back to the Evac Hospital. There ensued a "hair raising" ride in a downpour in a jeep with no brakes. They watched tracers flashing overhead; one nurse carried an M-16, the driver a .45 pistol. "Much later," Tanaka wrote, "when I reviewed the slides of our day on the rifle range and saw a picture of this nurse I had entrusted my life to, and how poorly she aimed the M-16, I would have pulled rank and taken over, had I known what a bad shot she was."

They did treat enemy soldiers at their hospital. One day, a "little wisp of a boy" she guessed was sixteen years old "and surely not more than 100 pounds" was brought in to be interrogated because he had been identified as a squad leader. He was also suffering from fragment wounds in his skull and abdomen. The interrogation lasted an hour, after which the doctor tried to treat his wounds. It took four men to hold him down so that the medical personnel could start an IV and insert a catheter to prepare him for surgery. "He probably thought we were torturing him," Tanaka wrote. She added that many of the nurses and corpsmen were bitter about having to care for the enemy, "but many of them, especially the young ones, are victims of circumstances, and I can't help but feel compassionate toward them."

On September 1, she was promoted to Head Nurse of the 24th Evac Emergency Room. That day, they received sixteen Vietnamese soldiers and two Vietcong. Two days later, on Election Day, Vietcong guerrillas attacked voting booths with mortars, killing or injuring many civilians and children. On the 15th, her ER was alerted to receive fifty casualties from a battle.

On September 19, she wrote a group letter that began, "This business of being a Head Nurse in Vietnam isn't exactly a Crown of Glory. Haven't had a day off to speak of since I became heir to this job three weeks ago." Worn down by her demanding schedule she had developed a case of laryngitis, for which she was "getting all kinds of medical advice." She had taken to wearing a sign that read, "Don't talk to me unless you HAVE to. I'm saving my voice for the Met," and signed it LARYNGITIS.

In the same letter she reported that her application for an extension had been approved and that she was requesting a transfer to the 3rd Surgical Unit in the Mekong Delta starting in February, around the time of her first anniversary of arriving in country.

In the meantime, she was dealing with everything from a doctor who was being verbally abusive to the Vietnamese patients (he was transferred) to an expectant mother dying of a head wound (the operating room crew came to the ER and delivered her baby by Caesarian before she died).

She did manage to slip in some R&R: a trip to Thailand in November, and the next month a trip to Hawaii, to see her brother Frank and celebrate their birthdays. Christmas was a mixed bag. Bob Hope and his troupe came to the Long Binh amphitheater for a show; she sent her staff to see Hope while she stayed behind to cover. They all had dinner in the mess hall after the show. Then after dinner, "all hell broke loose." GIs from other units who had come to eat at their mess hall began coming back in droves, all of them with severe symptoms of food poisoning. "It turned out to be the reconstituted eggnog," she wrote.

In 2½ hours they admitted seventy-five patients, and there weren't enough litter stands, so some patients were left on the floor. It might have been a comic scene if it weren't such an unholy mess. Tanaka enlisted a new nurse who was to begin work the next day and who had never started an IV before. It was a baptism under fire of a very different kind.

On New Year's Eve Tanaka made a bet with a male colleague that she could drink him under the table. After ten drinks, she spent all night throwing up, and when she reported for work on New Year's morning, she was still drunk and learned that the general was going to visit the ER at 0800. She recalled, "The staff made every sobering concoction they knew how to make and poured them down me to sober me up in an hour. The general was prompt. I saluted him, spun around, and headed for the sink so as not to puke on his clean boots. Never again!"

On January 13, she was awarded a Bronze Star. "I'm not sure why," she wrote, "I think they give it to every head nurse." When she heard that she was going to receive the medal, she insisted that she would not accept it unless her ward master also got one, since he was "the one who did most of the work." As a further reward, the army gave her thirty days' leave.

Her brother Art was an Army engineer stationed in Germany. They had planned to travel together in Europe, but his leave was cancelled at the last minute. They managed to see each other for a weekend. Meanwhile, she toured England with friends, did Paris, Frankfurt, Nuremberg (where she saw her brother), Zurich, Amsterdam, and Brussels. The whole time she never looked at a newspaper, never watched news on television, so she had no idea what was happening back in Vietnam. Less than a week after she left for Europe, the Tet Offensive had begun. When she returned to duty on February 17, with the offensive over, "the staff rubbed it in by saying, 'Boy, you sure know when to take a vacation.'"

Her extension of duty had been approved, and she was to transfer to a surgical hospital, but her chief nurse, Lt. Col. Morgan, was leaving and asked Tanaka if she would consider staying on at the 24th Evac as a favor to her. Tanaka couldn't refuse her, and besides, some renovations and reorganization she had begun with her ward master were not yet complete, so she got to see them through.

Tanaka's memoir contains little detail about her last six months in country. She went to Hawaii in July for the wedding of her brother to a nurse she met in boot camp and had a last R&R in Tokyo (her inability to speak Japanese and cloudy weather dampened her fun). She returned to Vietnam just in time to clear post. At her exit briefing, "I was told by my chief nurse to put a civilian dress in my purse and to change clothes as soon as the plane landed on American soil, to prevent being spat upon and called a "warmonger" or "baby killer." I could not believe I was coming home to the same reception I received twenty-three years before, following World War II. This time I was NOT the enemy, but I was there saving lives, perhaps their loved ones."

She landed in Oakland, and she did change into civilian clothes as instructed. No one, she recalled, was allowed to meet her at that airport. She and four others pooled their money to pay for a cab ride to the San Francisco airport, from where the others caught planes home. Her friend Ann met her at the airport, and they went to the PX on Treasure Island for one last splurge: She bought her younger brother, who was about to marry, a wedding gift and ordered a new car for herself. "Can't beat the PX prices," she wrote.

For Carolyn Hisako Tanaka, perhaps the defining moment of her eighteen months in Vietnam came on November 6, 1967. That day her

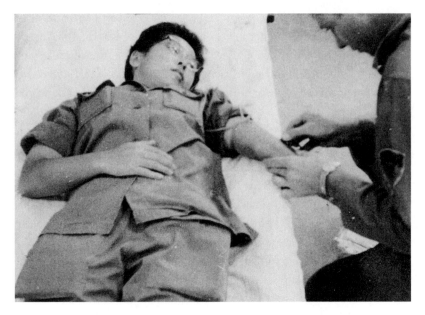

*In November 1967, Tanaka skirted Army regulations
to donate blood to a soldier so badly wounded he needed
36 pints before and during surgery.*

ER received a GI with massive wounds in his buttocks and pelvic area; he was also missing an eye and had a badly mangled hand. She recalled, "When I got off duty, everyone was scurrying around to find A+ blood for this patient who was still on the operating room table. I was told that they had a policy that nurses were not allowed to donate blood. I had cared for this patient earlier in the day and I was not about to let him die for lack of blood. I told them I was going on ten-day leave the next day, so they allowed me to donate blood. He received thirty-six pints of blood in all, including mine, and survived. That made a believer out of me, and I have been a regular blood donor ever since. I surpassed the ten-gallon mark in 1991, and this was before the blood bank had computers to keep records of donations."

CHAPTER FOUR

GROUNDBREAKERS

WARTIME CALLS ON MANY TO SERVE, AND SOME PEOPLE FIND THEMSELVES on the front lines of more than one struggle. For women and minorities, especially African Americans, a national emergency is an opportunity for advancement and for changing the culture of the military. World War II was a turning point in that struggle; it gave women their first real chance to serve in uniform, and it reminded everyone that fighting a war for freedom was meaningless without racially integrated armed forces to win that fight.

Augustus Prince was one African American for whom World War II provided an enormous break, while Bertran Wallace, who served in Korea, found himself fighting his own private war with officers who wouldn't give him one. Darlene Iskra joined the Navy with no intention of becoming a pioneer, and her breakthrough was nearly lost in the fog of war. And for Japanese Americans Norman Ikari and Yeiichi Kelly Kuwayama, World War II was a chance to prove their loyalty to the country of their birth, even as their own families suffered humiliation and hardship back home in the United States.

Darlene Iskra trained as a diver, defying men like one petty officer who said, "I'll be damned if I'll have some woman in my diving Navy."

DARLENE ISKRA:
THE UNSUNG PIONEER

"When I decided to join the Navy and change my life—it did!
It totally changed my life."

IT WAS A QUIETLY MOMENTOUS MOMENT, LOST TO THE GENERAL
public in the midst of preparations for war, but Darlene Iskra
remembers it well. She was making history for herself and for
many women who had served before her in the U.S. Navy. If
what followed was both anticlimactic and frustratingly incomplete, she
could still lay claim forever to the distinction of being the first woman
to command a ship in the Navy's long history.

Darlene Iskra was born in San Francisco and attended high school
and college there. While in high school, she had flirted with the idea
of joining the Navy, but her stepfather, who had served in the Navy,
advised her to finish high school and college before deciding on a military career, to avoid joining as an enlisted person. During her senior
year in college, she worked at a USO club in San Francisco as part of
an internship toward her degree in Recreation Management. She married a Navy man she met there, and four years later, when they decided to get divorced, they were stationed at the Naval Air Station on
Whidbey Island, Washington.

Iskra answered a blind classified ad recruiting middle management
candidates and found out that it was placed by the Navy. It was the late
'70s, there had been a big draw-down from the Vietnam War era, and

the Navy was trying new ways to reach potential recruits. "Ships at sea," she recalled in a 2002 interview, "that was foreign to me." A co-worker who had been in the Navy suggested she look into being a diver, and coincidentally, a new Navy program for women divers had just opened. She was twenty-seven years old and looking for something new. She would recall, "When I decided to join the Navy and change my life—it did! It totally changed my life. I figured they would teach me what they wanted me to know, and I would just do it."

Iskra attended Officer Candidate School, one of thirty women in a class containing ten times as many men. She never sensed any competition between the women. "We really bonded," she recalled of the "very stressful" sixteen-week course. She recalled steel garbage cans being rolled down the hall at reveille in place of a bugle and "a lot of harassment," though none of it sexual.

During OCS, Iskra tried out for the diving program and was accepted, as well as into Surface Warfare Officers School. She would later recall her excitement: "That was the first indication that I was going to sea!" After OCS, she was sent to the Naval Amphibious Base at Little Creek, near Norfolk, Virginia, and that's where she learned what the diving community was all about. Only two other women had been through the Dive School before her. It was a grueling time; the stress came from the physical training, while for Iskra the academics were a snap. Every morning, there were long runs, and as Iskra admitted, "I wasn't a runner. I was always at the back of the pack." She had a friend, Martha, who was younger and in better shape; they were the only two women in their class. Iskra once heard a chief petty officer mutter, "I'll be damned if I'll have some woman in my diving Navy," and Iskra did think about dropping out. But Martha wouldn't let her. "You can't quit," she told Iskra, "and leave me here all by myself."

After six months of Dive School, she went to Surface Warfare Officers School, where she spent four months learning the basics of navigation, seamanship, and engineering. This time the pressure was academic rather than physical. "I had two very challenging things my first year in the service," she recalled, "and when I got out of there I was very self-confident. It really changed my life. All through school I got As, but I never knew I was smart because there was always somebody smarter than me."

At the end of 1980, she was assigned to her first ship, the *Hector,* a repair vessel. There were plenty of opportunities for Iskra to work on her diving, which involved inspecting the hulls, propellers, and rudders of other ships for possible repair work. "Once I got on that first ship," she later wrote, "I realized that going to sea was fun. I had a good experience there. My department head and everyone up the chain of command was very supportive of having women on board. It made me want to stay in and make it a career."

After a year stationed in Alameda, California, and then at sea in Pacific ports, she was ready for new challenges. She had remarried, but that hadn't dampened her ambition. "I was on shore duty," she recalled. "I was not happy on shore duty. I wanted to move on with my career." She stuck her nose out and went to Washington, D.C., to see an assignment officer, who agreed to give Iskra's career a push.

Between 1985 and 1993, she was largely at sea—an unusually long time, but she had no regrets, because it provided her with the chance to, as she said, "maintain parity with my peer group." The only problem was that she saw little of her husband, a Navy SEAL; whenever she got some leave time, it seemed he was on an assignment. She served aboard three more ships—as operations officer on the *Grasp,* as executive officer on both the *Preserver* and the *Hoist*—and in the spring of 1990 she got the call to assume command of a ship. "Being a recreation specialist and a bit older than my cohorts," she would later write, "actually worked out well for me. I was more mature, and my skills in standing in front of a group of people, getting them to do things that they didn't want to do, came in handy in the Navy."

Iskra's new assignment proved a controversial move, not only because she would have been the first woman in that position, but because of her background training. "The diving community is not a major community in the Navy," she said. "But the surface warfare community is a major community in the Navy," and they had already lined up a woman of their own for the honor. But Iskra was actually in a position to take the command post sooner.

She would later admit that at the time "I didn't know all the political stuff that was going on." It was suggested she go to the War College in Newport, Rhode Island, before assuming command, but her advo-

*In December 1990, Iskra made history when she took
command of the USS* Opportune. *Her ship was on
duty during the Persian Gulf War.*

cates saw that as a delaying tactic and took the matter all the way up
to the Chief of Naval Personnel. His decision: Since Iskra had put in
more time at sea than her rival, she would get the nod. Following several months of training and briefings, she was scheduled to take over
her ship in January 1991, but the commander she was to replace was
diagnosed with stomach cancer. While Iskra and her husband were in
Philadelphia visiting his family on Christmas Eve 1990, she was notified that she was to assume command as soon as possible. On the day
after Christmas, she flew from Norfolk to Naples, Italy, where she took
command on Dec 27, 1990, of a ship named, appropriately, the USS

Opportune. "The first woman at sea thing, in command thing, didn't affect me until I got to the ship," when she saw a stack of congratulatory mail on her new desk.

The *Opportune,* like the *Hector,* the *Hoist,* and the *Preserver,* was an old salvage vessel of World War II vintage. For the first six months of her command, she was the only woman on board, during which time she made one thing clear to the men: "Don't treat me any differently; I am the commanding officer, and that's it."

She didn't have much time to get acclimated before her first major duty assignment. Three weeks after she came aboard, on January 17, 1991, the U.S. and its coalition began a massive air attack on Iraqi forces that had invaded Kuwait in November. She and the crew had known that war was imminent, but they did not know the exact date when the U.S. would strike at the Iraqi invaders. Now the Persian Gulf War was on. The *Opportune,* then docked in the southern Italian port of Taranto, was ordered to sail for the Suez Canal.

Just north of Egypt, outside the Canal, the *Opportune* was ordered to stand by, in case, as she later wrote, "the Suez Canal had been mined or ships were purposefully sunk to hinder ship traffic. We were there to ensure the canal remained clear." The communications systems on the ancient ship, while upgraded, still weren't exactly state of the art, so Iskra and her crew weren't able to monitor the progress of the war as closely as they would have liked. "People who saw what was going on on CNN knew more than we did," Iskra would later admit, adding that things were "pretty scary," especially given rumors that Saddam Hussein might employ chemical or biological weapons and that the *Opportune* was ill-equipped for such an attack.

Iskra admitted that it was a challenge to keep morale up while awaiting orders and news of the war. She ran frequent drills and tried to keep everyone as busy as possible. The most memorable moment of their deployment turned out to be something of a tension breaker. One day, three ships approached the *Opportune.* Iskra was summoned immediately to the bridge; she had been working out below decks and was still in her shorts and t-shirt. The convoy proved to be Soviet ships; a helicopter from one of them hovered off the starboard bow of the *Opportune,* and its senior officer demanded to see the commander. It took some explaining from Iskra that she was in fact in charge of the ship.

At the end of February, after the ceasefire was declared, the *Opportune* was released to go home. Although Iskra and her crew had spent the entire war in a standby position, when they returned to their home base in Norfolk in April 1991, it was to, as Iskra recalled, a "hero's welcome." The rest of her first command tour was anticlimactic. The following year, the *Opportune* helped another ship recover its lost anchor and towed it through the Panama Canal to hand it off to another ship that would take it to the West Coast for repairs. On the way back to Norfolk, they were held up by Hurricane Andrew, which hit south Florida with devastating force in August 1992. Again the *Opportune* was in standby mode, and this time the crew's mood turned anxious with the delay. Iskra admitted that the end of her tour was "very stressful."

She finally hit land for good in February 1993 and was assigned to an office job with the Bureau of Naval Personnel in Washington. She was then sent to the War College and then to Guam for two years as a liaison for the Pacific island nations, a posting that allowed her to literally get back in the water and do some diving. Finally, it was back to D.C. for a desk job that convinced her that she preferred to be at sea where "you have a job to do." In 2000, after twenty years in service, she decided to retire from the Navy and go back to school to get a graduate degree in military sociology.

"I really had no idea what the Navy had in store for me when I joined," Iskra would later write. "I had a B.A. degree in Recreation Management that was pretty much good for nothing. I was living in a depressed area north of Seattle. Had just gotten divorced, and had no hopes for any kind of job that would give me the financial security I needed as an independent woman. So when the Navy offered me a job, I thought it was a great opportunity to get out of my miserable situation and 'see the world.'"

Though it was frustrating not to be a more active participant in the action during a war, Iskra was in fact a woman in command of a U.S. Navy ship, ready to do her part to ensure success in the Persian Gulf. And if her subsequent postings didn't seem to capitalize on her pioneer's status, she still understands what the entire experience did for her, not just as a woman, but as a person.

AUGUSTUS PRINCE:
THE GRATEFUL PIONEER

"I learned...that I'm as good as anybody."

I T WAS A SMALL MOMENT IN A BRIEF MILITARY CAREER IN A WAR
filled with large and momentous events. But even sixty years after
it happened, Gus Prince still knows what it meant to him, a
young black man struggling for respect in a largely segregated
Navy, and how it likely shaped the rest of his life.

Prince was born in Philadelphia in 1926. His mother stressed discipline and education, even though she had attended school only
through the fourth grade. She would ask Gus and his two brothers if
they had finished their homework, and if they said "Yes," she would tell
them they could read the Bible. That was incentive enough for the
Prince brothers to really finish their assignments.

In spite of posting good grades in high school, Prince wasn't able
to attend college, because his family lacked the funds. So he went to
work at the Sun Shipbuilding and Drydock Company in Chester,
Pennsylvania, south of Philadelphia. His younger brother was already
in the Navy, there was a war on, and so he decided to enlist. Prince's
timing was fortunate. The Navy was finally opening up previously segregated areas to African Americans, and with his interest in "anything
that dealt with science," he signed up for radar school, becoming the
first black radar man in the Navy.

Breaking down barriers to attend radar training was one thing, but finding a ship that would take him on was another matter. Prince was rejected by several commanders who claimed they had enough radar men. Then he came to the *Santee,* a former oil tanker converted into an escort carrier. It was a ship Prince knew well; the *Santee* was a product of the Sun shipyard. He spoke with Lt. C.L. Fergus, who was in charge of radar on the ship. Prince asked him, "If I serve on your ship, will I serve as a radar man?" Fergus asked him, "Did you finish radar school? "Yes." "That's what you will be."

Prince was lucky in finding a ship that would take him, and he was also lucky to be joining the *Santee* in late 1944. The ship was in Los Angeles for repairs after a horrific series of attacks during the Battle of Leyte Gulf. On October 25, a Japanese kamikaze had crashed through the flight deck of the *Santee.* The plane ripped a 30-foot gash in the flight deck, killing 16 men and wounding 27. Sixteen minutes later, a torpedo from the Japanese submarine *I-56* struck the ship, flooding several compartments. Emergency repairs were quickly completed, and the ship returned to Pearl Harbor and then Los Angeles for further repairs.

The *Santee* left in March 1945 for Hawaii with Prince in his new slot. The only other black men on board were cooks and bakers, who slept in segregated quarters. Fergus insisted that Prince bunk with the rest of the crew. Prince wound up teaching algebra to some of the other radar men, and he spent his spare time training as a middleweight boxer. His duty station was the ship's Combat Information Center, where he monitored radar screens for activity and reported his findings to the bridge. He also drew bridge watch for hours at a time.

The *Santee* returned to action in the spring of 1945 for the campaign to take Okinawa. Once that island was secured, the crew got their orders for the invasion of Japan. They were to be part of "Operation Coronet," the northernmost invasion force, and they were issued cold-weather gear in anticipation of a long campaign. On the way to their staging area, they heard that a huge bomb had been dropped on Hiroshima. "We thought Tokyo Rose was kidding," Prince recalled upon hearing the news from Japan's top radio propagandist. Even after the second atomic bomb was dropped, on Nagasaki, the *Santee* was kept on hold, until the Japanese surrender gave them the green light to head back home.

Thanks to the GI Bill, Prince was able to obtain a degree in physics at Penn, and he eventually specialized in nuclear physics,

Augustus Prince, enjoying shore leave in 1944, the year he got his first break in the Navy with an assignment as a radar operator.

working at Brookhaven National Laboratory in Upton, New York, on reactors and reactor safety. He also consulted with Brookhaven on recruiting minority engineers and scientists from historically black colleges as well as from others such as Stanford and Michigan.

Even after sixty years, Gus Prince still tears up in telling the story of that simple encounter with a color-blind officer on the deck of the *Santee*. "I think the most important thing I learned [in the Navy] is that I'm as good as anybody," he recalled in a 2004 interview. "And I owe that to Lieutenant Fergus."

BERTRAN WALLACE:
TOO PROUD TO BOW

*"There were still people who had hidden
agendas because of the color of my skin,
which I had nothing to do with."*

S ERVING IN TWO WARS PLUS ALMOST THIRTY YEARS OF PEACETIME
duty didn't take the edge off Bertran Wallace, a proud man
who fought as hard against prejudice within the Army as he
did against the Germans and North Koreans.

In 1942, Wallace and two buddies he'd grown up with and roomed
with at Lincoln University in Jefferson City, Missouri, answered the call
for "pilots of color" to join the segregated Army Air Force's 99th Pursuit
Squadron, formed the year before. However, a run-in with a captain
who called him "boy" doomed Wallace's chance to serve with the 99th.
He joined an enlisted reserve corps, waiting for another opportunity.

In March 1943, he got it. Called to report for active duty, he was
assigned to the MP Battalion at Fort Riley, Kansas, an all-black unit
headed by white officers. Wallace recalled in a 2002 interview that he
was a member of Company A, an elite unit that whipped through a
thirteen-week basic training course in eight weeks. He was impressed
with one of his officers, a lieutenant from South Carolina, who "treated us with a great deal of respect" and "spoke often of our intelligence."

At Fort Devens, Massachusetts, he fell in with a group of eastern-
ers, many of them college students referred to within the all-black
group as "college niggers." He sailed on the *Queen Elizabeth* to Oran,
Algeria, where he guarded German POWs. Though he and his fellow

black soldiers were quartered in barracks separate from the whites, they did eat in a common mess hall, one of the first signs he saw of integration in the Army. They called their commanding officer, John Groom, "Gary Cooper" for his gentlemanliness. He encouraged them to form their own boxing, track, and basketball teams and compete with other units as a way of boosting their esprit de corps.

In June 1944, his unit was sent to Rome, which had been liberated by the Allies, to serve as security troops for five hotels where officers would spend their R&R time. He played with an integrated basketball team called the New Mexico Five. "It was a beautiful time," he recalled in his interview, "because for the first time in my life, growing up in Kansas City, born in Texas, I felt that our song, 'land of the free and home of the brave,' that indeed I was an American." They pulled duty on the same floor where white WAC officers lived, and there was never a hint of any shenanigans. "Our reputation," he recalled, "was outstanding."

One other vivid memory Wallace had from his wartime service in Italy was singing as part of a choral group at the San Carlo Opera House in Naples, backing famed tenor Richard Tucker. It was the first time a group of color had sung there.

He worked for a time on *Stars and Stripes,* the Army's newspaper of record, and decided after the war to pursue a career in graphic arts. He attended graduate school at Columbia University, and when President Truman integrated the armed forces, he saw an opportunity to become an officer. He was commissioned a second lieutenant, but a run-in with a lieutenant colonel set his career back. As the Korean War began to heat up, he thought he might find a better opportunity for his talents there. He had asked on an application form not to be assigned to a base in the South; in his interview, he admitted that he had a "difficult time handling prejudice there, because I think all human beings are equal in the sight of God." Nevertheless, he was sent to MP School at a base in Georgia, where he did have some problems with white officers.

Wallace had become close to a white officer from South Carolina, and they shipped out together to Korea, with Wallace winding up at a POW command in Kojedo. He was the only officer of color in his MP unit. "There were still people who had hidden agendas," he recalled, "because of the color of my skin, which I had nothing to do with." He was made orientation officer. It was a huge compound, housing over 13,000 prisoners. Tensions among the prisoners ran high, and in April 1952, when a riot broke out, Wallace was approached to help quell it. He was insulted to be singled out for that duty just because he was a person of color.

The prisoners were also agitating to turn American soldiers against the war by erecting signs that read, "Oppose the War for Peace!" and "The War Mongers of the Wall Street Drives You to the Place of Death." Any prisoner who expressed pro-American views was subject to murder by his fellow inmates; when the compound was dismantled, workers discovered a number of buried corpses.

Even in Korea, Wallace could not escape racial tensions. A captain he ran into at the camp spoke disparagingly of "nigras," referring to their buckteeth and talent for dancing. Wallace had to bite his tongue around a senior officer like that. "I used to climb up on a mountain," he recalled, "go under a tree and ask God to forgive him and to give me the strength before I kill him." Later, when the same officer gave him an order to be somewhere else in ten seconds, Wallace nearly lost it. He lunged at the man, his fingers clutching for the man's throat, but he stopped short of actually touching him. "All I could hear was my mother's voice," he recalled. "I proceeded to tell him how sick he was and that I was going to help him, and I was going to pray for him."

After that episode, he was transferred to a peripheral security detail. Whenever he saw the captain, he made a point of not saluting him. Five years later, at Fort Gordon in Georgia, he spotted the officer. Realizing that he still harbored hatred for the man, Wallace went back to his barracks, "got down on my knees and prayed to God to throw this out of me, because this is not a good feeling."

In Korea, when another officer came down hard on a recruit just arrived in camp who had accidentally fired his weapon—the captain wanted him court-martialed—Wallace came to the recruit's defense. Shortly after that, he was relieved of duty and sent back to the States.

Although he enjoyed some good assignments during the rest of his career, starting an advanced MP school and working for the Inspector General, Wallace finally left the military because "I could not handle the overt prejudice," feeling that he had been passed over one too many times for promotions.

"I am an American," he told his interviewer. "I don't want to be called anything else than that." Bertran Wallace was willing to look past the color of another man's skin, and it still pained him to know many men cannot do that.

NORMAN IKARI:
EAGER FOR A FIGHT

"The first thing I think about is I better not move.
They might finish me off."

THE DEMANDS AND PRESSURES PLACED ON YOUNG JAPANESE American men who served their country during World War II while their families were confined to detention centers can't be understated. And for men like Norman Ikari, who served with the 442nd Regimental Combat Team, that pressure was intensified, since the 442nd, also known as the "Go for Broke" outfit, fought in some of the European Theater's most intense battles.

Norman Saburo Ikari was the third son (which *saburo* means in Japanese) of immigrant parents. His two older brothers were born in Japan, before his parents emigrated to Seattle, Washington, where his father opened up a laundry and dry cleaning business. His older brothers quickly adapted to their new country, acquiring bicycles and then motorcycles to make their way around Seattle.

During the Depression, with the Ikari family business suffering, they decided to move to California, encouraged by the two oldest sons, who were already living there. Mr. Ikari and his sons opened a cleaning shop in Montebello, a suburb southeast of downtown Los Angeles. The family looked for a house to rent, but when they showed up at one prospective residence, the landlady took one look at them and burst into tears, claiming the neighbors would never allow a Japanese family to move in. They eventually found a home,

Norman Ikari at Camp Grant, Illinois, 1942,
where he did his basic training. He was not
issued a firearm in training, which he thought was intentional.

conveniently located across the street from the local Japanese Congregational Church.

Norman was a good student but minimally talented at athletics. He attended a Japanese language school every day after his regular classes; he recalled that the school was many blocks from his home, and he often had to walk back in the dark. He hated the school, mainly because it was just more work. He and his Jewish friends, who had to attend Hebrew school in the late afternoons, would commiserate about their academic burdens.

Ikari graduated from high school in 1936, but the family could not afford to send him to college, so, like a lot of other Nisei (second generation Japanese Americans), he got a job in a fruit and vegetable market. Then he got involved in the baby chick business, which was another magnet for young Nisei. The idea was to separate at birth female and male chicks, to ensure that a farmer buying chicks in quantity from a hatchery was getting only egg-producing females. He and a buddy staked out a territory in northwest Ohio and worked out of Toledo, traveling to hatcheries. The money was good, but the work was exhausting. Nevertheless, he was able to save enough money to return to Los Angeles in 1939 and enroll in the City College. Between semesters, he would go back east to earn more money in the chick business.

He was living in Los Angeles on December 7, 1941, when he heard the news of Pearl Harbor. There were some unpleasant episodes at school in the ensuing days, but he completed his final exams for the semester. All around him, other students were being drafted. He went to his draft board and registered, and on January 20, 1942, he was drafted.

In the wake of Pearl Harbor, Ikari's family split up. His father requested and was granted repatriation to Japan; his mother and his two younger sisters were sent to the relocation center in Poston, Arizona. One of his older brothers was assigned to Manzanar, a camp in California, the other to Poston. A younger brother moved to Colorado to join his girlfriend and her family living there.

Although the U.S. government classified all Japanese men of draft age as 4-C, non-draftable, Ikari had joined the Army before that policy was enacted, and he was allowed to stay. He underwent basic training at Camp Grant, Illinois, and was assigned to the medical replacement training center. He was never given a gun to carry or even to train with while he was there. He noted in his interview that he didn't think it was a coincidence.

He did get a pass to visit his mother in Arizona. He heard but couldn't confirm that Nisei soldiers couldn't get passes to go to Manzanar. Although he was in uniform for the entire trip, he did suffer some harassment, first at the gate to the camp, where he was challenged by an MP to produce his pass. Then when he and a buddy accompanying him went to the nearby town of Parker to buy a case of beer to share with residents of the camp, a bartender chased them out of the tavern. On their way out, they ran into an Indian on the street who was also in uniform. The soldier told Ikari, "Guys like us will never be welcome in places like this."

After completing basic training, everyone in his unit shipped out except for the Nisei soldiers. He was assigned to the station hospital, because he was a pre-med major in college. With his academic background, he was given responsibilities in the hospital's laboratories, and he learned a lot while he worked there for nearly two years.

In February 1943, President Roosevelt authorized the formation of the 442nd Regimental Combat Team, an all-Nisei outfit that would serve in the European Theater. Working in the lab at Camp Grant, "I felt like I was sort of out of things," Ikari recalled, and in November 1943, he applied for a transfer to the 442nd. To do so, he had to give up the sergeant's stripes he'd earned at Grant and was busted down to private. He recalled that about 100 Nisei were left behind at Grant, though they were later assigned as replacements in the 442nd after the team took heavy casualties.

"The Army," he recalled, "was just trying to round up Japanese guys from any place." They even selected men who were only one-eighth Japanese and reassigned a Nisei who was training as an aviation cadet in Texas. ("What a comedown," Ikari remarked.)

There were 3,300 men in that initial pool, about 2,500 of them from Hawaii, the rest from the mainland. Friction between the two groups sprang up, and it was "not just a verbal kind of thing," he recalled; there were "brawls and fights." The islanders were more extroverted and fun-loving; they shared everything with one another. There were also language differences; the mainlanders spoke a more precise English, which caused the islanders to call them "sissies." Meanwhile, many of the mainlanders, Ikari included, couldn't understand the islanders at all, their English was so heavily laced with Hawaiian vocabulary. Things got so bad that soldiers from E Company (Ikari's outfit) served on guard duty with fixed bayonets to protect their men from their rivals in M Company.

Finally, the commanding officer called together the entire regiment and read the riot act to them. He was especially upset about the behavior of some of the regiment's members while on leave in the nearby town of Hattiesburg, Mississippi, particularly toward local women. Ikari remembered his final words: "How are we going to fight together in combat when you're doing this fighting here?"

As Ikari heard it, what helped to unify the team was a little bus trip

Ikari at Camp Shelby, Mississippi, March 1943,
where he was part of the newly formed 442nd
Regimental Combat Team.

by the islanders to a Japanese American internment camp. The islanders had rarely experienced any discrimination in Hawaii, but the experience gave them an appreciation for what their fellow Nisei were going through, and things did calm down in Camp Shelby.

Ikari worked for a time in supply, then in the spring of 1944 shipped out through Newport News, Virginia. A month before he left, General George Marshall paid the unit a visit at Shelby to encourage the 442nd. The rumor was that they were headed for the Panama Canal and the Pacific, but their ship headed east for the Strait of Gibraltar and Italy. They landed north of Anzio and received their first combat orders on June 26.

But before he went into the line, Ikari was given a temporary assignment with a unit called the Special Police. He wore a helmet emblazoned with "SP" and was told to serve as a road guide for the advancing troops. It was "ridiculous," Ikari recalled, because he was new to the country and had no idea where anything was.

After a week of SP duty, he asked to rejoin his company, which had left for the front. In his travels to catch up to E Company, he saw a lot of jeeps coming in the opposite direction, carrying men on stretchers; they were all Germans, and many of them were dead. He caught up with Easy Company on the reverse slope of a hill and found his sergeant. "Better get yourself an M-1," was his advice. A few minutes later, someone handed him a rifle. As night fell, Ikari nodded off, and then awoke with a start—his company was gone. He worked along the hill sideways, "hoping to bump into somebody," and finally located some familiar faces.

Ikari recalled from those first days in combat the screaming of the German 88mm shells, the most feared ammunition in the Nazi arsenal. His sergeant went without a helmet, he claimed, to be better able to pick up the first sounds of an incoming shell and warn the rest of the men. Ikari's other memory: "It seemed like all of our combat was going uphill," that Germans always occupied the higher ground.

One day in the hills east of Pisa and Livorno, he was the number two man on an advance patrol and was actually coming down a hill when he "felt like someone had hit me with a lead pipe or baseball bat across both legs." His number one man ran for help, and he was left alone on the side of that hill. He recalled, "The first thing I think about is I better not move. They might finish me off. So I didn't move; evidently the bullet had pierced my femoral artery. I felt myself starting to pass out. I thought, This is not good. I reached down and tried to grab my leg. My fingers just slipped into a hole in my leg. I was yelling for the medics. I said a few prayers."

He heard someone approaching and then could see a soldier with a red cross on his helmet bending over to examine him. It was one of the company's medics, Yeiichi "Kelly" Kuwayama, accompanied by a Hawaiian soldier. "I can remember every word Kelly said to me to this day. When he bent over, he said, 'Why didn't you put on a tourniquet?'" In the next moment, their position began to get blanketed with mortar fire. Kuwayama told him, "We're taking an awful chance," but he and the Hawaiian managed to carry Ikari back to safety.

The doctor at the aid station told him, "You should feel lucky; I've seen guys come in without their legs," not exactly reassuring words. He was seriously hurt, with bones shattered in both legs and compound fractures. He spent four months recovering, first in Rome and then in Naples, starting out in a double cast, then a single, then confined to a wheelchair, then on crutches, and finally walking with a cane.

Late in 1944 he was assigned to the 15th Medical General Laboratory in Naples. It seemed like a dream job, but it was in the veterinary section, so he wasn't motivated to learn much.

After three months, he was rotated back to the States and given a twenty-day furlough before he had to report to his next duty station, at Camp Ritchie in northern Maryland. He visited his mother in Arizona and then headed east. At Ritchie, a training center for intelligence officers, he was told that he would join other Nisei soldiers in a demonstration team; they would don Japanese Army uniforms and participate in exercises to prepare for the invasion of Japan. "We were shocked and disgusted and angry," he recalled. A high-ranking officer tried to talk them into doing the job as "one last gesture of your patriotism." Several Hawaiian Nisei were so angry that they went AWOL; Ikari heard that they headed out for New York City and just disappeared. When he and a buddy refused the assignment, they were handed brooms and made janitors at the camp.

In August 1945, with the Japanese surrender, "there was no more need for us on this crazy duty," Ikari recalled. He traveled to a separation center at Fort Bragg and soon rejoined his mother in Los Angeles.

Norman Ikari wants to keep alive the memory of what he experienced in World War II for younger generations of Americans, who may only vaguely know the story of the Issei (first generation Japanese immigrants) and Nisei. He speaks frequently at schools and believes that "to talk about the camps is only part of the Japanese-American experience." Being a decorated member of the 442nd—the most decorated unit of its size in the history of the U.S. military—is a badge of honor he does not wear lightly.

YEIICHI KELLY KUWAYAMA: NOT PLAYING IT SAFE

"I think each time I went out into no-man's-land was an event."

F OR MOST SOLDIERS ALREADY SERVING IN THE U.S. ARMED Forces on December 7, 1941, the attack on Pearl Harbor was a call to battle. But for a Nisei (second-generation Japanese American) like Yeiichi Kuwayama, the opportunity to join the fight was delayed by mistrust. Kuwayama insisted he could do more for his country than serve Stateside, and he got his chance to make a contribution by serving in combat as part of the most decorated unit of its size in the entire war.

His parents were both born in Japan and emigrated to the U.S. in 1909 (his father) and 1913 (his mother). They married in 1913 and settled in New York City. Yeiichi was their third of five children and first son, born in 1918. Senzo, his father, was an entrepreneur who owned a store from which he sold arts goods to retail customers and Japanese provisions to stores and restaurants in the New York area.

Until Yeiichi reached the age of twelve, the Kuwayamas lived on East 59th Street in Manhattan. In 1930 when they moved to the Woodside neighborhood of Queens, there were no other Asians living nearby, but Yeiichi's friends were a mix of second-generation Irish, Italian, and German American kids. Yeiichi and his siblings attended a Japanese language school on Saturdays, but he said the school was not well-run and he learned little from the experience.

Yeiichi Kelly Kuwayama, January 1944. He was drafted in early 1941, and after the Pearl Harbor attack, knew he was in for the duration.

Yeiichi attended public school and was expected, like all of his siblings, to attend college, even though neither of his parents had an education beyond high school and were not vocal about what they wanted their children to do. "They really left it up to the individual child to set his own goals on what he or she wanted to do or be," he wrote in a short memoir. His older sister (the eldest sister had died in

1918) attended New York University, and Yeiichi went to Princeton; his younger siblings went to Skidmore and Williams.

He wrote, "My family's outlook and planning was that we were free agents. My father bought [a] cemetery plot in 1918 when my sister died, so he expected that he and his family would be buried in the U.S.A. He did not expect his children to take up his business after him. New York City was a city with people from all over the world who were constantly changing occupations and lifestyles, so he was permissive as to what his children did. My father had no feelings of ethnic purity. We as a family were not conscious of racial ties at that time during war and pre-wartime."

Even in the late 1930s, with war looming, Yeiichi's parents did not discuss politics with their children, though, with so much of his father's business tied up with Japanese trade, it was difficult to ignore the increasing tensions between Americans and Japanese immigrants. As Yeiichi recalled, "I was probably eleven or twelve years old, before we moved to Woodside. I was asked by a Japanese visitor in case of war which side would I fight for. I said the U.S. I had been saying the Pledge of Allegiance at school, and even at that young age I knew my deficiency in the Japanese language. My parents made no comment either way when I responded. I think they expected it, since my father had bought his cemetery plot in the U.S."

Kuwayama graduated from Princeton in 1940, the year the peacetime draft was initiated. He was working for the Japanese Chamber of Commerce in New York when he was drafted, and he reported for duty in January 1941. "My Japanese ancestry was not a question before, during, or after my induction into the U.S. Army," he wrote. "I did not expect or want to be treated any differently than any other American." Most of his fellow draftees were men, like him, in their twenties, a mix of professionals and laborers.

The Army was clearly unprepared for this influx of personnel. There were no uniforms available, and the men were issued World War I outfits with wraparound leggings and riding boots. They were quartered in tents, even in the middle of the winter, with only a wood-burning stove for heat. Rations were so scarce that for a time they ate only two meals a day.

He was assigned to the 244th Coast Artillery in Brooklyn, and he encountered his first incident of anti-Japanese prejudice. "I found myself in a tower with a map of New York City Harbor with locations of the Coast Artillery batteries and cross-fire into the ships channel. We had a general inspection and the general asked my name, and I said, 'Private Kuwayama, sir.' The next day I was shipped out to a Quartermaster Company located in Madison Barracks, New York, and assigned the job of requisition clerk. Although we were not at war, and Pearl Harbor was a year away, I was quite sure that because my name was Japanese I was shipped out from New York Harbor Defense and to a job of requisition clerk for auto parts in northern New York near Lake Ontario."

His family accepted his being drafted and visited him when he was stationed in New York City, but not when he was moved north.

On December 7, Kuwayama had just returned to his barracks from maneuvers in North Carolina when the news of the Japanese attack on Pearl Harbor was broadcast on the radio. He then realized he was not getting out of the Army any time soon, that he was in for the duration. After the U.S. entered the war, his family's movements were restricted, under a general order from New York Mayor Fiorello LaGuardia. The FBI visited them once, to confiscate a Japanese archery set and a radio, which were never returned. His father closed down his business, whose fortunes had been dwindling, and the family managed to get through the war years on savings.

Kuwayama wrote, "My parents felt, I suppose, 'shikataga nai'—it just can't be helped."

During his first two years in the Army, both before and after December 7, Kuwayama was transferred many times, always to administrative and service units. He picked up the nickname "Kelly" from a sergeant who never learned how to pronounce his last name. But he never received any formal training in what he was assigned to do; his experiences required learning on the job. At the Station Hospital in Fort Ethan Allen in Vermont, he taught himself operating room procedures from a manual and then taught them to other recruits. He rarely saw any other Nisei, largely because after Pearl Harbor, they were forbidden from serving in the U.S. Armed Forces. That changed on February 1, 1943, when President Roosevelt signed an order opening up military service to Nisei, and the all-Nisei 442nd Regimental Combat Team was born shortly thereafter.

At Ethan Allen, a Japanese American chaplain named Yamada

Kuwayama in Italy in February 1945,
after his unit, the 442nd Combat Regimental Team,
had distinguished itself in battles
in France and Italy.

approached Kuwayama and two other Nisei, asking them if they'd like
to join the new 442nd. They agreed, but when Kuwayama reported for
duty, he found that there was a surfeit of medical sergeants like him.
For Nisei who were already in the Army before Pearl Harbor, medical
units were a popular dumping ground. He was sent to an evacuation

*Kuwayama (center) and members of the 442nd
present a check to President Truman toward a memorial to the late
President Roosevelt, September 1945.*

hospital in Texas, but just before the 442nd shipped out for Europe, he was reassigned to them, as a field medic with Company E.

They sailed over on a Liberty ship. A running poker game didn't interest him, and the stench below decks of men suffering from seasickness drove him to sleep on deck. They landed in Naples, which already had been taken, and there was a delay in their getting into action. Meanwhile, they attended an opera ("an interesting experience," he told an interviewer in 2003), inspected the damage done to the city by the fighting, found out how valuable their cigarettes and chocolate were to the locals, and couldn't help noticing the openness of prostitution, "which was new to us."

The first time Kuwayama saw dead soldiers was on a bridge—two Americans who had been on advance patrol, and two of the enemy. The 442nd's first combat experience came in June 1944, north of Rome, when the Germans shot over the infantry and hit regimental headquarters, killing a popular captain. In their first firefight, they were pinned down, but after that they settled into a routine: "it was one hill after another. The Germans would put a machine gun on top of a hill with one or two people and that was it." The 442nd would direct their artillery to the top of the hill, and either the Germans would be hit or move on to the next hill. Occasionally, the Germans would mount a real resistance, setting up artillery and troops to take a stand. Then the 442nd would have to hold for a few days, and "their artillery would hone in on our positions, and we would have quite a few casualties."

Their biggest supply problem was water; in the hot Italian summer, one canteen wasn't enough for one day. The Germans "knew we had to get water" and targeted the water pumps and wells in the mountains. As Kuwayama recalled, "I always admired guys who came around and collected our canteens to fill with water and then returned them to us. It was a dangerous mission just to get water."

As soon as they were in sight of Pisa, he got leave and went back to Rome to play tourist, taking in the catacombs and the Coliseum. Upon his return, the 442nd was told they were going to be reassigned to the invasion of southern France. Their anti-tank people had already gone in with glider troops; the rest of them went up in trucks toward the Rhone River, near Lyon. They fought a fierce battle for Bruyeres, which they took with, as Kuwayama recalled, "quite a bit of casualties."

In October, they received their most dangerous assignment, a rescue mission involving the 141st Infantry Regiment in the 36th Texas Division, which became known as the "Lost Battalion." The battalion was surrounded by the Germans in the Vosges Mountains near Biffontaine, France. Between October 26 and 30, the 442nd fought valiantly to break through the German lines. "We didn't know how many they were going to rescue," Kuwayama recalled, "we knew it was a tough mission." (The count was 211 soldiers.) They had to deal with cleverly concealed machine gunners, who didn't open fire on the Americans until they got very close, lest they give away their position by their own gunfire; and with tree bursts, which happened when Germans would shoot artillery into tops of trees, and limbs and shrapnel would come raining down on the soldiers.

Kuwayama was wounded during this mission, in which the 442nd, by one account, suffered over 800 casualties, nearly half of its

men. On October 29, he was tending to a wounded soldier when
he was hit, he thought, by shrapnel from a German grenade, though
one member of his outfit saw a bullet hit his helmet, go all around
it and drop down. "I didn't see that at all," Kuwayama said. When he
was wounded, he was closer to G Company than his own; they took
him back to an aid station on a jeep. The battles in the Vosges
Mountains were unquestionably important, Kuwayama, said,
because this was the entryway into the backside of Germany. "So
tactically it was important," he said, "but whether it was worth that
many casualties, I'm not sure."

His job was to answer the call for "medic" from anyone in the field.
He didn't wear a red cross on his helmet, because that might give away
their position, but he did carry a flag with the cross on it; he kept it
furled until he went into the field. His principal job was to stop bleeding either by tourniquet or pressure, to put sulfur into the wound, and
get the man to a stretcher-bearer. "I think," he wrote in his memoir,
"each time I went out into no-man's-land was an event."

After the rescue of the Lost Battalion, the 442nd was so decimated that they were given extended R&R in the Maritime Alps, a secure
area between Italy and France. Kuwayama spent a month or so in hospitals in that area and managed to get down to the French Riviera and
enjoy the hotels and restaurants of Nice.

The 442nd then returned to Italy, starting at Spezia and working
their way over the Apennine Mountains into the Po River Valley. It was
during this campaign that the Team's most famous member, Daniel
Inouye, the future senator from Hawaii, was wounded and lost his arm.
They were still in Italy when the war ended in Europe.

With his service dating back almost four years and his citations
(including a Silver Star for his actions the day he was wounded),
Kuwayama was immediately eligible to be rotated back to the States.
He was discharged from the Army at Fort Dix, New Jersey, and was
back in New York when he heard the news of the atomic bombs being
dropped on Hiroshima and Nagasaki. On August 15, 1945, he was in
Times Square for V-J Day, just another man in civilian clothes.

"The record of the 442nd," Kelly Kuwayama said, "is that any mission we were assigned, we accomplished." The spirit of the 442nd,
whose slogan was "Go for Broke," earned it more commendations

than any unit of its size in the history of the American military. Some may call that circumstance ironic, but for Kuwayama and his Nisei brothers in arms, they were only serving the country in which they were born and had sworn allegiance to those many times in their school classrooms.

CHAPTER FIVE

SURVIVORS

THE VULNERABILITY OF MEN AND WOMEN SERVING THEIR COUNTRY IS vividly recalled in the selections that follow. We begin with two riveting tales of survival at sea, in which Harold Lippard recalls the attack on the USS *Franklin* and Giles McCoy relates the sinking of the USS *Indianapolis*. Every sailor who survived these incidents could tell his own story of heroism and perseverance.

Other dramatic tales of survival in the Veterans History Project come from prisoners of war. At the mercy of their captors, they cannot know what to expect. As Americans in the custody of Germans (Harold Riley, Johann Kasten, and Milton Stern), Japanese (John Stensby), Koreans (José Mares), Vietnamese (John McCain, Roger Ingvalson), and Iraqis (Rhonda Cornum) would learn, civility often took a back seat to expediency and cruelty. The terms of captivity related here range from a week to five and a half years, but in each instance, the prisoner tapped on reserves of fortitude, patience, and resourcefulness.

HAROLD LIPPARD:
COOL UNDER FIRE

"I wasn't as cocky. It was a pain to go back into battle."

H E HAD NEVER BEEN ON A BOAT BIGGER THAN A ROWBOAT, SO when Harold Lippard boarded the huge aircraft carrier USS *Franklin*, he might have had an excuse to be in awe of it. Later, in battle, Lippard was to call upon all his Navy training to keep his composure in the midst of one of the worst catastrophes in U.S. naval history.

A self-described "dumb little farm boy" from Statesville, North Carolina, Lippard was the youngest of eleven children. After graduating from high school, he worked on his family's farm and took other jobs. By 1942, he recalled, though married with his first child on the way, he was "tired of being called a 4-F" and enlisted in the Navy. He did his basic training in Pensacola, Florida, the first time he'd ever been away from home. Asked what he did in boot camp, Lippard replied with a grin, "Anything the fellow said."

He was assigned to the Norfolk Naval Hospital and applied to be a storekeeper, but was placed in the medical corps. He learned how to give inoculations and basic first aid, then went to an aviation medical school in Portsmouth, Virginia. His first shipboard orders were for the newly commissioned aircraft carrier USS *Franklin* out of Norfolk.

Lippard was amazed to find himself aboard a "floating small city" with a crew of nearly 3,500. The *Franklin* displaced 27,100 tons, was 872 feet long, and could hold more than eighty aircraft. The carrier sailed through the Panama Canal and on to San Diego, where her 40mm antiaircraft guns were installed. They would not have fit through the canal locks if mounted.

In June 1944, she sailed via Pearl Harbor for Eniwetok in the South Pacific. Lippard had his head shaved in the time-honored ritual for crossing the International Date Line. The problem was "it never grew back." A medical officer with a mustache had half of it shaved off.

The *Franklin's* first big action came on July 4, off Iwo Jima. Lippard remembered an ominous feeling as they approached the island, in part because he could see Mount Surabachi, the immense, brooding volcano on the island's southern tip, from more than fifty miles away, well before the rest of the tiny island appeared. In preparation for the U.S. invasion, which would take place in February 1945, the *Franklin's* guns pounded Japanese installations and her planes bombed the island.

Even before entering into combat, Lippard saw casualties. The flight deck, he soon learned, was a dangerous place to be. If you weren't careful around the planes, a strong gust of wind or back draft could blow you into a spinning propeller and shred you to ribbons; Lippard saw that happen more than once.

Two days later, the *Franklin* struck Guam and Rota to soften them up for their invasions; she then lent direct support to enable safe landings for the first assault waves. October found her in support of the upcoming invasion of Leyte in the Philippines, and it was here that she ran into serious danger. Four Japanese bombers swooped down on the *Franklin*, and she narrowly missed being hit by two torpedoes.

Then a Japanese plane hit the *Franklin's* deck in what looked to be a suicide attack, among the first of what would later become an epidemic of kamikaze attacks. The plane hit the deck about 100 feet from where Lippard was standing, slid across the deck and into the water on the starboard side.

Later that month, on the thirtieth, off Samar, one of the Philippine Islands, the ship came under more serious attack, by three planes determined to crash into her and do maximum damage. One missed the *Franklin* and went into the water, the other missed the *Franklin* but did hit another ship, the *Belleau Wood*. But a third one managed to dodge the *Franklin's* guns and hit the flight deck, crashing through to the gallery deck, killing fifty-six and wounding another sixty. After that hit, the ship had to return for repairs to the Puget Sound Navy Yard in Bremerton, Washington, arriving there in late November 1944.

Lippard and his buddies had been listening to Tokyo Rose, whom he admitted "put on a good show" in terms of the music she played. She had warned them that the Japanese Armed Forces were going to find a way to sink the big aircraft carriers that had been so instrumental in turning the war around for the American Navy.

In Bremerton he got a thirty-day leave and made his way back to North Carolina to see his baby for the first time. For the trip, the cooks onboard the ship furnished him with some grapefruit juice, while he laid in a supply of medicinal alcohol to pep up the juice. What Lippard had seen in his first few months in the Pacific had shaken him. He admitted, "I wasn't as cocky," adding that "it was a pain to go back into battle."

For the return trip to the front, the *Franklin* packed some new rockets. But she never got to use them.

They left Bremerton on February 2, 1945, sailing for Okinawa, the last big island battle before the planned invasion of Japan. On March 15, the *Franklin* rendezvoused with several other ships in support of the upcoming invasion, and on March 18 she commenced action against the island. The Japanese knew that once the Allies took Okinawa, their planes would be within easy striking distance of the homeland.

On March 19, the *Franklin* was within fifty miles of Okinawa, closer than any U.S. carrier had come during the war. Just before dawn, a Yokosuka D4Y dive bomber came knifing through the cloud cover. Twenty-five planes had already left the *Franklin* on the dawn patrol, but there were still many more parked on deck. The dive bomber managed to drop a pair of 500-pound bombs, one right on the centerline of the flight deck, the other aft. The first bomb penetrated through two more decks, the second set off explosions among the considerable ammunition onboard.

Lippard recalled that he was the only corpsman on deck at the time, and his main concern was giving first aid to as many men as possible. Fires had consumed all of the planes, their ammunition and bombs were exploding, and he thought the ship was going to sink. Not surprisingly, he said the scene "scared the hell out of me." What he recalled of those minutes and hours after the crash was reacting and not thinking—just like a well-trained sailor. Luckily, sick bay was still secure, so they were able to use those facilities without interruption.

At one point, he went to get a stretcher for a severely wounded man, and an explosion forced him over the side. He was in the water for four hours or more, taking care, as best he could, of injured men who had fallen or jumped into the water themselves. Whenever he could, he recalled, Lippard administered morphine to the men.

The ship was dead in the water and listing badly to starboard, with no working communications. But miraculously, she never sank. She got a tow from the USS *Pittsburgh* until she could get up enough speed on her own, proceeded to Ulithi, a base in the South Pacific, and then to Pearl Harbor for cleanup before sailing to the Brooklyn Navy Yard for repairs that could only be handled in that shipyard. They arrived in New York on April 28, 1945. The war was almost over in Europe; it was definitely over for the *Franklin*.

The final death toll on the *Franklin*, according to Lippard, was 832; some sources put it at 724, but in either case, it was one of the greatest disasters in the history of the U.S. Navy. The voyage home must have been among the saddest for any crew; Lippard remembers putting the last body to rest at sea just off the coast of New Jersey.

In spite of what he'd been through, he considered making a career out of the Navy, but according to Lippard, a new "shavetail" (slang for ensign or second lieutenant) came in and "just tore things up," and he didn't want to deal with the political repercussions. He agreed to stay in the reserves and was called up during the Korean War, only to spend his eighteen-month tour at a naval air base in Virginia running a dispensary and handling routine assignments. After all the action he saw on the *Franklin*, that was the "best duty I ever had," he said.

GILES McCOY:
THE ULTIMATE SURVIVOR

*"I didn't want to end up in the belly of some shark,
and neither did the other guys."*

AFTER SURVIVING THREE OF THE PACIFIC THEATER'S MOST harrowing campaigns and a kamikaze attack, Marine Giles McCoy thought the worst was over when his ship returned to the States for repairs in the summer of 1945. But that ship, the heavy cruiser USS *Indianapolis*, had one more mission to perform, a special delivery to a tiny island 5,000 miles away. The aftermath of that mission was an event whose horrible consequences still reverberate.

McCoy was barely into his teens when the U.S. entered World War II. Born in 1926 in St. Louis, Missouri, he saw two older brothers go off to fight, and neither came home. Nevertheless, he wanted to make his own contribution to the war effort, even if he wasn't old enough to sign up. "My mother didn't want to sign [for me], and my dad was a World War I veteran, and he didn't want me to go," McCoy recalled in a 2002 interview. "I had to beg them. All my buddies out of high school were going into the service. I liked the Marine Corps and I thought that I would get into some action. So that is what we did; I went down there and finally [my mother] came along with me and signed the papers for me and cried all the way."

McCoy's stint at boot camp at the Marine Depot in San Diego earned him a reputation as a crack marksman. "After I fired on the range I made a mistake of firing too good," he recalled. "Out of a top possibility of 250 I shot a 248. The major in the Marine Corps came up to me and said, 'Where is this McCoy at?' I said, 'Right here.' He said, 'We are going to make a sniper out of you. We don't have any, and you are going to be one of the first ones.' I said, 'Why are you doing that to me?' He said, 'Look at your firing score.'"

"I didn't like the job," McCoy later admitted. "It was a nasty job. I almost got court-martialed a couple of times, once for not shooting two Japanese boys. They weren't any more than ten or twelve years old. I had a sergeant with me as an observer, and he told me to take those boys out. I told him, 'I'm not going to do it. I wasn't brought up that way and I didn't come into this war to shoot kids. I've shot men, and I haven't liked it, but I'm sure as hell not going to shoot those boys.' He said, 'Well, I'll get you court-martialed.' I said, 'Sergeant, you do what you have to do, but I'm not going to shoot them. Here's my rifle, but I'm not going to have that on my conscience; I've got enough on my conscience.'"

This was on Pelelieu, an island in the Palau group east of the Philippines. It was September 1944, and U.S. forces were slogging their way through the Pacific, taking back one island at a time from the Japanese. McCoy's unit was involved in the capture of Pelelieu, to protect General Douglas MacArthur's flank as he fought his way back to the Philippines. The island was honeycombed with fortified bunkers in the cliffs that allowed Japanese defenders a great advantage. Scaling those cliffs and taking out gun emplacements took seven weeks of fighting in terrible tropical heat, and U.S. forces had lost 1,750 dead, with over 8,000 wounded. According to at least one source, Pelelieu exacted the highest casualty rate of any amphibious landing during the war.

McCoy almost made it through that invasion without a scratch, but near the end of operations a Japanese sniper wounded him. "I was shot through the groin and through my leg," he would recall. "I was trying to stop the bleeding and decide how badly wounded I was." A sergeant who had taken McCoy under his wing during the first landing on Pelelieu kept saying, "Do you see him? Do you see him, McCoy?" And McCoy told him, "Hell, Sergeant, I'm busy trying to stop my bleeding." "Get that damned stuff stopped and pick him up;

Giles McCoy at boot camp in San Diego, 1942.
His scores on marksmanship tests there earned him a job
as a sniper in the Pacific Theater.

he's moving!" replied the sergeant. "I looked and I found him," McCoy remembered. "The Jap made a stupid mistake; he got up and moved, and when he moved to try and get into a better position to finish me, as soon as I got him in my scope it was over with. I clicked off a round and the sergeant said, 'Did you get him?' I said, 'Sergeant, you know that I don't miss at this range.' He said, 'OK, now go and stop that damned wound.'"

McCoy was evacuated to an island called Pavuvu, north of Guadalcanal, where sanitary conditions were non-existent ("It was filled with rats and land crabs, and it was really bad.") He was sent back to Pearl Harbor for further treatment, and when he was well enough to return to action, one of the officers looked at his record and said, "You've done enough, son. I am going to put you aboard the USS *Indianapolis.*"

"It was a beautiful ship," McCoy recalled. "Once you have been in the Marine infantry, and all of a sudden you get onboard a clean ship like the *Indianapolis,* and you can take a shower every day, and your food is not filled with bugs, and you can eat food without gritting your teeth because of all the sand that comes in with it—it was really a pleasure. I thought I was in heaven." He became a "hot shell man" on one of the eight five-inch/.38 caliber guns; he would catch the hot shell casing when it was ejected out of the chamber of the gun. "You can't let them bounce around the deck, 'cause they will hit somebody and break a leg." After he caught the shell, he would put it into a net with the others, and he never dropped a single shell.

The *Indianapolis* was off to Iwo Jima, where McCoy's skills as a sniper were in great demand. As at Pelelieu, the Japanese occupied the high ground, especially on Surabachi, the mountain that dominated the island's southern tip. McCoy was among a group of eighty Marine snipers assigned to protect the regimental assault on the mountain, picking off any Japanese soldier who showed his face.

The *Indianapolis* moved on to Okinawa, where it was to shell the beach at Naha, on the southeastern end of the island. They were close enough to land their own shells, but the Japanese guns returning fire weren't powerful enough to reach the ship. Then a suicide plane hit them. "It hit on my side of the ship," recalled McCoy. "I was on the port side where my gun was. I was catching shells as the gun was going up and shooting straight up. I was jamming them into the deck and kicking them away from me. All of a sudden there was no more shells coming. I thought, 'What's wrong here?' I looked around and my gun crew was gone! They were all lying on the deck right off where I was throwing the shells; they saw the suicide plane come right down to us. It hit about fifty feet from our gun emplacement. In fact, I went back to the fantail where it hit—it hit on the main deck aft—and I got a hand on the plane to help push it over the side, because we didn't want it to catch fire. I could see the Japanese pilot that was plastered up on the dash of the plane; the Navy boys were already wiggling it, and then we pushed it on off the side and got rid of it and it didn't ignite. It put a big hole in us, and we had to creep back to Guam."

The *Indianapolis* lost nine men in that attack, and it had to return to the United States for further repairs. While McCoy was waiting, his mother got word of his being back, and she insisted on bringing out one of his five sisters to visit him. They stayed in Vallejo, California, in the eastern portion of San Francisco Bay, while the *Indianapolis* was being fixed up on nearby Mare Island. McCoy and his crewmates got wind of a mission for their ship back to the South Pacific. "As we were pulling out of our repair dock," McCoy recalled to his interviewer, "I told my mother and sister goodbye, and then we went down to Hunter's Point in San Francisco. We pulled up alongside of the dock there, and we should have known that there was something big up, because there was Marines in motor launches out in the Bay area and there were armed Marines all over the dock. Anyhow, my mother and my sister were still up in Vallejo, and so I asked my executive officer, Commander Flynn, if I could call my mother. He said, 'No, I can't even tell my wife that I'm not coming home for supper!'"

Two large crates were loaded onto the *Indianapolis*, and a twenty-four-hour Marine guard was assigned to them. "We were making all kinds of nasty jokes for the admirals and the officers," McCoy recalled. "All the guys were taking bets [on] what it was, but we didn't know that it was that desperate. The captain told us Marines that we had to guard this with our lives and that we couldn't let anybody come in there that wasn't authorized. My statement to him was, 'Sir, what the heck, we are going to be out in the middle of the ocean. How can anybody come in here and get in?' He said, 'I don't care. None of the enlisted men or officers who are not authorized are to go in there and mess with those crates. You are not to allow anybody to tinker with them unless they are authorized.'" Two scientists were also on board,

McCoy has remained active in the Indianapolis's *survivors organization.*

and they were assigned to periodically check on the condition of the crates. The ship and its mysterious cargo were bound for Tinian, a small island in the Marianas chain.

As McCoy recalled, "The *Indianapolis* still holds the record as far as I understand for a surface vessel on the trip from the States to Tinian, which is about 5,000 miles. We averaged between 29 and 30 knots; most ships can't even do that many knots. The *Indianapolis* could do 34 to 35 knots; very few destroyers or any of them could keep up with us when we were opened up. The *Indianapolis* was a good ship; it was a happy ship. I know that sounds strange, but you kind of base a combat ship on, 'Did you have a happy ship or was it a bitch of a ship?' Ours was a happy ship; Captain [Charles] McVay was a great skipper, and we all had tremendous respect for him. He was top drawer as far as any of us were concerned. There were times when he even came down and got into the mess line. I remember one time I gave my spot to him and he said, 'You've been standing in line waiting there, I'll get behind you. You get in there and get your food.' If he didn't like the food he called the cooks out and he said, 'Do you expect these men to eat this garbage? You improve that and you do it by tomorrow!' He was that kind of a man. He wanted a good ship, a well-disciplined ship, but he wanted everything to be done just perfectly. He didn't tolerate, 'I don't remember.' He didn't understand that, and that is why he and I got along so well together. I had a tremendous respect for him."

The cargo the *Indianapolis* delivered to Tinian was the atomic bombs destined to be dropped on Hiroshima and Nagasaki. The crew still didn't know that even after they dropped off the two crates and headed to Guam. Captain McVay had requested a destroyer escort for the late July voyage, but he was denied.

At 12:14 A.M. on July 30, 1945, the USS *Indianapolis* was torpedoed by Japanese submarine *I-58*, commanded by Mochitsura Hashimoto, in the Philippine Sea. The first torpedo destroyed the ship's bow; the second hit amidships on the starboard side, adjacent to fuel tanks and an ammunition magazine. As McCoy recalled, "I was three decks below; I had changed the watch a half hour early. We had a brig watch; we had two of our sailors, a cook and a baker, who had misbehaved in San Francisco, so they got a deck court-martial. They were going through a ten-day sentence, so we had to stand watch twenty-four hours a day on them. They were [supposed to be] on bread and water, but they never did; they had the best food. All their buddies from the cooks and the bakers brought food down, and they brought enough for the Marines that were on guard. I had my share of it. They took care of their men and us, too.

"I changed the watch a half hour early that night because it was so hot below deck. The *Indianapolis* had no air conditioning, and it was 118, 120 degrees during the day; it was awful hot at night, you could hardly sleep. So I changed the watch, and PFC Davis was the guy that was on duty; he just got back to the Marine compartment when the second torpedo hit. It hit right below the Marine compartment, and so he just got back in time to get killed. When the second hit, then it blew up our eight-inch magazine, which was amidships, and then it threw me from one side of the compartment to the other, and men and bunks came down on top of me. I squirmed out from underneath all of it. All the lights and controls went out. So I crawled back to my battle station where the brig was, and I had an electric battery-operated lantern. I turned it on, and guys were hollering, wanting to get the bunks off of them. Fellows had broken arms and broken legs and broken ribs. So we started getting them out. I got my two prisoners out, and I told them, 'I can't let you go topside. I want you to stay here and help me get these men out from underneath these bunks. They did; they did a great job. They stayed right with me, and we hauled these guys out. As we would get them out, we would get them to go topside if they could make it.

"Then a chief petty officer stuck his head down and he said for everybody that was able in the compartment to get out because he was going to close and 'dog the hatch.' When they 'dog a hatch' onboard a ship to make [a compartment] water tight, that means that it is sealed permanently. They close it from above and they put a metal pin in it where you can't open it again from below. I know that my two prisoners left me right when he hollered. The second time the chief came by—the chief knew me because I had done work for him—he said, 'McCoy, you get your butt out of there because I'm dogging the hatch.' I came topside and I said, 'Chief, let me go back down there again. There are still men down there that can't get out. They are buried underneath bunks and such.' He said, 'That's where they are going to have to stay, son. I'm not letting you go back.' That is the part that still bothers me, even in my old age. I can still remember hearing those fellows holler, trying to get out. That was going to be their tomb."

McCoy managed to grab a life jacket; there was no time to man the lifeboats, the ship was sinking so quickly. He began walking down the side of the ship toward the keel. "I knew that I had to get away from the ship," he recalled. "When I got to the keel I just squatted down and slid on down into the water and started swimming away. When I looked back, the ship was standing on her nose and the propellers were still going around and men were still jumping off the fantail, many of them hitting the propellers.

"I started swimming, and the ship sucked me on down. I don't know how far I went down; I went down until my head felt like it was going to blow open. Then I caught an air bubble and came back up in the air bubble to the surface. When I looked back, there was nothing left but a big old mountain of foam, and the *Indianapolis*, which was our home, was gone. You could feel her still exploding; I could feel the explosions under the water hitting me in the groin as I was trying to get my life jacket on." The ship sank in twelve minutes. Of 1,196 men on board, approximately 300 went down with her.

The seas were rough, it was pitch dark, and there was a huge oil slick on the surface of the water. McCoy swallowed some of the oil and got violently ill. "I came across another group of men," he recalled. "One of them was a bosun's mate who was a good friend of mine, that I had done duty with; his name was Gene Morgan. Gene was straddling a five-inch powder can; he didn't have a life jacket. I got up to him, and he recognized me. I said, 'Gene, you can't survive on that powder can. We don't know how long we are going to be out here.' He said, 'Well, that's all I got!' We had to wait until a dead body floated by with a life jacket on; I took it off the body and said a prayer to it and let it go. I put it [the jacket] on him and then I left him."

A group of men floated by clinging to the remains of a life raft that had been damaged by the second torpedo. McCoy's buddy Gene passed on joining the group. "They'll pick us up tomorrow," he told McCoy. "It may not be tomorrow," McCoy said.

At daylight sharks came. "A couple of guys got hit by sharks and got taken down," McCoy remembered. "We did everything wrong. We kicked our feet and tried to get them up out of the water, and we climbed on top of one another because we knew they would come underneath you and come up after you. I kicked seven of them in my days [in the water]. I never had any training on sharks; I was just told you had to try to keep away from them. If you got hit by one of them, you were pretty well going to die, because it would attract a lot more sharks. I found out that if you kicked them in the eyeball, it really hurt them, and they would leave you alone. You could see thirty, forty, fifty feet down into the water and you see them thrash back and forth after you hit them. They just couldn't stand that. The other ones would come back, but not those."

McCoy found himself trying to pick up everyone's morale. "I kept trying to encourage everybody that within forty-eight hours they would be picking us up out of the water," he recalled. "I kept telling a lot of the guys that were wanting to give up—guys started giving up quick—'You can't die, you got to stay alive, you've got a family at home, hang in there.' I said, 'I don't have a family, I just have a wonderful mother and a bunch of sisters and my father and I want to stay alive for them if I can. Some of you guys got families.' So we tried to help one another, and as the days went on and nobody showed up, we realized we were not going to be picked up out of the water. We were going to eventually die. I didn't want to end up in the belly of some shark, and neither did the other guys.

"It was easier to die than it was to stay alive; to stay alive you had to work at it, but to die all you had to do was quit, just give up. We kept trying to encourage the guys. They wanted the easy way out; they had all [the suffering] they wanted. We tried to tell these guys, 'Don't die! There is a light; they are going to pick us up out of the water tomorrow. They are going to give us water and there are going to be doctors to take care of us, so don't quit, stay alive!' Some of them listened, some of them did not.

"I prayed so hard to God. I was brought up in a religious family; I was Catholic and my mother was a very devout Catholic. I promised God that if he got me out of this that I would go back home and I would study and I would do something with my life. I would not kill any more of his people. I would become a doctor; that is what I did.

"When I got back home, I told my mother what I had promised God, and she said, 'Well, son, you better get started!' She said, 'You can't expect your dad to help you; he can't afford it.' I said, 'No, I think the government will help me get through. I'll work real hard even in school and I will work in the summertime, but I'll get through. The GI Bill will help pay my way.' It did. I will always be in debt to my government."

Shortly after 11:00 A.M. on August 2, the fourth day of their ordeal, the *Indianapolis* survivors were accidentally discovered by Lt. (jg) Wilbur "Chuck" Gwinn, who was flying out of Pelelieu in his PV-1 Ventura on a routine antisubmarine patrol. As McCoy described it, "He came into our area and he had a trailing wire [radio antenna] problem. They put out a trailing wire with a weight so that they could send a better [radio] message back to their land base. His trailing wire weight had broken off and it was banging up against the fuselage, so he was afraid that it was going to damage the plane. He went back and opened up the bomb bay doors and got down on his belly and cranked it in by hand to keep it from damaging his plane. When he did he

looked down and saw the oil slick and thought that there was a crippled submarine [there]. So he pickled—when they fused their bombs
they called it 'pickling'—his bombs and started a bombing run down
to the oil slick. The closer he got to the water, he could see all these
heads bobbing up and down and sharks all around. He backed off and
knew that it wasn't a submarine; there were too many men for a submarine. Then he radioed back, and that was the first message that went
back. It was just accidental that he found us."

Radioing his base at Peleliu, he alerted, "many men in the water."
A PBY seaplane under the command of Lt. R. Adrian Marks was dis-
patched to lend assistance and report. Enroute, Marks flew over
the destroyer USS *Cecil Doyle* and alerted her captain. The captain of
the *Doyle*, on his own authority, decided to divert to the scene.

"When [Marks] got there," McCoy recalled, "he couldn't believe
what he saw with all the men and all the sharks. He landed his PBY
in the water. He wasn't supposed to do that; he could have got court-
martialed for it. He got permission from all his crew members, and he
put the plane down in a trough (we were having ten- to twelve-foot
seas all the time). He got it into one of the troughs and started picking up survivors; he wound up picking up fifty-six. He filled his fuselage and was still picking up men. Marks' crew were real strong and
very brave in doing what they were doing; they would pick up survivors and put them on the wing and punch a hole in the wing and
tie them on with parachute shrouds to keep them from sliding off into
the water. He gave everybody a little bit of the water that he had; he
had three gallons of water on board. He kept them on all that night
and took them off the next morning and put them on the *Doyle*."

When the *Doyle* arrived on the scene that night, it stopped in the
water for fear of running over survivors. The *Doyle's* captain pointed his
largest searchlight into the night sky to serve as a beacon for other rescue vessels, and the men in the water knew they had been saved. Several
other ships would come into the area, among them the APD *Ringless,* a
small destroyer converted into a personnel carrier, under the command
of Captain Meyer. The *Ringless* picked up Captain McVay, who, according to Giles McCoy, was one of the last men out of the water. McCoy's
group was the very last one to be rescued. He is pretty certain that he
was the last *Indianapolis* survivor taken out of the Pacific Ocean.

"When the *Ringless* first came up to us," McCoy remembered, "I had everybody tied together, because your life jackets didn't last forever. They soaked up water after seventy-two hours. All of us, our chins were just sticking up out of the water because our life jackets were sinking. I tied everybody together so that they couldn't drop their faces in the water and drown. I tied myself to the group too at the end. When the *Ringless* came by, I hollered at them, 'We don't have any knives, somebody will have to cut us apart.' Two sailors dove in right away." He added, laughing, "They saw these five sharks that had been around us all day long; they turned around and went right back to the ship. Then two more sailors came in and they swam out and cut us all loose.

"I remember when I got onboard the *Ringless*. I was Mr. Macho. I told all the guys with me that I was a tough Marine and I would take care of them as long as I had life in me, and I wouldn't let them drown and I wouldn't let the sharks get them. Anyhow, I came up with the idea that I could walk into one of the compartments where they had bunks. I stood up and my legs gave out and I fell right flat on my face. I couldn't get up, so I remember I turned on my side and kissed the deck. Everybody laughed and thought that was funny. Finally a couple of guys got me into a stretcher and put me in a bunk."

Out of the nearly 900 men who went into the water after the *Indianapolis* sank, only 317 were still alive for the rescues of August 2 and 3. Some of the survivors were taken to Pelelieu, others to the island of Samora. While McCoy was in Pelelieu waiting for the hospital ship *Tranquility* to take him to Guam, he went blind. A corpsman was checking on his legs, which had water ulcers from where the straps had rubbed them raw, and McCoy told him, "I can't see you. All I can see is just an outline of your head." The corpsman summoned a doctor, who told McCoy that he was sun blind from the glare off the water; his retinas were inflamed, but his vision would recover in four or five days. It did.

In the Base 18 Hospital on Guam, Captain McVay paid him a visit one day and asked him to be his orderly, whose duties included driving the captain's jeep. "I drove him back and forth to CINCPAC," McCoy recalled, "which was the mountain where Admiral Nimitz and all of them had their headquarters on Guam. CINCPAC means

Commander In Chief, Pacific. After one trip he said, 'You know what, McCoy? I think they are going to try and hook me for the loss of the ship.' I couldn't believe it. That's all he ever told me; he never did confide in me. I said, 'I don't know how they can do that, sir. Gosh, you are a survivor just like us. That was an act of war. Hell, we know we got sunk by torpedoes, but it was an act of war.'

The story of the *Indianapolis* has been told many times, perhaps most memorably (and succinctly) by Quint, the shark-hunting captain played by Robert Shaw in *Jaws*. For McCoy, it was a tragedy compounded by a miscarriage of justice. Captain Charles B. McVay III was indeed court-martialed late in 1945. It was decided to bring Mochitsura Hashimoto over from Japan to testify. McCoy was also a witness at the court-martial in Washington, D.C. "When it was my turn to go into the court-martial area to testify," he recalled, "they sat me right next to Hashimoto. I couldn't believe it! I just was so upset! I even said so, and Captain McVay liked that. I said, 'Who is this guy here? He is Japanese.' They said, 'Well, he is the one who sunk you.' I said, 'How can you do that?' When I got through with my testimony I went back and I told the rest of the guys, '"You know, they got that Japanese bastard that sunk us. You are going to have to sit next to him when you testify.' That upset everybody, too."

McVay was convicted of "hazarding his ship by failing to zigzag." Of the decision, McCoy spoke for many survivors when he said, "We all felt that it was such a terrible thing to do." Although over 350 Navy ships were lost in combat during the war, McVay was the only captain to be court-martialed. Controversy over the verdict never went away, thanks to the activism of men like Giles McCoy. In 1960, he organized a reunion of *Indianapolis* survivors, and McVay came. "I asked him for permission to try and get him exonerated," McCoy remembered. "He refused me. He said, 'No, I was the commanding officer and I will take my punishment.' I said, 'Well sir, it is unjust.' He said, 'That's all right, that's the way the Navy works.' So he wouldn't give me permission. Then in 1964 we were getting ready for the '65 reunion (we had them every five years), and I called him and said, 'Skipper, will you give me permission to try to get you exonerated?' He said, 'I can't go to the reunion because my wife is dying, but I am going to give you permission, but it isn't going to do any good. Don't work too hard on it, because the Navy won't back off.' I said, 'But you will allow me to do it?' He said, 'Yes, go ahead.'"

McCoy worked at clearing McVay's name, even after the skipper committed suicide in 1968. He continued to hold regular reunions, though reaction among the other survivors was mixed about those events. Some of them, he recalled, "thought that was wrong, bringing it back. They didn't want to go back. A couple of them got pretty harsh in their letters. Boy, they really called me something! They got me upset enough that I contacted a psychiatrist at Missouri University, because I went to school there. I told him what I was doing about getting the reunion started, and was I wrong? Because I didn't want to do anything that would hurt the guys. He said, 'No, that would be the best thing that ever happened to them. They need to talk about it. You go right on and do what you are doing.'"

The campaign to clear McVay's name was given a huge push by an eleven-year-old Pensacola, Florida, boy named Hunter Scott. In 1996, he saw *Jaws* and wrote a school report on the *Indianapolis* tragedy. He got in touch with McCoy and many other survivors. Scott's youth attracted much media attention to McVay's cause, and finally, in October 2000, legislation was passed and signed by President Clinton expressing the sense of Congress that Captain McVay's record should reflect that he was exonerated for the loss of the *Indianapolis* and for the deaths of her crew. In July 2001 the Navy Department announced that Captain McVay's record has been amended to exonerate him.

"I was just overjoyed with the fact that we got him exonerated," McCoy told his interviewer in 2002. "I just wish that he was alive to understand that we didn't give up on him, that we stayed with him. That is what I tried to get the Navy and all to understand, that combat people just don't forsake other combat people. We stay there and we fight for honor. That is what was violated with Captain McVay; his honor was violated. It was up to us to fight to get his honor back. That is what we did, and I am proud that we did."

Before McVay's final vindication, McCoy had one more meeting with Mochitsura Hashimoto. On December 7, 1990, on the forty-ninth anniversary of the attack on Pearl Harbor, survivors of the *Indianapolis*, including McCoy, convened in Pearl Harbor. Hashimoto, who had become a Shinto priest, attended the ceremonies. The encounter is recorded on a web site (www.ussindianapolis.org) devoted to survivors of the *Indianapolis*: "Speaking through a translator, Hashimoto told McCoy, 'I came here to pray with you for your shipmates whose deaths I caused,' to which McCoy, apprehensive about encountering the man who had caused him so much pain and sorrow but touched by Hashimoto's comment, replied, 'I forgive you.'"

RHONDA CORNUM:
DOING SOMETHING HONORABLE

"I would have been afraid, except that I was so grateful to be alive."

I N A CONFLICT AS BRIEF AND LOPSIDED AS THE PERSIAN GULF WAR, it may be surprising that there were actually American prisoners of war. Rhonda Cornum was one; she served with an attack helicopter battalion as a medical officer, went down in a helicopter crash, and for seven days was held by the Iraqis. She drew on her training as both a soldier and doctor to survive her brief but painful ordeal.

Cornum told an interviewer in 2003 that she had grown up "under a barrel" in upstate New York, where she was unaware of world events and knew only one person who had been in the service: her grandfather, who had fought at Iwo Jima—"not that he ever talked about it." She noted, "It was a real shock to everyone when I joined the Army," but on reflection she realized that her grandfather's personality had influenced her decision. "I was just so impressed with his work ethic, his integrity, his faith."

Her early ambitions were to be a veterinarian or scientist; she loved pets and above all she loved doing research. In her undergraduate years, begun at Wilmington College in Ohio, she had prepared for veterinary school, but after two years she transferred to Cornell and realized "there were things a vet did that I didn't want to do."

While doing her graduate work at Cornell in biochemistry, she married a fellow student, whom she described as "one of those back-to-the-land people." They raised a daughter in an isolated cabin while she worked on her Ph.D. In her second year of graduate school, she gave a talk in New Jersey on amino acid metabolism. A representative for the Letterman Army Institute of Research in San Francisco approached her afterward and told her, "You know, we need someone to do the research you just presented. The only deal is you got to join the Army." She recalled, "Well, I was looking for a job. I had to do some non-profit thing to fulfill my fellowship payback." And she saw going into the Army as "a great opportunity." She went to San Francisco, was impressed with the research facilities at the nearby Davis campus of the University of California, and decided to make the commitment.

She and her family moved across country in the summer of 1978. She was commissioned a first lieutenant and made captain six months later. Her six weeks of officer basic training at Fort Sam Houston in Texas were a shock, if only because it was "the first group thing I ever really did." In high school, she had never played any team sports, preferring to show dogs and horses. But she found that she enjoyed the camaraderie.

Back in San Francisco, she spent four years stationed at the army base on the Presidio, home to the Letterman Institute. Her marriage ended, and her military career stalled a bit; she had hoped to make major, but there was the problem with her short stint as a lieutenant. She had never led a platoon, never been on a battalion staff or served as a company commander.

There was another problem. Though she wrote as many papers as anyone in her department, she was making only half as much in salary because they were physicians and she was not. That "irritant," as she described it, prompted her to enroll in medical school. She had decided to stay in the Army, but her only other choice at that point would have been flight school, which she found less hospitable to women. Between 1982 and 1986 she attended medical school at the Uniform Services University in Bethesda, Maryland. In her first year, she met a fellow student who became her second husband.

She understood going into the Uniform Services University that she would owe the military seven years of service once she graduated, which meant she was now committed to the Army for her career. After a one-year internship at Walter Reed Medical Center in Washington, D.C., there came time for a decision. Her husband, Corey, had ambitions to be a flight surgeon for a fighter unit. She decided that if she wanted to spend time with him, she would have to follow his lead. At that time, in 1986, the Army was still allowing flight surgeons to fly helicopters, so they went to train on a TH55, which she recalled was "probably the most fun thing I've ever done."

At Letterman, she recalled, the atmosphere wasn't strictly military. The institute was a combination hospital and research facility, and she didn't wear her uniform off-base. ("It was a time when the military wasn't very popular," she recalled.) Before she went to medical school, she decided she needed a deeper immersion into military culture, so she got her Expert Field Medical Badge at Fort Ord, California, and then, as part of her drive across country to Maryland, she stopped off for three weeks at Georgia's Fort Benning to attend Jump School.

Out of medical school, Cornum was assigned to Fort Rucker in Alabama, where she made major and was appointed chief of the base's primary care clinic. Though she'd never run a clinic, she learned the ropes quickly. After three years at Rucker, where all the Army's helicopter training was being conducted, she got an important call. The United States was responding to Iraq's invasion of Kuwait, and the Army was mobilizing units to go overseas. She had been working with pilots of Apache helicopters, and the head of their unit, Colonel Bill Bryan, asked her to join them for Operation Desert Shield. "What was I going to say?" she told her interviewer. "If he thought his unit was going to be better if I went, then I was surely going."

Her departure in August 1990 was "very sudden." She was with the 229th Attack Helicopter Battalion, attached to the 101st Airborne, serving as flight surgeon with five medics to back her up. Their assignments were to tend to any illnesses and to go along as needed on evacuations or search and rescue missions. Originally based in Dhahran, Saudi Arabia, they moved closer to the front as the action began moving northward.

In the first five months before they were deployed, they were stationed at Dhahran's King Fahd Airport, an unfinished facility that was virtually deserted. They lived in a parking garage with no electricity or running water. "People were aghast" at the living conditions, she recalled, but it reminded her of living in the cabin during her graduate school days.

The Saudis looked at her and the other female soldiers "as American soldiers and not as women." She went into Dhahran to a hardware store to buy plywood and a saw to build some personal things and noted that Saudis had never seen a woman buy a saw before.

Before the ground war began in late February, her unit did some reconnaissance work. They did lots of flying in Blackhawk helicopters and "got shot at a few times." She recalled, "I knew people were expecting it to be bad" when her unit of 335 people were issued 75 body bags, but she also noted that "everyone was pretty highly motivated."

On February 27, she flew her 27th mission, to pick up a downed F-16 pilot with a broken leg. He had landed near where he'd been shot down, so as her helicopter approached his position, the same Iraqi anti-aircraft guns shot at them, blowing their tail off. They were only fifteen feet off the ground, and they crashed nose in, flipping the craft.

It was late afternoon when they went down. Cornum remembers that when she regained consciousness, it was dark. She couldn't feel anything and nothing around her was moving; she thought for a moment that she was dead. Then she tried to move but couldn't turn over. Her stirring prompted other movement inside the wreckage. She opened her eyes to see five armed Iraqis with their guns pointed at her. "Well, I guess I'm not dead after all," she remembers thinking.

They pulled her up, pulled off her helmet, and her hair fell loose—"at which point it was pretty obvious" that she was a woman. Her sense was that the Iraqis were more excited that they'd shot down anything than with her being a woman.

In the crash, she had broken both arms, blown out a knee, and suffered "a couple of other minor" injuries. When she was pulled up from the wreckage, one of her arms was dislocated. She was dragged into a bunker. All the officers spoke English, and a lieutenant looked at her and asked, "What are you doing here?" "We had a wreck," was her answer. She was feeling weak and nauseated; she found out later that she had lost about a third of her blood volume from her wounds.

"I would have been afraid," she recalled, "except that I was so grateful to be alive."

Taken to another area, she saw one of her comrades, Sergeant Dunlap, and was happy to know she wasn't the only survivor from the crash. (In fact there was a third survivor as well; five men died.) At one point, several Iraqi soldiers held revolvers to the backs of the prisoners' heads as if to suggest they were about to be executed. That moment passed, and a captain arrived to interrogate them. When he asked what unit they were from, Cornum didn't mind telling him, because of the identifying patch on her uniform sleeve.

Before she was deployed it had occurred to her that she might be taken prisoner. When a couple of pilots asked what might happen if they were captured, she told them, "We'll come and get you." So she figured her job was to "stay alive until they come and get me."

She and Dunlap were thrown into the back of a pickup, and with no way to brace herself, since her arms were broken, she landed in great pain. Dunlap, who was uninjured, placed his legs over hers to brace her and keep her from bouncing around. Along the way to their destination, which turned out to be Basra, American planes flew overhead, strafing the road. The Iraqis jumped out and took cover in a ditch. She thought, "Crap, it will really piss me off if I survive this wreck and get shot by an Apache or A-10 or something."

In Basra, she was placed alone in a room that was about 10 feet by 12 feet, empty of all furnishings except for a bench. It was a long time before she got any medical treatment, but her background in medicine became crucial to her survival. "Knowledge," she said in her interview, "even if it's bad news, is better than wondering." When she felt the need to urinate, she thought, "At least I know I have enough blood volume left that my kidneys are working." On the third day in her cell, someone came in and trussed up her arms. She was able to get Sgt. Dunlap to redo the job, giving him instructions on how to do it right. The next day she got a splint, and the day after that she was taken to a hospital for professional care. She was "pretty impressed" with the hospital, "considering they had three hours of electricity a day."

After her hospital visit, she was put on a bus to Baghdad. On board was Captain Andrews, the pilot that she and her crew had been sent to rescue. She thought, "Well, we got him; we're just going the wrong way."

In her first days without any care, she dealt with her discomfort by setting her pain threshold higher, figuring "there's nothing I can do about it, so there's no sense in complaining about it. I focused on things I could have some impact on," simply not contemplating the possibility of torture or even interrogation. As for the prospect of release, "I could not conceive after what I'd been briefed on, that they were going to let us sit there for years. Months, maybe." She knew the

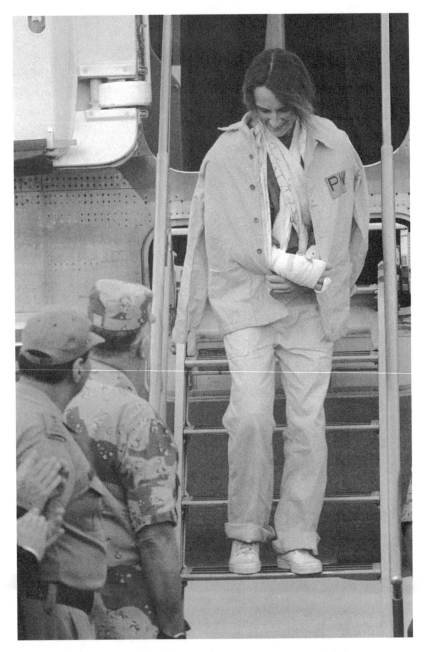

Cornum returning from her brief ordeal as a POW.
Her injuries, including two broken arms,
were sustained in the copter crash.

war was nearly over before she went down (the ground war ended the following day), and she was certain that she and any other American prisoners would be repatriated. Of her cohorts in the U.S. armed forces, she thought, "They were either going to get us back or they were going to turn Baghdad into green glass."

She was interrogated once in Basra by someone using what she called "the nice guy approach," and again in Baghdad, with a spotlight shining in her face, by three men who were polite. "There wasn't a lot of incentive for them to be aggressive," she recalled.

She was provided with some food, but it was difficult to eat with both arms fractured. She lost fifteen pounds in less than a week, though she had little trouble sleeping. "A surgeon can sleep anywhere," she noted.

Cornum was disciplined during her captivity. She kept track of the days and the time of day, and she started a little physical therapy program for her injuries. She and two Iraqi women, who were more or less her keepers, began to teach each other their respective languages, using an Arabic-language edition of *People* magazine. She also sang a lot. "It gave me something to do," and she figured it was a way of letting other prisoners, who might be released before her, know that an American woman was being held. Cornum's repertoire included show tunes from *Evita* and *Cats*, and songs by James Taylor and Cat Stevens.

A week after she'd been captured, she was awakened in the middle of the night. Her two keepers blindfolded her, stuck a toothbrush and tube of toothpaste into her hands, and led her to a bus, which took her to what turned out to be the lobby of a hotel. When her blindfold was removed, she could see that she and other POWs were being handed over to the Red Cross. There were twenty-six of them in all, and once the exchange was complete, they were offered single rooms, which they turned down. They had all been in solitary and were eager for the company, so two large rooms were commandeered. Spaghetti and chocolate were on the repatriation menu. When she asked someone if she should eat that rich food, she was told, "You may get diarrhea and you will probably throw up, but it's worth it."

Her husband was also serving in the Gulf. He was watching television when General Norman Schwarzkopf, commander of Operation Desert Storm, announced the end of the ground war but cautioned about unresolved situations, mentioning that a helicopter with the

101st Airborne had been shot down, its occupants still unaccounted for. Her husband thought, "That's got to be Rhonda."

Cornum felt no animosity toward her captors, save for two soldiers. One of them stole her wedding ring, which she had on a chain with her dog tags. And a second soldier molested her in the bed of the pickup truck.

"I've looked at [my experience] as a positive thing," she said thirteen years later. "It makes you more confident about facing anything else. I have been a different and better commander." Though she's flattered by the attention she has received from the POW community, she doesn't feel that the Persian Gulf prisoners suffered nearly as much as those in other wars.

"For me," Rhonda Cornum noted, "the Army was a great awakening to the real world." It took her from a sheltered world of academia and taught her valuable lessons about teamwork and perseverance and duty. After she joined the Army, her grandfather, who had served in the Pacific in World War II but had never talked about those days, opened up to her about his time in the service. "He told me there were worse things than dying; there's living with dishonor. That's probably the most important thing he said." As her helicopter crashed in the Iraqi desert on that February day, her thoughts were of her grandfather: "At least I'm dying doing something honorable."

ROGER DEAN INGVALSON: THE MAN OF FAITH

"People ask, 'How did you survive?'
And I say there's one word, and that's faith."

IVE YEARS AS A PRISONER OF WAR HAD A PROFOUND EFFECT ON
Roger Ingvalson, and it was a decision he made at the
moment of capture that informed his years of brutal captivity.
He intuitively understood that remaining mentally focused
and steadfast in his religious faith would offset anything the North
Vietnamese could throw at him. Thirty years after his release, he admits
that some physical ailments have caught up with him, and that at least
one aspect of psychological torture still haunts him. But as he talks
about his experiences, it's clear that he has made a certain kind of peace
with the past.

Ingvalson, the youngest of six children, grew up on a southern
Minnesota farm. He was three years into college when the United States
entered the Korean War and, anticipating he would be drafted into the
Army, Ingvalson chose to enlist in the Air Force. His older brothers and two
brothers-in-law had all served in World War II. While they were fighting in
the Pacific, his most vivid memory was of not hearing from them for
months on end, but he was inspired to emulate their commitment to serve.

After three years of completing various assignments around the
country, Ingvalson got his wings at Spence Air Base in Georgia. He
knew that meant a commitment of another four years to the Air Force,
but he was hooked. "I never hesitated," he remembered in a 2003

Roger Ingvalson and the F-105
he flew during combat missions over Vietnam.
Shot down in May 1968, he spent five years in captivity.

interview. "I never cared about how long I would stay in. At that point I decided to make it a career." He received his combat training at Nellis AFB in Nevada, with orders to go to Korea. After three years of being shuttled around the country he was primed: "When you first start flying fighters, your ego starts skyrocketing. Basically it's a tiger school. You gotta be a tiger. And to be a good fighter pilot, you gotta feel like you're the best. If you don't feel like you're the best, you probably aren't. But I had no fear. I was ready to go into combat and shoot airplanes down. It was an exciting time."

On his way overseas, his orders were abruptly canceled. The war was winding down, and this eager recruit had to refocus his energies. Over the next few years, Ingvalson gained experience flying intercept missions, first out of California, checking out civilian aircraft that had suspiciously strayed far off normal flight patterns, and then out of Iceland, tracking Soviet military aircraft. "Never did have any problems as far as harassment," was his laconic memory of the latter assignment. He also trained on supersonic aircraft in Indiana, acquired more combat training in Georgia, and in Florida tested F-105s, which would become the Air Force's choice among aircraft for bombing missions in Vietnam.

As American military involvement in Southeast Asia began to escalate in the early 1960s, Ingvalson helped to write tactical procedures for fighter pilots who might be needed in that war. Early in 1965, he received orders to go overseas again, this time to Okinawa. From there, he was off to Thailand, from where he began flying missions into North Vietnam: strafing and firing rockets at ground targets, tangling with Russian MIGs, and dropping bombs. He flew about twenty-five missions, but because of his wife's medical condition—she was suffering from multiple sclerosis—he was excused from more. Then in late 1967, the Air Force ordered Ingvalson to return to Thailand, this time for a commitment to 100 missions. Before he left, however, he was allowed to take his wife and seven-year-old son back to the States, where both could be taken care of by her family.

Ingvalson would recall in an interview thirty-six years later, "As a fighter pilot flying in combat, because of my pride I would never leave a target unless it was destroyed or at least on fire." Weren't you ever afraid, asked his interviewer. His answer: "No fear—that could be a problem." On May 28, 1968, flying over Dong Hoi in the southern portion of North Vietnam, Ingvalson was to take out a convoy of Russian-made trucks with his plane's 20mm cannon. It was his eighty-seventh mission. He was making sure that the entire convoy was destroyed, flying very low—about thirty feet off the ground—at over 500 miles per hour, when an explosion rocked his plane. Smoke filled

Ingvalson's plane in mid-flight, firing its load of rockets.
Asked if he were ever afraid, he replied,
"No fear—that could be a problem."

the cockpit, and he blew off the canopy to clear his vision, turning on the afterburners to gain some altitude and speed. The plane climbed a little, but then he sensed he was losing control, and his training kicked in: he hit the ejection button.

When a pilot ejects at that speed and at a low altitude, he's subjected to severe windblast that often results in severe trauma. Ingvalson was knocked unconscious, but his parachute opened automatically. Just before he hit the ground, he regained consciousness in time to see a group of Vietnamese rushing toward his landing spot. When he hit the ground, he did a quick body check and was amazed to discover he had suffered no broken bones from his risky ejection.

In his interview, Ingvalson described what happened next, as though he were reliving the moment. "Now I go back to my religious training as a child: Always involved in church activities, but I was not a Christian, and immediately I realize that this had to be a miracle. I knew that Jesus

Christ performed miracles, and that had to be a miracle that I was not injured. And so right then and there, with the enemy coming toward me, I bowed my head and prayed to God that Jesus Christ would take over my life. Because of that decision, I'm sitting here today."

Within five minutes, Roger Ingvalson was a prisoner of war. His first group of captors—local civilians—beat him and led him away. Walking in a dry riverbed, they encountered four soldiers, who stopped and aimed their guns at the American pilot. It was a bluff, but, as Ingvalson would later come to understand, it was part of the psychological torture he was to endure for five years. His first prison was a local cave; after about ten days, he was loaded onto a truck, which traveled only by night. Ingvalson was grateful that during the day, his captors kept the vehicle concealed; otherwise, American planes may have strafed or bombed it, unaware of its cargo.

He was taken to "a bamboo-type prison," where his legs were shackled, and he lay on a dirt floor for another ten days. One day, June 20, he realized it was his fortieth birthday. "You know," he told his interviewer in 2003, "people say, 'Life begins at forty.' I thought, There's something wrong here someplace." A navy pilot badly hurting with internal injuries soon joined him. The man begged for some kind of medical attention; finally, their captors gave him a large pill, and within a half hour he was dead. Ingvalson figured the North Vietnamese simply didn't have the medical personnel or supplies to take care of its seriously ill or wounded prisoners.

Ingvalson continued his journey on a truck. "Every day I was escaping death, just making it," he recalled in his 2003 interview. "Friendly bombs were going off around me; we should have been hit, but the Lord was taking care of me." One bright moonlit night, he was waiting for a ferry to cross a river; the bridges had been bombed by American fighter pilots like himself. Three U.S. bombers appeared in the night sky, circling around his position. He waited for the explosions, the concussions, the mayhem, but they never came.

By the time he reached his final destination, it had taken him twenty-eight days to travel 250 miles. He was at the infamous "Hanoi Hilton." Its official Vietnamese name was Hoa Lo, after the portable earthen stoves used by the site's original inhabitants, before the French colonized their land at the turn of the century and built the facility. The Hilton began housing American POWs in 1964.

Ingvalson spent the first twenty months of his imprisonment in solitary, periods of loneliness broken by interrogation sessions. The questions he was asked were mostly technical. At what altitude did bombers come in on their missions? (The answer would help the North Vietnamese calibrate their antiaircraft guns.) One interrogator insisted that Ingvalson provide him electronic schematics for his plane. He kept insisting that he was "just a dumb pilot who only knew how to turn the engine off and on." After a couple of days of Ingvalson sitting on a stool outdoors in cold weather with almost no clothes on, his interrogator produced the schematics he was asking about—he only wanted his American captive to confirm the information.

"You learn to lie," Ingvalson recalled. "As a prisoner of war it was proven in Vietnam that they can break you; they can torture you to a point where you're gonna talk. So you learn to lie about things, and you make up formulas, giving them numbers that are not accurate."

His first cell was tiny—four feet by seven, with stocks on the end of the bed in which his legs were confined, though not for too many hours a day. He was moved to a larger cell, but his furnishings and amenities were Spartan: a bed made of hard teakwood, a can for his waste, a small teapot and cup, a tube of toothpaste, a toothbrush, and mosquito netting. Meals were "a bowl of weeds—they would call it greens"—once or twice a day.

He had worried about being confined to solitary, wondering how he would pass the time. There were no writing materials. He spent a lot of time walking laps around the room, doing calisthenics. "You learn to exercise your mind as well as your body," he recalled, and he took to studying the behavior of his cellmates: various creatures such as ants, spiders, and, "my best friends," the tiny gecko lizards, who skittered along the walls and ceilings with suction cups at the ends of their legs.

He was taken regularly out of his cell to a washroom. One day he found a small piece of wire there, then he found a screw head, so he fashioned a drill to make a hole in the door of his cell. He made it high enough so that his Vietnamese captors would not notice the shaft of light coming in; he stood on his overturned waste bucket to peer out, where he did see other prisoners moving about. One of them, a crippled young man, he later found out, was John McCain, who had been shot down in October 1967.

Another day in the washroom he found a banana leaf, which he smuggled back to his cell under his pajamas. He stripped out two pieces of fiber from the skin and began doing daily weaving exercises with them. He built houses in his mind. He did math problems. "I figured out what my monthly military pay was, and I figured if that money was put into a savings account with daily interest. I got so good at it, I was multiplying a three-digit number by a six-digit number."

He made a point of keeping track of the days, of marking family birthdays. In five years of captivity, he was moved nine times, and over thirty years later, he could still remember each of those dates.

The interrogations eventually stopped, but the Vietnamese weren't ignoring him. "Physical torture is tough," he noted, "but mental is worse because physical is only temporary." Night after night in solitary, he heard a baby crying somewhere. It began to haunt his dreams and waking hours. Later, he found out that his captors were playing an audio tape— and it worked. "To this day," he admitted, "I can't stand to be around my grandchildren, my babies, to hear them when they are crying, especially if it's a hurting cry. I'll never be relieved of that mental torture."

He wasn't sure if his family knew he was alive until one day he received a letter from them. His wingman had circled around and saw Ingvalson get captured. Later, a photograph of his capture was taken

Ten months into captivity, Ingvalson received his first letter from home—
and his captors recorded the moment with a TV camera.

and distributed by the Associated Press. Ten months into his captivity, he was led into an interrogation room. A big stack of letters was sitting on the table. They were all from his mother. Ingvalson noticed a TV camera in the corner of the room recording his tearful reaction as he read through the letters.

Twenty months into his stay at the Hanoi Hilton, he was moved to a cell with three other POWs. They said he didn't stop talking for two weeks. All of them had been shot down after him, but they had been imprisoned together. He wound up living with six other prisoners. One day, the door opened and a Bible was tossed into their cell. Ingvalson found there was one other Christian in that cell, so they began reading it together.

Four days later, he was called into an interrogation room, where he was told that his wife had died. "Normally you wouldn't believe what they tell you, because the Communists are the world's greatest liars," he recalled. "But if we ever got any news from home from them, it was always bad news. And I knew my wife was in critical condition." He later learned that she had died twenty days earlier. A group of clergymen in the States had petitioned Hanoi to release him for her funeral, and that's how his captors found out that she passed away. He returned to his cell, crying, and took up the Bible and began reading Scripture with his Christian comrade. He took the presence of that Bible as another sign, that God was giving some hope and comfort by having that book there.

That night, he dreamed of his wife. In all his dreams of her while in captivity, she had always appeared crippled, just as he had left her. That night, after he cried himself to sleep, she appeared whole and healthy. God, he believed, was telling him that she was now in heaven and restored to good health.

In the Hilton, the prisoners set up simple communications systems to pass along information or just to stay in touch. They developed a box code, a five-by-five square containing all but one of the letters of the alphabet. K was omitted, and C was its substitute. A letter was signaled in pairs: "B" was one tap followed by two (first row, second position), "Z" would be five taps, followed by five more. The prisoners learned that their teacups were sound resonators between cells. A sender would press the open end of the cup to the wall and tap on its bottom; the receiver would place his cup on the other side of the wall to get the message. There were abbreviations: "TD" meant today, "YD" was "yesterday," and "GBU" was "God Bless You."

Their toothpaste tubes, they discovered, had zinc in them, which could be used like graphite in a pencil. On scraps of toilet paper in the washroom, they would leave messages for each other. "We'd drive the Vietnamese crazy," he recalled. "They said the ingenuity of the Americans just amazed them."

Late in 1972, over 4½ years into his captivity, Ingvalson was moved with 208 men, half the Hilton's prisoners, in seventeen trucks, to a stone dungeon near the Chinese border. The POWs suspected something good was about to happen, and they began to establish a priority order for prisoners to be released: sick and wounded, followed by civilians, and then proceeding by date of being shot down, oldest to most recent.

The Paris Peace Agreement, whose final draft was initialed on January 23, 1973, stipulated that all prisoners of war be notified within three days of their imminent release. Ingvalson recalled that the document was actually signed on January 27, and on the thirtieth, his captors assembled all of the Hanoi Hilton's "guests" to inform them of their imminent freedom. In March, Ingvalson went home.

Military officials weren't sure what to expect when these men were set free. "Basically," recalled Ingvalson, "our minds were in better shape than they expected." Eating for him was a bit of a problem, as he had broken five teeth on stones that were in his rice rations, until he finally learned to swallow the rice rather than chew it.

Roger Ingvalson stayed in the Air Force for two more years; his first assignment, once he had recovered and put on some weight, was teaching young pilots at a base in Alabama. He spent his weekends in Chattanooga, Tennessee, visiting the widow and parents of his best friend, who had been shot down and killed seven months before his own capture. "To make a long story short," he told his interviewer, "I married my best friend's widow."

The adjustment was tough at first on his son, who was thirteen when Ingvalson returned from captivity. "The worst mental pain," he remembered, "was thinking about him when I was in prison," especially after he learned that the boy's mother had died. But Ingvalson's second wife, who had three teenaged sons of her own, adeptly blended the families together.

"People asked me if I ever worried about dying," Roger Ingvalson recalled. "And I said I didn't. Because I knew if I died I was going to heaven. And I had that perfect peace. People ask, 'How did you survive?' And I said there's one word, and that's *faith*. Faith in God, faith in our great country we knew would not abandon us, and faith in our fellow prisoners of war."

JOHANN KASTEN IV: THE MAN OF CONFIDENCE

"Without any hesitation, I pushed the loaf of bread
to the center of the table and stated,
'We are all Americans; we don't differentiate by religion.'"

H OW DID A SECOND-GENERATION GERMAN AMERICAN WIND up in one of the worst POW camps in the Second World War? And what was that same man doing in Hawaii only eight days before the Japanese attack on Pearl Harbor?

Johann Kasten's memoir tells an amazing story. It begins with his grandfather, Johann II, a citizen of Bremen, Germany, who was befriended by a Mr. Hackfield, a German émigré living in Honolulu who owned that city's largest department store, Ehler's, as well as a shipping line and plantations. On a trip back to Bremen, Hackfield told Kasten, "When your son finishes his schooling, send him to me." In 1906, that time came, and Johann Kasten III set off for Hawaii, stopping briefly in San Francisco right after the famous earthquake and fire that had ravaged the city.

Johann III, according to his son, "rose rapidly through the ranks of Hackfield and Company to an executive position." After fulfilling a seven-year contract with Hackfield, he returned to Bremen to marry his sweetheart, and the two spent their honeymoon riding the Trans-Siberian Railroad before taking a boat to Japan and a ship back to Honolulu.

Three boys were born in quick succession to the Kastens; Johann IV, nicknamed Hans, was the middle one, born on August 18, 1916. After Germany was defeated in World War I, "life in Honolulu became

Hans Kasten cut a dashing figure in uniform. His Nazi captors, however, were not impressed, especially when they learned he was a German American.

very difficult for the German community," Kasten wrote. Although there was no internment, as with the Japanese on the West Coast during World War II, Germans did see their businesses confiscated. Hans's father had become a U.S. citizen, and in the early 1920s, he moved his family to Milwaukee, where many Kasten relatives owned businesses. Hans's father soon became a banking executive, and the Kastens added two girls to their family. All of the boys went on to the University of Wisconsin, where Hans majored in art and minored in music. He took a course in gemology in anticipation of employment with the Alsted Kasten Jewelry Company of Milwaukee.

In 1936, Hans's father took him and his brothers out of college and sent them to the University of Heidelberg, where they spent two years in the elder Kasten's homeland. In 1937, they were staying at a new youth hostel in Bavaria named after Adolf Hitler, the Third Reich's Führer (Supreme Leader), who appeared for the opening ceremonies. Hans and his brothers were introduced to Hitler as "*Deutsche Americaner studenten.*" Kasten wrote, "Little did I know then that I would be his 'houseguest' in 1944-45."

In 1939, at the ripe old age of twenty-three, Kasten recalled, "I retired from college and the jewelry business and sailed to Hawaii to see the South Seas," adding, "everybody talks about what they are going to do when they retire, but when they finally retired, they were too old to enjoy it."

From Hawaii, he sailed several hundred miles south to Palmyra Island, a U.S.-controlled atoll, where he stayed until mid-1941. (The island, now owned by the Nature Conservancy, is operated as a wildlife refuge.) Upon his return to Hawaii, he was asked if he would be interested in a construction job in the Philippines with the Hawaiian Dredging Company. It would require him to leave in November, and he decided to accept the job and come out of "retirement."

Kasten left for the Philippines on November 29 aboard the USS *Chaumont*. Having crossed the International Date Line, it was December 8th when they received news of the attack on Pearl Harbor. The Philippines had been bombed by the Japanese that same day, so the ship immediately changed course for the Fiji Islands to take on supplies and then head for Brisbane, Australia. The *Chaumont* arrived in Brisbane on Christmas Eve, and Kasten spent a week there "while the powers that be decided what to do with us." They were finally sent to

Sydney and put aboard a troop transport ship "that had just discharged thousands of U.S. troops" and was headed back to the U.S. On their departure from Sydney, they manned the guns on board because they felt they were in a war zone. Kasten took the .50 caliber anti-aircraft gun on the aft boat deck, and his buddy, Gus Figaredo, fed him ammunition.

In the middle of the Tasman Sea, south of Australia, a "misguided" Japanese plane bombed them. One bomb hit the deck below Kasten's duty station, and when he came to in the ship's sick bay, he had sixteen stitches in his forehead. The ship docked in Wellington, New Zealand, for repairs and then continued to San Diego, where they were berthed for a couple of days before setting out for Samoa with a contingent of construction crews. On January 24, the U.S. Marines had landed on Samoa to secure the island from Japanese attack. The crews aboard Kasten's ship had been hired to build an airfield at Tafuna for emergency use.

According to Kasten, "The U.S. Navy ran the island in what I considered a pretty lousy way, throwing Samoans in jail for the least offense. I spent a lot of time getting them out." He and two American buddies learned to speak Samoan. When the airfield was finished, the Navy asked the three of them to stay and run the port, "because they were having so much trouble with the Samoans."

They worked in three shifts; Kasten took the day shift. There was one memorable attack on the island; Kasten recalled that one night a Japanese submarine fired shells over a mountain into Pago Pago, but the only structure hit was Shimasaki's General Store, owned by the only Japanese on the island.

Kasten befriended the native Samoans, and their top chief, Tufele, a graduate of the University of Hawaii, summoned him to the council house to give him the title "*Tuanuutele.*" "The name," Kasten wrote, "means 'with the big as well as the small.'" Tuanuutele was a legendary island chief who rode on a shark but mingled with the small fish as well—in Kasten's words, "a very democratic guy apparently."

The three American civilians were living quite comfortably, "better than any of the Navy officers." The Naval commander, a man named Crumpaker, "spent all his R&R in our house." Kasten assumed he had few problems because he and his cohorts had bothered to learn the language and none of the Navy men had; they just referred to the Samoans as "gooks."

One day a Navy messenger delivered a letter to them from a captain offering them commissions as full lieutenants in the Navy. Kasten wrote, "We took this up with Commander Crumpaker on his next visit and we were told in confidence that the brass in the Navy was upset with our living so well and being so favored by the local population, that they thought that we would jump at the chance to get commissions so easily, and when we did they would move us out of our house into the BOQ [Bachelor Officers Quarters] and give us a bad time." They declined the offer. This angered the captain, who then sent them a message announcing that because Samoa was in a war zone, all civilians were to be evacuated from the island. (There was no mention of the native Samoans in the message.)

Kasten and his buddies sailed for San Francisco. On reaching the States, he flew to Milwaukee and "immediately went to the draft board and volunteered." They sent him away because, "as they stated, 'I had already been out there.'" On his third visit to the draft board, in September 1943, they took him as a volunteer.

"When I enlisted," Kasten wrote, "my father merely agreed with my decision. However, after the war, it was a different story, as he refused to accept all the terrible things that were done to me by his people—Germans."

He was sent to Fort Sheridan, Illinois, and then assigned to training at Camp Plauche, Louisiana, for duty with the Transportation Corps. In the middle of his training, he was abruptly assigned to be a teacher in the OCS (Officer Candidate School). He asked for a transfer back to his original unit because "I did not volunteer for the Army to become a teacher."

Back with his unit, he shipped out to England early in 1944. On their arrival in northern England, the transportation soldiers were assigned to work in the rail yards. Kasten soon uncovered a scheme by some of the NCOs to divert certain boxcars to a siding and sell the contents on the black market. He and a buddy, John Kopczinski, decided they wanted nothing to do with that set-up and requested a transfer to the infantry. Their company commander "thought we were crazy and tried to dissuade us," but he finally gave in. They trained at Tidworth Barracks, and Kasten turned out to be "the best marksman in the company."

"The next thing we knew," Kasten wrote, "we were onboard a landing craft headed for Omaha Beach." He lauded the film *Saving Private Ryan* for re-creating an accurate picture of that day's "bloody mess." He wrote, "The first fifteen minutes [of that film] were so real that I was seriously affected for three days," adding, "Today, for the life of me, I still don't remember how we made it up the cliffs."

Kasten recalled his unit fighting their way across France "for innumerable days." In December of 1944, his unit was given a rest near the town of Clervaux, on a ridge overlooking the Our River. The Germans had been retreating, but now they launched one last major counter-offensive. "The night the Battle of the Bulge started for us," wrote Kasten, [was] Christmas Eve, when the Germans came swarming over a small bridge spanning the Our River." He was manning a Browning Automatic Rifle, which he described as "a small, portable machine gun," and his buddy John Kopczinski was carrying the ammunition for the gun. Not an hour into exchanging fire with the Germans, Kopczinski was hit by two bullets and paralyzed. He was the last man to be evacuated before the company was overrun and taken captive.

It was dark, and in the confusion Kasten managed to slip away from his German captors and find his way back to company headquarters. The first sergeant took him to the commander, a second lieutenant who was hiding in the basement. He asked Kasten if he spoke German. "Fluently," was Kasten's reply. The officer told him, "You stay here so when they capture us you can talk to them." Kasten told him he had just escaped captivity and had no intention of being taken prisoner again.

When he and the sergeant returned to the first floor, the Germans burst into the building, and the two Americans leapt out the window and took off for battalion headquarters. The sergeant knew it was located back in Clervaux, and they finally reached the town and reported in. They were ordered to occupy an old castle in the middle of town. German Tiger tanks soon appeared and focused the firepower of their 88mms on the castle. There were sixty-two Americans in the castle, and when they ran out of ammunition and food, they radioed headquarters for help, only to find that everyone had pulled out, assuming the soldiers in the castle would cover their retreat.

They decided to surrender, first setting free some German prisoners who were being kept in the castle's basement. The first night of

Kasten's captivity he dug graves in an apple orchard for the Germans killed in the battle for the castle. The prisoners then began a seven-day march to Germany; there was no food or water offered, and the men ate snow for nourishment. "Many men," he recalled, "died from wounds, fatigue, and hunger."

One night in a small town, the only building big enough to accommodate them was a church. The Germans had arranged in advance for tubs of ersatz coffee to be distributed to the prisoners, and Kasten was on one team assigned to carry the tubs into the church. A woman in the house he was assigned to slipped a large sandwich into his pocket, muttering that she had an uncle in Texas. "I will forever be grateful to the uncle in Texas," Kasten wrote. "That sandwich to a starving man was equivalent to a bar of gold today."

They arrived at a rail yard and were loaded into boxcars that had previously held horses, so the hay inside was filthy with manure. When the cars began moving, Kasten organized his section of the car so that men could alternate standing and sitting down. One man died standing up, but conditions were so crowded he didn't have room to fall.

At a stop in Limberg, Germany, American bombers swooped in on the train, and two of the cars were blown apart with much loss of life. They disembarked from the train in Bad Orb and were marched up a mountain road to a place called Wegscheide, a camp that had once been a summer home for German children but was now a POW enclosure, Stalag 9-B, holding mostly enlisted men from Russia, Serbia, Italy, France, and America. Eventually the camp would hold over 4,000 prisoners.

There were fifteen barracks buildings. Each barracks elected a leader, and the fifteen leaders elected an overall leader, the *Hauptezondsman*, or Chief Man of Confidence, who would deal with the German officials at the camp on behalf of the prisoners' interests. "I was the unlucky one to be elected," Kasten wrote—unlucky because of subsequent events.

Each barracks building at Stalag 9-B had, as Kasten recalled, "one faucet, no heat, broken windows, and an outdoor latrine where you had to sit and balance yourself on a pole." Russians ran the kitchen, and the food was terrible; Kasten recalled that the Americans installed their own men to cook, though they had little to work with: bread with undissolved lumps of sawdust and a soup with mystery ingredients.

Shortly after his arrival, all the officers and NCOs were transferred elsewhere. Two chaplains, one Catholic and one Protestant, remained, as did a dental officer with access to only "the most primitive equipment."

Kasten organized an MP brigade, a list of interpreters, and he selected two assistants, Joe Littell and Ernst Sinner. Both spoke German; Littell had been an exchange student in Germany in the late 1930s, and Sinner was born in Germany and had emigrated as a youth to the U.S.

There was bartering between the American and Russian prisoners, sometimes not on the up and up. The two groups were separated by a five-foot walkway with barbed wire on both sides. Kasten recalled a GI throwing a cigarette packet across the corridor as a Russian threw him a watch at the same time. "The cigarette package was empty and the watch had no works inside." Nevertheless, Kasten wrote, "Life in the camp ran fairly well, all evils considered."

One night two prisoners decided to raid the kitchen. They were surprised by a pair of guards, but the prisoners overpowered the Germans and beat them severely. The next morning, the commandant of the camp announced there would be no food for anyone until the perpetrators were turned over. The prisoners' investigator identified the men and turned them in. "Surprisingly," Kasten wrote, "the two men were not executed."

One morning, the chaplains came to Kasten with a problem. One of the prisoners had told them he had been forsaken by God and he only wanted to die, that he would not move from his bunk. Kasten went to see the prisoner and heard the same line. He pulled out the man's wallet, showed him a photo of his family and told him, "Your family is expecting you back, and if you haven't the guts to live for yourself you have to live for them." The man repeated the reply. Two days later, he was dead.

Kasten was summoned another day to the commandant's office and informed that representatives of the Swiss Red Cross would be inspecting the camp, and he was to tell them only specific facts about their conditions. The next day, the four-man delegation showed up, and in a private meeting Kasten asked if he could speak in confidence. Assured that he could, he laid out all of the camp's shortcomings and violations. The Red Cross workers then met with the commandant, and they repeated everything he had just told them in confidence.

"From the looks on the faces of the Germans," Kasten wrote, "I could foretell my fate."

"The following morning I was summoned to a small second-floor conference room. There were eight chairs, and in front of one of the chairs was a loaf of bread—very obviously a bribe for something coming. When we were all seated, the senior officer started, 'Kasten, we want the names of all the Jews in the American camp.' Without any hesitation, I pushed the loaf of bread to the center of the table and stated, 'We are all Americans; we don't differentiate by religion.' This infuriated them, so they jerked me out of my chair, started slamming me around, and then hurled me down the straight flight of steps from the second floor to the street."

He made his way, limping, back to his barracks, where he summoned the barracks leaders and told them about the Red Cross betrayal and what had just happened. His final instructions were, "Something is bound to happen, and soon, and none of the men should admit to being Jewish."

That afternoon, the entire camp was assembled on the parade ground, with the fifteen barracks leaders lined up in front, and Kasten and his two assistants in front of them. An officer stood on a platform and ordered, "*Alle juden ein schritt vorwerts*" (All Jews take one step forward). No one moved. The officer jumped down from his platform, grabbed a rifle from a guard and rushed toward Kasten. "I was convinced he was going to shoot me," Kasten recalled, "but instead, holding the barrel, he swung the rifle like Babe Ruth, and with all his strength crashed the butt against my chest." Kasten flew back about fifteen feet and lay on the ground dazed, trying to catch his breath. Meanwhile, the guards went down the lines and pulled out every prisoner who, Kasten wrote, "looked Jewish." They came up with eighty men, well short of their quota of 350, so they began to pick out the troublemakers, including Kasten and his two assistants.

Told they were going to be working on a farm, the prisoners were loaded into boxcars and spent four days riding with no food or water to Berga, the site of a slave labor camp, an establishment strictly forbidden by the Geneva Convention. A German officer, Lieutenant Hack, greeted him, "We know all about you, Kasten." The Jewish men who had been transferred selected a prisoner named Goldstein as their leader, but the Germans forbade a Jew from holding that position, so Kasten's position in Stalag 9-B carried over.

"Very rapidly, things went from bad to worse," Kasten wrote. The laborers were digging seventeen tunnels into the mountains along the banks of the nearby Elster River, where an underground factory would be constructed, safe from any bombing runs. Their daily routine was to rise before dawn, march to the tunnels, and work without food or water for twelve hours at a stretch. Men soon began dying of exhaustion and malnutrition.

Kasten requested a meeting with Lt. Hack, and he brought along Joe Littell. They emphasized that the camp was in violation of the Geneva Convention and that Hack was going to answer for this brutality some day. The German's reply: "You were brought here to work, and that's what you will do." He asked to see Kasten's dog tags and read his full name: "Johann Carl Fredrich Kasten." Hack told him, "You are a German, and you have come here to destroy the Third Reich. You know, Kasten, there is only one thing worse than a Jew. Do you know what that is? It's a traitor who betrays his country, and you are a traitor. Incidentally, we have something special for you. We have just received two new dogs that are trained to tear you apart, and tomorrow we are going to turn you loose to see if they could get you."

Immediately after Kasten and Littell returned to the barracks, Hans told his two assistants that he was going to try to escape that night. They insisted on going with him, and after some resistance, he agreed. That night, before all the barracks buildings were locked, they slipped into the crawl space beneath their building. They had taken some food, and Kasten decided to bring six sticks of dynamite and blasting caps, which had been stolen from the construction site. They crawled to the perimeter barbed wire fence, and the two assistants squeezed under the wire. Kasten went last, and he was halfway through when they saw a guard approaching on his rounds. As Littell wrote in his memoir, *A Lifetime in Every Moment*, he was fearful that the guard would fire on them, detonating the dynamite, but somehow he didn't notice them and walked right by.

As they collected their wits outside of the fence, a siren went off. It was an air raid, and all the lights in the camp were doused. Although the guards came rushing out of their quarters, in the complete darkness they couldn't see the escapees, and Kasten, Littell, and Sinner took off running.

They traveled by night, heading west with the stars, living on sugar beets they liberated from mounds the farmers had made to feed their cattle. Kasten managed to shave off his beard, and they cut the brass buttons off Littell's and Sinner's coats; his was a reversible, and he wore it with white on the outside, his Army olive drab inside.

After several days, they came to a town and tried to rent a room at an inn. The innkeeper told them that since bombing had begun, citizens were using his inn as a shelter, and it was full. They tried another inn up the street but got the same story. They decided to order beers, but when a German officer began eyeing them suspiciously, they got up to leave. As they reached the door, the officer demanded to see their papers, and Kasten tried to bluff him: "Who are you that we have to show you our papers?" The man backed down and suggested they try an inn up the street owned by a friend of his.

As they walked with him up the street, the German asked again to see their papers. This time, Kasten's bluff didn't work; when he told the German, "Call the police; we will show them our papers," that is what he did.

Two policemen showed up, followed by a contingent of Gestapo agents, and Lt. Hack was summoned. He confronted Kasten, assaulting him again with a rifle across the chest. Guards beat him into unconsciousness, and Littell and Sinner had to carry him to their cell.

They were taken through the town, as the citizens spit on them and threw horse manure at them, to the train station. Their next stop was the punishment jail in Stalag 9-C at Bad Stulza, part of the Buchenwald complex. They were assigned to three solitary-confinement cells. While Littell was given books to read, Kasten was treated as a saboteur; his daily interrogations were punctuated by beatings.

One day, the officer supervising his interrogation sessions suddenly said, "*Also shluss damit, ershiessen*" (Finish with it, shoot him). The execution was to take place in five days. "The five days," Kasten wrote, "were for added torture to know you would be dead shortly."

On the third day, Kasten recalled, "the German guards began to run away, and shortly thereafter the U.S. military arrived, cut the fence open, and we had a great reunion." It was April 10, 1945.

As Littell wrote in his memoir, he lost track of Hans Kasten that day and didn't see him again for two months. Kasten wrote that he had gone into town, "liberated a Mercedes Benz" and went looking for Lt. Hack. It proved to be a futile search, and he finally collapsed from exhaustion, his weight down to ninety-six pounds. He was taken to a hospital at Camp Lucky Strike near Le Havre, France, and was shipped back to the U.S.

During his ordeal as a prisoner, Kasten suffered numerous injuries whose effects would plague him for the rest of his life, but he had never given an inch to his captors. Littell's memoir reported that shortly after he and Sinner and Kasten were recaptured by the Germans, a Gestapo colonel struck Kasten in the face several times during an interrogation, but Hans wouldn't flinch. Littell had feared they would be shot on the spot, but the defiant look on Kasten's face seemed to impress the colonel, who ordered them into solitary. "I firmly believe," Littell wrote, "that in the few minutes that had just transpired, Hans Kasten, without saying a word, had saved our lives. Never was I prouder of anyone! Never was I prouder to be a citizen of the United States!"

JOHN McCAIN:
THE INEVITABLE WARRIOR

*"I was privileged to observe a thousand acts of courage
and compassion and love."*

W HEN JOHN MCCAIN DESCRIBED HIMSELF TO A HISTORIAN in 2003 as "the luckiest person you will ever interview," it came at the end of a conversation that focused on his five-and-a-half-year ordeal as a captive of the North Vietnamese in the infamous "Hanoi Hilton." But McCain arrived at that conclusion without a trace of irony. His destiny was to serve his country in the military, and like any intelligent warrior, he knew the risks involved in going to war. That he was alive and well thirty years after his release, and serving his country in another capacity, might be considered more than a stroke of good luck.

McCain was the third John Sidney McCain in his family to serve in the U.S. Navy. His grandfather (1884-1945) was a World War II Task Force Commander in the Pacific Theater, an aviator whose forces had great success in retaking the Philippines. His father (1911-1981) rose from a WWII submarine commander to become Commander-in-Chief, Pacific Forces, during the same time his son was serving in Vietnam. Both senior McCains achieved the rank of Admiral.

"I resisted it from time to time," McCain said of the lure of the Navy, "but I was pretty sure that was what was going to happen." He attended the Naval Academy, which instilled a set of principles: "adherence to a code of honor, dependence on your comrades, a class system

John McCain, (front, right) with his squadron in 1965–1966,
when he was serving as an instructor.
A year later he was flying missions in Vietnam.

where you're loyal to your classmates, and then of course a reverence for and a desire to emulate leaders that you're taught about: John Paul Jones, "Bull" Halsey, Teddy Roosevelt." He had no doubt what he wanted out of a Naval career: to be a pilot, which he thought "was the most glamorous and exciting life that any person could ever choose. It was always my goal."

He came of age during the Cold War, but like his father and grand-father, he soon had his own shooting war to serve in. By 1967, he was on duty as a Navy pilot at Yankee Station, a fixed location in the China Sea for U.S. aircraft carriers that were daily launching planes to attack targets in North Vietnam. As McCain described it, a typical day there might consist of routine launches of one or two planes every forty-five minutes or so, or Alpha strikes, in which practically the entire air wing from his carrier (and sometimes other carriers) took off on a mission.

More than thirty years after participating in the war, the typically blunt McCain was still expressing frustration at the way it was waged from the air, describing the "futility" of watching Russian freighters unload SAMs (Surface to Air Missiles) in the North Vietnamese port of Haiphong, seeing trucks move them into position, and then later having to dodge those same missiles. "We couldn't touch them," he said, claiming the target selection process was "foolish" and worse, in that he saw so many of his comrades get shot down and killed or captured.

On July 29, McCain was in his A-4D Skyhawk, ready to take off on a mission from the deck of the USS *Forrestal*, when something went horribly wrong. A Zuni rocket loaded into an F-4 across the deck from him already had been electronically connected (a procedure supposed to take place only just before takeoff), and when the pilot fired up his engines, a large charge of stray electricity ignited the rocket. The Zuni flew across the deck, striking the 400-gallon fuel tank beneath McCain's plane. However, he managed to get out and throw himself clear just before the spilled fuel burst into a fireball. An immense conflagration was set off, with bombs and armaments exploding. McCain saw the pilot in the plane next to his try to escape the flames, but he didn't make it. That pilot was among 135 sailors who died that horrible day.

Three months later, on October 26, McCain was part of an Alpha strike designed to take out the Hanoi Thermal Power Plant. Not surprisingly, he and his squadron mates came under heavy fire; at that point, Hanoi was, according to McCain, the most heavily defended place in history. He rolled in to bomb the target, and just as he released his bombs and started to pull back on the A-4's joystick, a SAM took his plane's right wing off. McCain ejected quickly but violently, striking his knee against the canopy as he went out, as well as breaking both his arms. He parachuted into Truc Bach Lake, and, fighting off the pain in his arms, used his teeth to inflate his life raft. A group of Vietnamese quickly intercepted his raft and pulled him into shore to a group of waiting civilians. "The crowd was rather angry, which was understandable," he recalled. They hit him repeatedly, breaking his shoulder with a rifle butt, and he was bayoneted at least twice. Finally, some soldiers arrived, who photographed him with an old woman giving him tea and then took him to the Hoa Lo prison, aka the "Hanoi Hilton."

Built around the turn of the century by the French colonial government, Hoa Lo occupied an entire city block in downtown Hanoi. Its walls were four feet thick and twenty feet high, topped by broken glass and electrified barb wire. American GIs gave it its new nickname, and they also dubbed certain areas with colorful monikers like Heartbreak Hotel and Little Vegas.

McCain was kept in solitary confinement for over three years, under conditions he would describe as "pretty poor." The guards were tough, and meals were soup once or twice a day with a piece of bread. The flavor of soup rotated: four months of pumpkin, then four months of cabbage, followed by four months of a soup with greens "that looked like clipped grass." If it were a good day, he might find some meat in the bowl.

McCain was not a model prisoner, even though at first he wasn't beaten or tortured. He admitted to acting out, if only because he wasn't being interrogated more aggressively. Able to communicate with whoever occupied the cell next to his by tapping in code on the walls, he had little else to occupy his time or mind. Any news he heard from the outside was usually through omission; the Battle of Khe Sanh was going on at the time of his capture, and his captors kept telling him how the Americans could not hold out there much longer. When he stopped hearing about Khe Sanh, he suspected (rightly) that the American forces had triumphed.

Starting in mid to late 1970, McCain noticed an upturn in conditions, but he also ran into trouble when he refused early release. Without access to anyone but his next-cell neighbor, McCain was on his own in this decision. He said later that he was following the Code of Conduct established for the U.S. Armed Forces after the imprisonment of GIs during the Korean War, which stated that sick and injured prisoners should be released first, then prisoners in order of capture. He knew there were men in the Hilton, like Everett Alvarez, the first American taken prisoner by the Vietnamese, in 1964, who should be ahead of him, and he didn't think his lingering injuries were bad enough to earn him a spot in the front of the line.

Then too, McCain was keenly aware of his propaganda value to his captors, as the son of an admiral in the U.S. Navy. "It wasn't an easy decision," he would admit, and he certainly did not know at the time that he would be there for another three years. Even though he endured eight or nine months of beatings for his stubbornness, in the end he called it "the wisest decision I ever made."

*On October 26, 1967, McCain's Skyhawk was shot down
over Hanoi; he ejected and landed in a lake,
where civilians and soldiers "rescued" him.*

In 1971, McCain was moved to a larger cell with other prisoners, and the second phase of his captivity began. The camaraderie he developed with the other "guests" at the Hilton comforted and inspired him. "I was privileged to observe a thousand acts of courage and compassion and love," he would recall. "It is a great honor of my life." The men were allowed to organize classes in history and mathematics, to put on skits and plays. They also amused themselves by making fun of the daily propaganda broadcasts of a Vietnamese woman named Trinh Thi Ngo. Radio Hanoi piped in her show to the Hilton on loudspeakers. She played the latest American pop music, interspersed with crude appeals in English to the prisoners to cooperate with their captors and tell them what they wanted to hear.

"Humor," McCain noted, "is vital to one's resistance and mental stability." They dubbed Trinh Thi Ngo "Hanoi Hannah," and they chose nicknames as well for their guards, calling the camp commander Slope Head. McCain said that communication and a sense of humor keeps your captors from becoming large and powerful and intimidating. "If you laugh at them," he said, "it puts them more back to their normal size."

There was still little news of the outside world, other than claims by the North Vietnamese of a growing antiwar movement in America and elsewhere. "Anywhere in the world someone burned an American flag," he recalled, "we would hear about it." During his captivity, he dismissed these claims as "blatant propaganda," but when he arrived back home in America and learned that they weren't exaggerated, "it was probably my greatest surprise."

In March 1973 the Hanoi Hilton began to empty its cells. The men suspected something was in the works when they were given new clothes, better food, and, for the first time, reading material. Then they were divided into three groups, arranged by order of capture. One day, McCain recalled, a bus pulled up outside, and his group was loaded onto it. At the airport, they saw a group of Vietnamese and Americans seated together at a table; names of the prisoners were read out, and they all boarded a plane for home.

The first stop was the Philippines, where they underwent three days of medical tests. Then the men were transported to the Stateside duty station from which they were assigned to serve in Vietnam, in McCain's case, Jacksonville, Florida.

"It took me about forty-five minutes to readjust," he told his interviewer thirty years later. He still had physical problems from injuries that hadn't been properly treated, but he claimed never to have had a nightmare or a flashback. For that, he credits the last two years in the company of his comrades. "It wasn't as if I just walked out of three years of solitary confinement into the outside world."

McCain was physically unable to continue flying, but he did stay in the Navy until 1981. His last assignment pointed the way toward his future. Along with James Jones, who would later become Supreme Allied Commander, Europe, McCain was Navy liaison to the U.S. Senate. "I saw how impactful a hardworking member of the Senate could be, so I aspired to be one." The year after he retired from the Navy, he was elected to the House of Representatives from Arizona, and four years later he was elected to fill the Senate seat of the retiring Barry Goldwater.

Ernest Hemingway's novel *For Whom the Bell Tolls* has been an inspiration for John McCain. Robert Jordan, the book's doomed protagonist, is fighting in the Spanish Civil War for the Loyalist side. McCain described him as "a man who was dedicated, selfless, brave, capable, but also stoic. He recognized the cause he served was a flawed one, but he still served it even to the point where he was willing to sacrifice his life, even if the particular enterprise, the blowing up of a bridge, would have no effect on the conflict. He still went out and did it. His final words were, 'The world is a fine place and worth the fighting for, and I'll hate very much to leave it.'"

"My idea of honor," McCain continued, "is to serve a cause greater than your self-interest. There are lots of good causes, and you can serve them in many ways. You don't have to serve in the Spanish Civil War as Robert Jordan did. You can serve them in your own community and even in your own home."

This is what has animated John McCain's life, and what leads him to believe, as he also told his interviewer in 2003, "I've been very fortunate in my life." Not only did he survive that horrible fire on the deck of the *Forrestal* and five and a half years as a POW of the North Vietnamese, but he has been given two opportunities—twenty-three years in the Navy and over twenty-two years in the U.S. Congress—to serve a cause greater than his self-interest.

JOSÉ MARES:
THE STUBBORN SPANIARD

"This actually happened. This is the truth. And if I by any chance can get any young person to have a love for his or her country as much as I did, that's what I want them to do."

NO AMOUNT OF TRAINING COULD HAVE PREPARED EIGHTEEN-year-old José Mares for what he would encounter as a prisoner of the North Koreans and Chinese during the Korean War. What Mares drew on for survival was physical courage, patriotism, and a stubborn belief that his ordeal was only temporary. His mantra—"There's got to be something better"—sustained him through brutal punishment and the death of his best pal.

Mares, the youngest of nine children, was born in Prescott, Arizona, which is, as he described it in a 2003 interview, "a little cowboy town" north of Phoenix. His father, who worked as a hospital orderly, was of Spanish descent, his mother Mexican. Several of his older brothers and his father all volunteered to serve in World War II. Just before America entered that war, the family had moved to Albuquerque, New Mexico, and nine-year-old José started hanging out in what was then called "bad company." He was closest to his oldest brother, who "always told me I could do something more with my life than running around with gangs." Young José heard his brother, but he didn't listen. "I was looking for something," he would recall. "I figured there had to be something better than this."

At the age of seventeen, José was hauled before a judge on a criminal matter. He was given a choice: join the Army or go to jail. José's

*José Mares, an 18-year-old recruit in 1950,
at Fort Lewis, Washington, where he learned to
string wire for field communications.*

father asked to sign the papers for his enlistment, and the teenager did-
n't object. José told his interviewer that he realized he had been given
an opportunity, and he was ready to take it.

He was sent to Fort Chaffee, Arkansas, where he worked hard and
"kept his nose clean"—except for a little misunderstanding that
involved a pack of cigarettes and a rifle he was carrying. The other
soldier wound up with a bullet wound courtesy of Mares, and José
wound up with a broken arm. They also wound up in adjacent hospital beds. At Fort Lewis, Washington, Mares was given training as a

field wire foreman, a job that involved stringing wire for field telephone communication.

In June 1950, the North Korean invasion of South Korea pulled the U.S. into a war less than five years after the conclusion of World War II. Mares didn't hesitate to ask to ship out, recalling the advice of his father and older brothers: "If there was anything we need to be, it was faithful to our country. We need to do all we can to conserve it and fight for it. We heard that there was a country in trouble, and they asked for volunteers, and I volunteered because there was a problem."

As he left Fort Lewis for Korea, he also recalled another piece of advice one of his brothers gave him about serving in combat: Don't get too close to anybody, "because if you do, you might get hurt in the long run."

Mares's ship landed in Pusan in August 1950. He didn't have to wait long for action; the 2nd Infantry, also aboard the ship, asked for volunteers to help clear the docks, on which there was so much fighting that it literally wasn't safe for the U.S. Army to disembark. "I went into fighting mode," Mares recalled, "because of the fights that I had had as a young person." He admitted, "I took a lot of unnecessary chances."

Mares was assigned to the 38th Field Artillery Battalion, working with a forward observer, whose job was to push into no-man's-land and scout for locations to direct artillery fire. One day, his observer didn't return, and Mares was asked to take his place. He was reluctant to take the job, but his buddies urged him on, saying they'd rather work with him than some unknown quantity. He was given a battlefield commission and the perks of the job: a jeep, a driver, and a radio man. Mares picked for his driver Wally Walker, a kid from Chicago he had become pals with. The two spent a lot of time talking about what they were going to do when they got back from Korea. One day in late October, Mares wasn't able to go out into the field, and he asked Wally to go in his place. Wally didn't come back.

Three weeks later, José Mares was spending his first Thanksgiving away from home. It was a rainy day, and he was sitting on a log, flanked by two officers, trying to enjoy the Army-issue turkey dinner, when they were startled by what he recalled as the sound of trumpets. (Chinese troops used bugles to communicate and announce an attack, in a tradition dating back to the legendary war strategist, Sun Tzu.) The air filled with harsh sounds of weapons fire; Mares saw the man to his left get shot in the head, the man to his right shot in the chest. He jumped behind the log for cover and heard someone—he thought the commanding officer—shout, "Every man for himself!"

Mares took off and met up with four other GIs. They agreed to stick together and try to make it back to American lines, but with no compass they got turned around and headed north. Mares instructed the men to stay in fighting mode, that if they had a chance to do some damage to the enemy to take it. Along the way, they managed to detonate several ammunition dumps. "The adrenaline started pumping again," he recalled, "and I felt like we were doing something." They traveled only by night, hiding during the day under piles of leaves. One of the soldiers developed a cough, and about five days into their flight gave them away. North Korean soldiers bayoneted the coughing soldier in his hiding place. Before Mares could be taken prisoner, he bent his rifle barrel against a rock, rendering it useless to his captors.

He and his buddies were stripped naked and led down a mountain to a camp miles away from where they were discovered. They were held in a house where the Koreans interrogated them one at a time. Each prisoner's hands were tied behind his back, the rope was thrown over a ceiling beam, and the prisoner was yanked off his feet, suspended, to be beaten when he didn't give a satisfactory answer. One night, Mares was taken out by a river and was interrogated by having water from the nearly frozen stream poured over his head. "They didn't care for us at all," was his comment fifty years later.

Mares may have thought he caught a break when his captors gave him a pair of pants and a pair of shoes, but then came his most harrowing experience. He and his three buddies, none of whom had given the North Koreans any information of any use, were bound and blindfolded and led to the bank of a river. They were made to kneel in a line; Mares sensed that he was third in the row. A North Korean loudly asked the first man in line for the size of his unit and what its mission was. When the GI barked out his name, rank, and service number, the Korean pulled out a .45-caliber pistol and shot the soldier in the head. Mares felt the man's blood splatter him, and he heard the corpse fall into the river. He would later recall his thoughts: "I wonder if I can do that. I don't know if I got enough nerve to do that. I love my country, I love what I am doing, but I don't know if I can do that."

The Korean repeated his questions to the man next to Mares, with the same results. "I didn't know what I was going to do," Mares would recall. "I really didn't. But as he asked me the questions, I just bellowed out; I gave him my name, rank, service number." He could feel the heat of the gun's muzzle next to his head, and then "all of a sudden—and I know this is God's planning—I hear some screeching of some brakes on a truck, and I could hear some language I'd never heard before." It was a group of Chinese officers; they told the Korean that there would be no more killing of prisoners. The Korean got so mad he began to pistol-whip Mares, and the beating permanently deafened him in his right ear.

He fell into the water, and the Chinese, assuming he was dead, laid him with the two murdered POWs in a cage. They hung it over a rafter back in the POW compound so "everyone could see what would happen if you didn't cooperate." After a time, Mares came to, and a Chinese guard saw that he was breathing. The cage was cut down, Mares fell out, and his captors washed him up and gave him a little bit of sorghum, telling him, "Sorghum is what we feed to our pigs."

Mares's family had been notified on Christmas Day 1950 that he was officially listed as missing in action since November 30. It was almost one year later, on December 19, 1951, that they received a telegram announcing that he was believed to be a prisoner of war.

Meanwhile, Mares was being shunted around Korea. At one point he was housed in an area west of Pyongyang known as The Caves. POWs were kept in a tunnel through which water flowed, packed in so tight with other ill and injured men that when someone tried to change position, everyone around him had to shift as well. If a prisoner died, the unwritten rule was his immediate neighbors could take what they wanted off the corpse, which would then be passed through the tunnel to the outside.

Mares managed to escape from his captors once and was free for four days. After he was recaptured, he was placed, naked, in a hot box. He couldn't figure out what they did to create the heat; all he knows is that by the time "you came out you couldn't hardly see anything." His captors told him they wanted an apology for trying to escape. "I told them I was sorry but that I was going to try it again."

In his second year of captivity, tactics switched from torture and deprivation to brainwashing. Prisoners were required to go to a library, and Chinese instructors, who spoke perfect English, lectured them on the fine points of the Communist Manifesto. They were given other books on communist ideology to read and were assigned reports to write. "Maybe I was just a stubborn Spaniard," Mares admitted, but he bridled at this forced education. One night, the library burned down. "It was such a pretty fire," he recalled. The next day, the guards came around sniffing the prisoners for telltale signs of their involvement in the arson, and Mares was judged guilty of the deed. He was stripped and brought before a panel of Chinese officials. Was he sorry for what he did? No, he wasn't. He was dropped into a hole with water to his knees, his meager rations thrown down to him. Trying to catch his food one day, he saw a cockroach crawl into his hand and immediately ate it. "There's got to be something better than this," he kept thinking. "I'm doing all I can for my country."

After a week or two, he was hauled out and told that he had been found guilty by a court-martial. His sentence was thirty years in a Siberian salt mine, and he was unlikely to ever go home again. He was transferred to another location where tough cases, called reactionaries, were housed.

At the other end of the prisoner spectrum from the reactionaries were the progressives, prisoners who told their captors what they wanted to hear. They were easy to spot; they were smoking cigarettes, had access to liquor and better clothes. But POW justice could be harsh. If a progressive was ever found alone, with no guards around, in an open latrine, his punishment would be swift and brutal.

Mares's next stop was across the Yalu River, in Manchuria, where he suffered "some of the worst interrogation I had in my life: beatings, whippings, spitting on you." One day, leaving the interrogation facility, he noticed a building atop a nearby hill. After several years in captivity, he had picked up enough Chinese to ask a guard about the building. "It is a hospital," said the guard, "and anybody who goes up will surely die." Mares had an instinct about the place and asked for permission to visit it.

Inside were prisoners lying on a bare floor, all in great distress. As he walked among them, some pulled at his clothes, begging for help. In the corner, he spotted what he would later describe as "a skeleton of a boy." It was Wally Walker. All through his own captivity, Mares had been asking about his buddy, and now he had finally found him.

"I reached down to him, and he said, 'Is that you, Joe?' And I said, 'Yeah, it's me.' And he said, 'Joe, I don't know if I'm going to go to

Mares (center) and fellow soldiers at Fort Lewis. His best friend, Wally Walker (left) underwent brutal treatment as a POW.

heaven or I'm going to go to hell. Can you help me?' I told Wally, 'We're in hell right now. And if we get to heaven that's good, but we're in hell right now.'"

Mares promised to get Wally some rice and sugar, and that once they were strong enough they were going to escape from there. He came back a couple of days later and was horrified to see rats chewing on Wally's flesh. He held the dying young man in his arms and put rice in his mouth. Wally pushed him away and repeated his question about going to heaven or hell. Before Mares could answer, Wally Walker died. Mares took his buddy outside and dug a grave with his hands. "That was a very hard time for me," he recalled in his interview. Did he feel responsible for Wally's death? "Yes, in that I couldn't tell him how to get to heaven."

On July 27, 1953, the United States, North Korea, and China signed an armistice, bringing an end to the war. Around this time Mares was brought back to Korea and told about the conclusion of the hostilities. But, he was informed, he would remain a prisoner, assigned to work-details in Panmunjon. He and his fellow reactionaries were taken to that city in August, and several weeks after they arrived a delegation of the Swiss Red Cross paid a visit. The prisoners were told in advance they

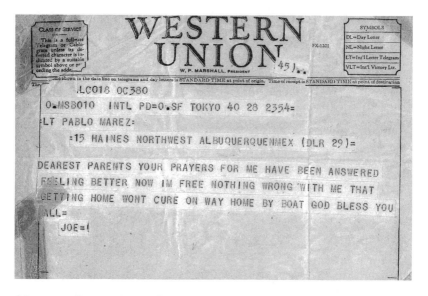

Mares sent his parents a telegram announcing his release from captivity in August 1953, one month after the armistice was signed.

could not touch any packages the Red Cross was leaving, nor could they say anything to the visitors. However, when one of the Red Cross officials asked Mares if he was indeed José Mares, he answered yes. The man recognized Mares because of a message smuggled out of a POW camp where Mares was a cook for a time. A flier was brought to that camp with a badly injured leg. Mares and another prisoner, who was an X-ray technician, knew that the man was going to die if his leg wasn't amputated. Mares asked some prisoners who were working outside the camp to bring in as many wild marijuana plants as they could; he dried the leaves and got some cigarette paper to roll them into. After the flier was sufficiently high from smoking the homemade "anesthetic," and several prisoners were enlisted to hold him down, Mares used a homemade tool to amputate the man's gangrenous leg. Another prisoner who was a fair carpenter fashioned the man a wooden leg, which was hollow. When the camp got word that the maimed GI was going to be released in a swap of seriously ill and injured prisoners, Mares and others placed some written material inside the leg. Their camp had been hit several times by American bombers, but once they identified their position as a POW camp, the bombing stopped.

On the night of August 24, 1953, Mares was roused from his bed. It was 2 A.M. There was no explanation from his captors about what was happening. He was again stripped of his clothes, blindfolded, bound by rawhide strips on his hands and feet and tossed into the back of a truck. He thought, "This is it. They're gonna kill me." After a time, the truck stopped, and he was thrown out, onto a sandy surface. He heard rifle bolts clicking and ammunition going into chambers. Then he heard feet scurrying and the truck pulling away. The next sensation he had was of a man cutting his bonds and taking off his blindfold. The man asked if he was José Mares. He was a two-star general in the U.S. Army, and he took off his field jacket and covered Mares with it. "I looked up," Mares recalled, "and I saw our American flag flying in the breeze, and that made me feel so good inside that whatever I'd done I did for my country."

He weighed 96 pounds the day he was released. The day he was captured, 33 months earlier, he weighed 165 pounds.

Mares remained in the Army until 1971. He married a woman he fell in love with at first sight, and they had five children. He has only praise for his wife—"she's a champion"—because his readjustment wasn't easy. He had nightmares. He actively hated Koreans and Chinese. And he believed that his pal Wally Walker's blood was on his hands, because he had not been able to answer Wally's question about how to get to heaven.

In 1958, Mares was approached by the pastor of a local Baptist church, who sensed the soldier was in need of some peace and comfort. Mares brushed him off, but his wife began pestering him to consider attending the Baptist church. They were practicing Catholics, but when Mares approached his priest for advice, the man brushed him off, telling him to make an appointment with his secretary. Mares finally figured there was only one way to get rid of the persistent Baptist minister—to let him in. "I've been freed ever since," he recalled, adding that he had been a captive of sin, and that when he accepted Jesus Christ those chains fell off.

In his retirement from the Army, Mares has become a missionary, taking his message to Central and South America (in both Spanish and English), as well as to churches and to high schools, where he would talk about a war that students his age when he enlisted had only read about. He also came to understand that "God has made a plan" for him and Wally Walker to someday be reunited, "and that will be one of the rejoicing times."

José Mares told his interviewer, "People ask, 'Why are you waiting until now to give your testimony?' Well, it's because of my beloved wife and my children. My wife said, 'How else are people going to know about people like Wally Walker? How else are people going to know there's a heritage here, that you're leaving something behind?'

"This actually happened. This is the truth. And if I by any chance can get any young person to have a love for his or her country as much as I did, that's what I want them to do."

HAROLD RILEY:
THE LAST PRISONER

"I believed the excitement and thrills of military action could be better appreciated from close contact, with real fighting."

As Harold Riley revealed in his memoir, what attracted many men like him to serve in World War I was the notion of emulating gallant fighting men. Riley became an ambulance driver, a pilot, and a prisoner of war, but his memories of the war were less than romantic.

In April 1917, when the U.S. entered the war, the twenty-two-year-old Riley was living in California with his parents and sister. In his memoir, which he wrote in 1931 from a journal and from memory, he recalled, "I did not want to stay on the sidelines, feeling I should get into it for all I was worth," adding, "this attitude was fostered by a selfish viewpoint, I must admit, as I believed the excitement and thrills of military action could be better appreciated from close contact, with real fighting."

To qualify that point, Riley wrote that he wanted to be an officer, to "wear a good-looking uniform and lead the attacks, just like the officers were described in the news and later shown in post-war movies." Because so many young men like Riley were applying for those positions, he decided to return to his native Minnesota, thinking he could use local connections to accomplish his goal. He was turned down for one officers' camp and put on a waiting list for a second one.

The impatient Riley soon discovered another route to his ambition: volunteer for the Norton-Harjes Ambulance Corps. Once in

France, he could enlist in the French Army; he saw this as his best chance to become a pilot in the Air Service. He had only to personally finance transportation to France.

The one drawback to this plan was his family. His parents had returned to Minnesota, and en route his father was diagnosed with diabetes. Harold assessed the situation: There was little he could do for his father, the family's finances were in fine shape, and, after all, as he wrote, "war was war." His parents told him they would not stand in his way if he wanted to enlist.

What he was doing finally hit him hard when he said goodbye to his father, knowing that he might not see him again. "This was my first taste of war and what it meant," he wrote. "Up to this point in time the whole thing was a lark, like preparations for a big trip to some place where a bunch of fellows were going to have a big time."

He left for Europe on June 20, 1917, on the ship *Chicago*. Before boarding, he had seen the ship as some grand liner, but the following morning he realized it was "just a plain ship, and an old one at that. It lumbered over the seas like an old, swayback horse."

His shipmates included two sons of former President Roosevelt, Kermit and Theodore, Jr., and the future writer John Dos Passos, another recruit for Norton-Harjes, which was an amalgamation of the Harjes Formation of the American Red Cross and the American Volunteer Motor Ambulance Corps, organized in 1914. The chief inducement then for many American college men was that they could get to the action in France without waiting for America to enter the war or get its Army organized. There, the American Red Cross could help them enlist in the French Foreign Legion, which didn't cost them their citizenship.

After the *Chicago* landed at Bordeaux, Riley took a train to Paris, which suitably impressed him. There he visited the Flying Service offices in hopes of enlisting, but reports were discouraging, even for joining the legendary Lafayette Escadrille, a group of American and French pilots who since 1916 had been fighting the Germans under the French flag, well before America entered the war. His instinct was to hold back before joining the French Army and hope for a better situation as a pilot.

In a few days, his unit of Norton-Harjes drivers was rounded up and taken on a slow train to the town of Châlons-sur-Marne, which Riley described as the location for a "well known champagne factory." They received their ambulances and drove to several different staging areas over the next couple of days, during which time he learned that "these ambulances were not made for speed or comfort."

While waiting for further orders, the men got acquainted. At night they watched the roads fill with traffic: food and ammunition being hauled to the front, the weary and injured being brought back.

Not long after he arrived in France, Riley received word from Minnesota of his father's death. He only mentions it in the memoir, with no accompanying memory of his reaction.

Close by their headquarters was an airfield, and Riley took time to talk with the pilots. "What I saw," he wrote, "made flying take on an even more fascinating color, whetting my desire to fly." He decided that he would join that service as soon as he could get released from the ambulance corps.

They drove to a field hospital, where they were told, if they performed well, "we would be allowed the honor to be attached to the 25th French Division, one of their attack divisions."

They were located in Recicourt on the Paris-Verdun Road. In the morning he and his partner, a New Yorker named Eddie Doyle, took out Ambulance No. 16. The roads, he wrote, were "pretty sketchy," and pocked with shell holes. At a steep incline, he and Doyle got stuck. Coming at them over the hill was a group of French soldiers retreating from German artillery shells. The shells came closer and closer, and Riley and Doyle dived for cover in different directions. They finally reached their post and loaded up the ambulance with wounded patients.

One night, they were to evacuate patients from a field wound-dressing station and get them back before dawn. Near the top of a hill the ambulance kept stalling. He recalled, "With the silence of no motor I could hear the machine guns much too close, and flares seemed to magnify the rig and make it look like the largest thing on the landscape." Then German gas shells landed nearby, and Riley and Doyle had to account not only for their own gas masks, but for those of their patients. They decided to take the stretchers out of the ambulance, hoping the vehicle would start with a lighter load. He wrote, "We put the five stretchers on the ground behind the car when the brake slipped and the ambulance rolled toward these men. There being no block handy, I stuck my foot under the nearest wheel and held the rig until Doyle could get around to the side and reset the brake. Doyle hitched a ride back to the post to get help while I stayed with both the immobile men and immobile ambulance. In what seemed like an eternity he returned with a different car; we reloaded the wounded, and completed our mission." Riley then awoke the unit's mechanic and made him drive out to the stalled ambulance and tow him back to headquarters. The man drove so fast that Riley thought the experience was "as dangerous as being shot at by the enemy."

On October 17, 1917, Harold Riley was released from French Army service and sworn into the U.S. Army as a cadet in the Air Corps. He was eager to get into the air, and when he received orders to leave for Issoudon, he and his fellow cadets "thought we would get into a nice camp, have American meals, and start flying. With such a start we would be at the front by Spring at the very least." It didn't work out quite like that. At Issoudon, he was given so many menial chores to perform that "I was put in the frame of mind to desert." Then he was transferred to Tours, where, after several weeks of guard duty, he finally started getting flying lessons. He wrote, "The Frogs were the instructors and they were in no more hurry about flying than they were about anything else, so progress was slow."

Toward spring, they were placed under the command of the U.S. Army Air Service, and living conditions improved, as did the instruction. His own instructor was Reed Chambers, who was the same age as Riley but already had plenty of experience flying in the United States and in action along the Mexican border in 1916. He went on to become one of America's World War I aces, compiling seven victories.

After completing his basic requirements, Riley was given his commission and sent to Paris to await his next assignment. He arrived on March 30, 1918, the day before Easter. The city was in an uproar, literally, as German shells were finding targets there. "However," as Riley laconically reported, "it did not slow me down very much, and I had a good time as long as I dared stay there."

He returned to Issoudon, and, though he had his wings, there were still lessons to be learned, in how to use a machine gun, both in the air and on the ground. He had plenty of time to "monkey around" because there was a shortage of airplanes. Even with a scarcity of planes there was no shortage of accidents, many of them fatal. "There was never a flying day in the early Spring," he wrote, "that there was not a funeral conducted for some fellow who had been bumped off in training." Riley thought the air casualties that spring at Issoudon were as heavy as those in the air at the front.

One weekend a bunch of fliers took a train and wound up in Limoges, a safe distance from the quarters of any French and American armies, so they had the town to themselves. They met Mr. Haviland, whose family owned and operated the famous china factory. He showed them how his product was made and offered to ship a souvenir back home for each of the visiting soldiers. "No one was interested in his offer," Riley recalled, "which displayed the soldier's attitude at the time: If you survived the war, well and good, but why worry about the future, least of all a set of china."

Finally, he received orders to report to Columbes-les-Belles, the headquarters for organizing flight squadrons. He was assigned to a new Aero Squadron, the 24th, setting up between Toul and Nancy, overlooking the Moselle River. Their commanding officer was quartered in a small chateau, where the men ate their meals, and their barracks were across the road. "Here we were at the front," he wrote, "good quarters, wonderful food, beautiful surroundings, a chance to do the things we had trained for over several months. No more soldier's complaints."

Each plane carried two men, a pilot and an observer. Pilots got to choose their observers, and Riley selected a young man named Collins, with whom he worked well until Collins came down with influenza.

One day, he and his observer went up for a little spin, even though his gun hadn't been mounted. They ventured toward the front and then decided to head for home. As they were coming out of a cloud, they nearly ran into two German planes; "we were so close," he recalled, "I could have hit them with a fishing pole or a monkey wrench." He changed course quickly and ducked back into a cloud for cover, hoping they didn't see them and headed straight for home.

His missions involved flying over the lines as an observer or acting as protection for the 91st Squadron when they were photographing enemy positions. A flight usually involved one, two, or three airplanes; it was on the solo flights that they suffered the most casualties. Early one morning his roommate went up alone. He had dressed hurriedly in the dark and accidentally put on Riley's shirt, on which Riley wore his Chi

Psi fraternity pin. The roommate never came back to base, and the squadron assumed he was killed. In fact, he was forced to make a landing when his engine quit behind enemy lines, and he was captured and put into a prison near the Swiss border where, as Riley wrote, "he and a group of Americans spent the rest of the war, enjoying the food and wines, having a good time." Several years later, Riley received the fraternity pin in a letter from the ex-flier. "I am glad," he wrote, "he did not ask me about the dandy pair of Cordovan Riding Boots he had gotten when one of his friends was killed in a plane crash." When his roommate had not returned, Riley, being "his nearest relative," had inherited them.

On clear nights, they would watch American antiaircraft guns firing at German bombers. The enemy planes made a sound easily distinguishable from American planes, so the pilots could often hear them before seeing them illuminated in searchlights that panned the skies. When American batteries cut loose with a barrage, Riley noted, it was "much prettier and far more exciting than a good Fourth of July celebration." He never saw their artillery catch up to a plane during one of these night-time displays, but one day over Germany he saw an American plane take a direct hit. His succinct description of the plane's fate: "It was there, and it wasn't."

Riley suspected that all the observation work his squadron had been doing was in preparation for a huge offensive by the Americans. When the day and hour of the battle was finally announced, they were able to observe from the air progress that was so swift that "by noon it was a walk-away," and back on the ground they began seeing streams of prisoners being marched from the front.

Collins came down with the flu, and as Riley wrote, "this seemed to be a turning point of the war for me." Their last flight "turned out to be a flop" but ended fortunately. They were on their way back to base when their motor quit. They were over a hill at the time, and Riley had to choose between landing on top of the hill, which had once been fortified with trenches and barbed wire, or landing on the side of the hill, which was covered with little trees and brush. He chose the latter, and they managed to walk away from the crashed plane, which suffered only a broken shock absorber.

The weather was now turning murky, making high flying difficult, with low flying always more dangerous, as it exposed the plane to enemy fire. On a heavily overcast day, Riley's CO ordered him to go up and drop propaganda leaflets behind enemy lines. The literature urged German soldiers to agitate with their officers for a surrender and an end to the war. The CO warned Riley to make sure all of the leaflets cleared his plane, for if he were downed and captured in possession of this material, he would be treated as a spy and executed.

In the fall of 1918, Riley and his flight were ordered to report to Colonel William "Billy" Mitchell, commander of AEF aviation, at First Army Headquarters. The word was that the 91st Squadron was not getting the job done, and HQ wanted to give the men of the 24th a shot. In Mitchell's office he showed the fliers a map of where they would fly, over the Boise de Consonvoy, a heavily wooded area that was blocking the advance of the French Army. The Allies needed to know if anything was concealed there before the army would advance.

Riley wrote, "We thought this Headquarters work was going to be a nice turn of events, sitting around and having the rest of the First Army Aviation taking care of us." On October 8, 1918, he took on his mission with a new observer, Samuel R. Keesler, a young man he'd worked with before and trusted.

They made their observation on the Boise and were turning around to head for home when they discovered that four German planes had been tailing them and blocked their route back. Riley realized that his and Keesler's only chance was to try to outrun them. The enemy planes were positioned above him, and he aimed his plane directly beneath them, figuring as he passed under them, the Germans would have to turn and fly into the sun to pursue his plane.

The planes dived at them, and as one passed by Riley let him have it with his gun. "That German," he wrote, "never got back into the war." However, the other three planes managed to get off some accurate shots, cutting his rudder cables so he could do no more maneuvering. He sped straight ahead, hoping to make it back to their lines and pick up some support.

Now the enemy fire was finding them; Riley took a hit in the leg, and when he looked back he could see Keesler was wounded, too, though he kept firing away. The fabric was beginning to tear off his wings, but his motor was still purring along. Finally, the damage caught up to them, and he lost control of the plane. He recalled, "We were falling and the ground was coming up to meet us—far too rapidly. Just when I thought it was all over and what was not shot to pieces would be smashed to bits, the plane flattened out and we crashed on the ground, hard but not hurt." His first impulse was to get out, open the gas line, and set the plane on fire so that the Germans would have nothing to salvage. But he saw Keesler still in his seat, firing away at the German aircraft above them. Riley shouted at him but Keesler paid no attention, so he ran to him and pulled him out of the plane. The observer had been wounded badly and could not walk. As Riley pulled him away from the plane, a German bullet struck Keesler in the right hip and he went limp.

The Germans flew off but soon enemy soldiers appeared on all sides of them. An officer soon showed up and called for a doctor. In a shelter, Riley learned that Keesler's chances of survival were one in a thousand.

One soldier who was guarding them told Riley that he had been a waiter at Sherry's Restaurant in New York City before the war, that he was visiting family in Germany when the war was declared, and he was conscripted into the army. He intended to go back to New York after the war and told Riley he was happy to have an American to talk to.

After a time, they were taken to a field dressing station and separated. Keesler was taken into the main building, Riley into a small shed manned by several orderlies who "did not seem very friendly." Sirens and bells went off, and Riley figured there was an air raid in progress. He also realized the dressing station was located near an ammunition dump, and that his chances of survival if a bomb hit nearby were not favorable.

He was taken to the main building and examined. He saw Keesler being transported on a stretcher, but the young man did not respond when Riley tried to speak to him; he looked very pale. After Riley received a tetanus shot, he looked into the room where Keesler had been taken. The doctor informed him that it was too late for any help for his friend, that he had died. (Keesler Air Force Base in Biloxi, Mississippi, which was dedicated in 1941, was named for Keesler, a native of Greenwood, Mississippi.)

An English-speaking German lieutenant told Riley that he was going to be taken back from the lines to Montmédy. They rode in a Benz automobile with the top down. They made small talk, but the lieutenant did not formally interrogate Riley. Riley did learn that his

Harold Riley (right) and his observer Samuel Keesler.
The two were shot down in October 1918,
one month before the end of World War I.

captor was an Oxford graduate who had been flying on the Eastern Front when he was shot in the chest and had been reassigned to pick up downed American fliers and relocate them to hospitals or camps. "He was a pleasant fellow," Riley wrote, "whose company I enjoyed but would have enjoyed more under more agreeable circumstances. After my experience at the Dressing Station he seemed like an old friend."

Riley was left at a church that was being used as a hospital. The lieutenant said he would return in the morning, at which time Riley would be permitted to write a note telling of his condition, which the Germans would drop on one of the American fields. It was, Riley wrote, "a courtesy offered by both sides when possible, to shorten the time required to find out about missing aviators." The letters were placed in a can to which a long tail was attached; the tail coming down through the sky made it easy for those on the ground to spot the landing place for the can.

Riley was housed in a small room in the middle bed of three. On one side of him was a patient whose face was bandaged. He couldn't speak, so he wrote a note explaining that he was an American flier who had been brought in the day before.

In the morning, Riley awoke to find the American patient had been replaced by a German. The lieutenant showed up and gave Riley paper and pencil on which to write his note. He showed Riley strips of film with pictures of the American's home base and told him the exact number of planes stationed there, information Riley was sure he hadn't shared with the German.

His stay in the hospital was uneventful except for the revolving roster of patients in an adjacent room with five beds. Most of them were German, and he couldn't understand what they were saying. He kept hoping for a German patient to be assigned to his room so that he might try to learn his language. But, he wrote, "it seems mine was the death room, each new patient brought in being very sick, not one surviving while I was there, the Sisters bring a screen to place around the bed and soon I could no longer hear breathing."

Each morning at the same time, a German band would march up to the hospital, and after a short delay they would leave, playing funeral music to accompany a procession to the town cemetery. "If I closed my eyes," Riley recalled, "I could imagine myself in Issoudon during the preceding spring months when so many of our men were killed in training crashes, the same martial, funeral music leaving the same impression."

Being alone in an enemy hospital," he wrote, "was not a lark, but it left no unpleasant memories or experiences." The nuns were pleasant, the doctors agreeable, and he met no vindictive or vengeful soldiers.

A doctor took X rays of his leg and told Riley he would be sent to

Trier for surgery. A nun came for him a few days later, and two orderlies placed him on a stretcher, which was wheeled through the town
on a two-wheel cart to the train station. "As we went through town,"
he recalled, "I was subjected to many curious looks, such as given a
clown at a circus parade."

On the train he shared a compartment with Germans, but the language barrier was impossible to overcome, even after they tried French
with him. In Trier, he was taken to a hospital ward where the first person he saw was Alan Winslow, a friend serving in the infantry whom
Riley thought had been killed at Château-Thierry.

There was one other American and a Frenchman in the room, but
the French soldier soon died. He and Winslow went to the man's
funeral, where they met some French officers being held in a nearby
prison camp. They shared with their American compatriots canned
food and hardtack rolls, "the kind we used to throw at each other
when we were in Ambulance Section, but now tasted like cake in
comparison to the bread the Germans were providing."

Within a week of his arrival, his room was filled with American soldiers, which made for more pleasant socializing, although some of
them were badly wounded. He and Winslow did what they could to
take care of these patients. A lieutenant from the Carolinas named
Walker was in such bad shape and low spirits that they didn't think he
was going to make it. One day they came upon a black soldier whom
they discovered was from the same area of the South. They brought the
man back to their ward, and the two soldiers struck up a conversation
about what they missed back home. Riley recalled that he got a
Christmas card from Walker in 1930 saying "he was well and none the
worse for his stay in Germany, thanks to that Black."

Riley expected that he would have his leg operated on, but there
were so many patients with more pressing needs that it didn't happen.
One day he was in the operating room to have his dressings changed,
and a young man was brought in on a stretcher. Riley had never before
paid attention to what was happening at the other end of the room
when he was in there. "I began to feel weak when they gave him ether,
a little weaker when they made incisions in his leg down to the bone,
and was barely able to walk out of the room when they finished saw-
ing through the bone and tossed his leg into a big box where such

things were put. I tried to see him often after that, and when I left he was doing nicely but would still curl up and suffer terrible cramps in the foot of the leg that had been amputated."

One morning they were told to be ready to leave Trier that day. He and Winslow were taken to the train station that afternoon, and they discovered a great commotion there. There was talk about an armistice being signed. By the time the train pulled out that evening, it was packed with prisoners of all nationalities, "the most motley bunch I have ever seen." There were "American Negroes dressed in French uniforms, wooden shoes with hay in them for socks; all manner of others in tin hats, German hats, no hats, Russian boots, parts of American uniforms and some clothes that must have been brought in from the farms."

He and Winslow and a French lieutenant were the only officers on the train, so they were given a compartment with a window; the rest of the prisoners had no windows. The trip took three days and three nights, and they had only cabbage soup to eat. When the train finally came to its destination, they sat in an unheated barracks for several hours and then were taken to a hospital. They were in Königsberg.

Sallet, a Frenchmen they met there, said it was true, the armistice had been signed. And yet, they were deep in Germany with no one to assure them they would be repatriated any time soon. Sallet told them to be patient, as he had been captured the first year of the war with a broken leg that had been re-set several times.

Riley finally got his operation—and it proved to be an ordeal, as the ether had not quite taken effect when the surgeon began cutting. "There were times I thought I could not stand the pain without yelling," he recalled, "but somehow I got through it, but I know I crushed the hands of the orderlies who were holding me." The surgeon later told him he was lucky to still have his leg, that the fur lining of his leather flying suit had been driven deep into the wound by the force of the bullets, "which by all odds should have long before this caused a serious, irreparable infection."

The three of them were "sort of privileged characters" at this postwar hospital, allowed to get out of bed when they wanted to in the morning and to keep on their lights at night after the rest of the hospital was darkened. Still, Christmas came and went with no word on their release. Winslow, who was the most mobile of the three officers, decided to go into town and see how long they still had to wait. He met a French officer on the street who took him to another officer in charge of the repatriation of his countrymen. He was angered when he heard of three officers still being kept in the hospital, and he loaded Winslow into a big limousine "that had been used by Hindenberg when he was operating on the Russian front" and drove to the hospital. The next day, Winslow and Riley were freed; the unfortunate Sallet still had to stay because there were not yet accommodations for invalids. They were placed on a train headed for a port on the Baltic Sea, to catch a ferry for Denmark.

It took the better part of three months before Harold Riley was back in the States, by way of Copenhagen, Paris, Cherbourg, and Nice. He was discharged on March 17, 1919, and returned to St. Cloud, Minnesota, to be reunited with his mother and sister.

In the summer of 1920, a deliveryman arrived at the Riley home with a trunk consigned to "Mrs. A.L. Riley, Mother of the deceased Harold W. Riley." Inside were all of Harold Riley's personal possessions, except for those handsome cordovan riding boots he had "inherited" from his onetime roommate. In concluding his memoir, Riley wrote, "I often wonder who had those boots at war's end."

JOHN STENSBY:
THE SOLDIER WHO WOULDN'T
SURRENDER

*"I'm probably the only GI in the history of the
United States Army that sunk a warship single-handedly."*

U.S. SERVICEMEN GARRISONED IN THE PHILIPPINES IN December 1941 were among the first American troops to physically confront the Japanese army in battle in World War II. But by the spring of 1942, many of them had descended into a kind of netherworld where they would remain for the rest of the war. Held in brutal captivity by their Japanese conquerers, men like John Stensby found themselves tested again and again, with no way of knowing for sure how close they ever came to the end of their suffering.

As a nineteen-year-old in 1939, living in the small town of Hales Corners, Wisconsin, Stensby had to put off any dreams of attending college to find some way of supporting his single mother and her brood of younger children. When he couldn't turn up any work in nearby Milwaukee, he decided to enlist in the Army to be able to send home even a portion of his paycheck.

In a 2002 interview, Stensby recalled that he had little trouble adjusting to barracks life, and that basic training at Fort Sheridan, Illinois, was not exactly grueling, either. He noted, "The Army in those days gave you a rifle, took you out to the firing line, and showed you how to load it, lock it, and fire it. End of training. That's all there was."

Stensby was assigned to an antiaircraft company and put in charge of maintaining all their electrical equipment. In the fall of 1941, he shipped out to the Philippines aboard the *Hugh L. Scott*, a passenger liner converted to a troopship. A dinner menu Stensby saved from that voyage lists six courses, beginning with cream of tomato soup, continuing through a choice of a half-dozen entrees (including prime rib), and concluding with a selection of cheeses.

He arrived in the Philippines in late November 1941 and spent two weeks on Corregidor, the island fortress at the entrance to Manila Bay, before moving ashore on December 2 onto Bataan, the thirty-mile-long peninsula on the opposite side of the bay from Manila. Several hours after their Pearl Harbor attack on December 7, the Japanese launched a surprise air raid on the American air base at Clark Field, near Manila, and later on the Navy base at Cavite, the home of the American Asiatic Fleet, finding little resistance to their bombers after destroying the air base. Two days later, the first wave of Japanese soldiers made a dual landing on the island of Luzon, to the north and northwest of Manila. Twelve days after that, the Japanese army landed in force, with 43,000 troops put ashore at Lingayen Gulf, just north of Manila, and with another landing south of Manila; the two forces then began a pincer movement on American and Philippine Commonwealth troops under the command of General Douglas MacArthur.

Outnumbered and outgunned, Americans and their Filipino comrades fought bravely on Luzon, but on Christmas Eve, MacArthur evacuated Manila and withdrew all his forces to the Bataan peninsula, and he set up his headquarters on Corregidor, determined to hold out for reinforcements—which never came. On March 11, MacArthur and his staff abandoned Corregidor for Australia, to assume command of the Allied Forces in that area. Four weeks later, on April 9, Bataan's last, overwhelmed remnant of American and Filipino soldiers surrendered to the Japanese. "I did not get word of the surrender orders," Stensby recalled in a memoir. "The last orders given to me on the evening of 9 April by Colonel Massello, then Captain, Commanding Officer of E Battery, were to take my squad of six men, proceed to the forwardmost units, tell them to destroy all equipment when the Japanese forward units were sighted, and then return to our base camp." Stensby and his men accomplished their mission, but on their return had trouble negotiating the only road available to them;

Highway Two was jammed with fleeing civilians and Filipino army personnel. They finally arrived back at their camp at 6 the next morning to find it deserted.

Still unaware of the surrender, Stensby climbed a telephone pole to patch into a line to communicate with any American possible. He got a major on Corregidor who asked him, "What the hell are you doing there?" That's when Stensby found out about the surrender and that Corregidor was still determined to hold out. Rather than give in, he and his men decided to make it to Corregidor. Shedding every personal item and supplying themselves with bandoleers of ammunition left behind in the surrender of their comrades, the soldiers took to the jungle to try to make it undetected to the coast adjacent to Corregidor. They reached Manila Bay and found an abandoned houseboat with some supplies—cans of peaches and condensed milk—which they devoured, only to make themselves sick. Working along the shoreline, they found another abandoned boat, this one a 40-foot Chris-Craft type vessel with two engines.

The Japanese were shelling anything that moved in the bay, so Stensby and his men were amazed to make it nearly all the way to Corregidor before they came under fire, within fifty feet of North Mine Docks. They jumped overboard and headed inland, finding their old company holed up and assigned to man Battery Way, a 12-inch gun mortar battery. Captain "Wild Bill" Massello greeted them, "I thought you were killed or captured," and informed them they were likely the last Americans off Bataan.

For the next 26 days, Corregidor hung on, taking a terrible pounding from Japanese artillery; in one day, May 4, 16,000 Japanese shells rained down on the small island. For every shell the Americans launched, recalled Stensby, the Japanese came back with ten. As much as from the constant shelling, American forces were finally done in by hunger and disease, particularly pellagra from their poor diet. On May 6, Corregidor fell to the Japanese invaders, and Lieutenant General Jonathan Wainwright, the U.S. commander, decided to cease futile resistance and surrender after radioing both President Roosevelt and General MacArthur. As Stensby recalled, "We were kind of beat in every way, shape, or form" (he was down to 100 pounds), but he echoed the sentiments of many men when he noted, "We never surrendered; we were surrendered."

TOP PANEL

Dearest Son John ████████
████████████████████████
████████████ Everyone
is well. Hope you Recieved Some
of the 53 Letters I wRote.
                              Love
████ ████████   Mom'

Censored mail John Stensby received from his mother during his term as a POW. She wrote him daily, but he received only a handful of her letters.

The Japanese herded their captives into the 92nd Coast Artillery Garage Area, an open, unsheltered compound where there were no sanitary facilities, food, or water. Stensby recalled, "First thing, they had to let us know who was boss. And they didn't do it like we would do it. They did it the hard way. The easy way for them." Two POWs were ordered to move a pile of rifles, and when they refused they were shot on the spot. The same thing happened when a soldier didn't bow to his captors.

On September 20, his twenty-second birthday, John Stensby and his fellow prisoners were ferried across the bay to Manila. Stripped of all personal items, they were paraded through the streets of Manila, the Japanese showing off their captives to the citizens of the city. They were housed in the country's main prison, Bilibid, for a time before being marched to the POW camp at Cabanatuan, north of Manila.

This was not the infamous Bataan Death March, which had occurred in April. But once Stensby arrived in Cabanatuan he faced those same brutal conditions. He was placed in barracks and assigned to a ten-man squad with one simple rule: "If one escapes, they shoot the other nine." They were fed three ice-cream scoops of rice a day, actually better rations than they'd been getting on Corregidor during the siege, when there were two scoops of rice given out daily, one at 10 A.M. and one at 3 P.M. Still, Stensby concludes, "At no time in all the time I was a prisoner was our treatment what you might consider humane."

He was taken back to Bataan and put to work in the Mitsubishi Heavy Industries shipyard there. He and his buddies practiced covert sabotage whenever they could, and Stensby is proud to admit, "I'm probably the only GI in the history of the United States Army that sunk a warship single-handedly." He was working one day on the final section of a ship, welding the portion of the bow that would hit the water first when it was launched. Stensby made sure that his welding torch wasn't hot enough to seal the job properly. So, when he next went to work, "there was that ship, sunk in the waves." He and his buddies "must have thrown a thousand welding rods in the bay" to undermine their captors. He concluded, "They would have been a lot better if they'd turned us loose or shot us."

The Americans did like one Japanese welder there, a man they named Junior. But what appalled Stensby and his fellow captives were the Japanese boys, some as young as seven or eight, who worked there as slave labor. He later heard that some Japanese families, desperate for funds, sold their own children to Mitsubishi.

The next stop on his "tour of duty" was Formosa, now Taiwan. He was loaded into one of the infamous "hell ships" the Japanese used to transport their prisoners: old, rusting vessels whose holds were packed with sick and dying men. Every night, the prisoners would pass dead bodies up to the deck, and the Japanese would simply toss the corpses overboard. On Formosa, he was outfitted with a carrying pole with baskets hanging on each end to balance across his shoulders. He spent his workdays, which began before sunrise and ended after dark, hauling rocks from a riverbed up a hill to a rail line under construction.

Late in 1942, Stensby boarded another hell ship, this one bound for Yokohama, Japan, where he was to work on the docks. The Japanese had given their prisoners one summer-weight outfit, but winter was setting in, and he watched as "the cold claimed many [prisoners]." He contracted beriberi and pellagra, and watched his ankles swell to twice their normal size. For the next eighteen months he worked every day of the year except for Christmas and one Japanese holiday. In the spring of 1945, when the U.S. bombing of Yokohama reached its peak, Stensby and his fellow survivors were moved to Sendai, a town about 200 miles north of Tokyo, to work in a coal mine.

"One day in September 1945," Stensby wrote in his memoir, "we were about to head back into the mines when we noticed the guards were gone. Some Japanese were still there, and the camp commandant informed us that the war was over." An American plane dropped food, clothing, and a leaflet telling the GIs to commandeer anything they could for transportation and head down to Yokohama. "That was a fun thing in a sense," Stensby recalled wryly, as their "uniforms" were by now a ragged amalgam of Japanese clothing and air-dropped GI issue. On the road, they passed a group of Japanese troops who looked at them quizzically, not sure what to make of this ragged band of Americans. At a railroad depot, they found an idling train and engineer. Carrying rocks—their only choice for a weapon—they persuaded the man to take them to Yokohama.

The first thing they spotted when they arrived was a group of WACs, the only American women they'd seen in four years. Stensby and his disheveled band were directed to a local base, where they finally shed their vermin-lined clothing, which was immediately tossed on a bonfire, and they were sprayed all over for delousing.

The former prisoners were put on the first available ship bound for the States. On board, they were allowed to eat whatever the other men were having, which was a mistake—they all took ill. "That was the only thing [that made me] angry about being released," Stensby recalled. "They never should have done that." Their ship docked in California, and they were taken to a military installation for medical tests. After a couple of days, the men got restless; as they understood it, they were waiting to be repatriated to a base close to their respective hometowns. Stensby was chosen spokesman for the group; he warned the hospital administrators that he and his buddies would be leaving the hospital shortly, even if it were in their pajamas. Shortly thereafter, he was put on a train bound for Wisconsin.

He hadn't been able to communicate much with his family, and between American and Japanese censorship only the most innocuous information ever passed back and forth. His mother would claim that she wrote him every day, but he received only six or seven of her letters. When he reached the States, he called home to find that everyone there believed he had died in captivity.

Stensby told an interviewer that one of the most frightening moments of his ordeal was seeing a Japanese order of January 1944 that detailed how they were to liquidate their prisoners if the Allies ever directly threatened to liberate a camp. A copy of that order is in his collection in the Veterans History Project.

He did almost give in once. Working in the coal mines, despairing of his ordeal ever ending, he confessed to a buddy that the next day he was going to deliberately allow a coal car to run over his leg and injure him. He hoped the wound would keep him topside, on easier duty. He recalled, "Do you know, that night the war ended? One more day, I might have been wounded for life."

Like many a GI who survives horrific experiences, Stensby came to the conclusion that a higher power was in control of his destiny. During the action on Bataan, as Japanese attacked from the air as well as on the ground, he was in charge of a truck loaded with five men headed for Mariveles, at the base of the peninsula. They had just entered a creek, with six-foot banks on either side of them, when "voices hit my head, so loud, so intense, I yelled to stop the truck. A second or two went by, and down the stuff come," bombs falling all around them. The only safe place proved to be right where they'd stopped, in the creek. Had they gone on, they would have died. "Where did those voices come [from] that saved our lives?" John Stensby would ask himself many years later. His answer: "God watched over me."

MILTON STERN: THE LUCKY POW

Things I Must Do On Return Home:
Get Married & Start Family.
Try to Get In Touch with Other Members of Crew.
Visit New York City and Wally Kast.
Join Book-of-the-Month Club.

S HOT DOWN OVER HOLLAND ON HIS SECOND MISSION ON A B-17
Flying Fortress, Milton Stern survived betrayal by the Dutch
Underground, threats of execution and shipment to a concentration camp, and near-starvation rations as a prisoner in
one of Germany's most overcrowded POW camps. His two accounts
of his adventures—a secret journal he kept while a prisoner and an
oral history interview conducted nearly 60 years later—create a vivid
portrait of a man who surrendered only his body to the Germans,
not his mind or spirit.

Stern grew up in Rochester, New York during the Depression, graduating from high school in 1941. His Jewish family was keenly aware of
the menace that Nazi Germany, already occupying much of Europe and
at war with Great Britain, presented to America. Young Milton took a
job with Bausch & Lomb at their headquarters in Rochester, working
on rangefinders for the U.S. Navy. Despite a promotion to the optical
division—he was made a group leader for the assembly of instruments
used for eye exams of military recruits—Stern quit Bausch & Lomb on
October 28, 1941, and enlisted in the Army Air Force. "A lot of my
friends had already gone," he recalled in his interview, "and even though
I had a lucrative job, I joined the Air Force."

Stern was assigned to the 6th Air Squadron, but when he and a buddy heard that they were headed for the Aleutian Islands, they decided to test for the Air Cadets, hoping to be placed closer to the action. His friend qualified for fighter pilot training, while Milton qualified for bombardier, navigator, and pilot training. When he was told that the Air Force's greatest need was for navigators, "being a good fellow I said I would be a navigator."

By January 1944, Stern's unit, the 381st Bomb Group, was ready to ship out. That month, they were transported to Grand Island, Nebraska, where they boarded a brand-new B-17 for the trip to Europe. Most of the other planes in his group took the southern route, through Florida and across the Atlantic to Africa via Ascension Island, but Stern and his crew were assigned the northern route, jumping off from Goose Bay, Labrador. One hour out of Goose Bay, flying at night, they found themselves in dense cloud cover. Stern had been navigating by the stars, so he requested that the plane ascend, but the B-17 could not get above the clouds. So the resourceful young navigator told his pilot to descend to one thousand feet, and Stern read the waves in the North Atlantic for guidance.

Once stationed in England, Stern and his crew were assigned to fly daylight bombing runs over Berlin. Allied bombers had begun flying massive raids over the German capital in November 1943 in the face of desperate defenses by antiaircraft fire and German fighter planes. Stern's first mission had to be scrapped because of bad weather, but he got credit for it anyway. On March 6, his second mission was a success, and two days later, his B-17 was up in the air again for another run. Over Germany, flak exploded all around the plane, and one engine went up in flames. Pilots in the group were advised to drop to treetop altitudes to avoid enemy radar. "We just happened to come down over a German airfield," Stern recalled, and he and the bombardier, who both were up in the nose of the aircraft, decided to shoot up the field. They destroyed a half dozen planes on the ground "which was kinda stupid, because we were down there to hide."

Some of the aircraft they didn't hit managed to get off the ground and pursued Stern's plane west. "We started seeing windmills, and as a navigator, I decided we were in Holland," Stern remarked wryly in his interview. "I got on the interphone and told the rest of the crew, 'We're safe, we'll soon be over the North Sea.' I no sooner got the

Milton Stern as an Army Air Force Cadet, 1943.
He quit a lucrative job in a defense-related industry to join the service.

words out of my mouth when we were attacked by three
Messerschmitt 109s." Stern and his crew managed to shoot down one
of the German planes, but the other two inflicted heavy damage. The
plane was now flying at 50 feet, and the pilot ordered, "Prepare to bail
out," adding that he would take the craft up to a level where their
parachutes would have a chance to operate. At 400 feet, Stern jumped
out of the plane. He wound up hitting a tree, whose brittle branches
snapped off, and he landed softly on the ground.

He was immediately surrounded by a group of Dutch citizens. "I had a mad impulse to run and see what I could do," he would write in his journal, "for the Dutchmen said that only seven chutes left the ship. [The B-17 carried a crew of ten.] I realized that I would surely be picked up by the Germans at the scene of the wreck." Stern was urged to ditch his chute, and a teenager led him to a haystack with a hollowed-out center, where he could hide from the Germans. Around 9:00 that night, the young man returned with some food and coffee and news that the pilot of the B-17 had broken his leg upon parachuting to the ground and had been captured by the Germans.

Stern spent the next 80 days as a fugitive, though one with many friends. He was sheltered by the Dutch and Belgian Undergrounds in homes, barns, churches, and, for one night, on the grounds of a castle owned by a Frenchman who had flown with American ace Eddie Rickenbacker in World War I. He was reunited for a time with some of his crew and also met fliers from other nations. Above all, he was fortunate that the first people he encountered when he hit the ground were not only Dutch citizens but Dutch citizens willing to risk their lives to help him. "About 95 percent of the people were anti-Nazi," he recalled in his interview. He was denied shelter by only one person: a landlady who was frightened of Stern's appearance just after his landing. His face had been blackened by the rubber in his oxygen mask. "I think she thought I was a Negro [and] the Germans would punish her for taking in a black man," he recalled. "It was worse," he added, laughing, "I was Jewish!"

Stern did not stay long in Holland. On March 11, he traveled by train—he and his fellow fugitives pretended to be deaf-mutes so as not to be recognized as Americans—and then at night in a rowboat across the Meuse River into Belgium. After he arrived in Belgium, he missed two opportunities to be transported out of the country. The first time was to be by air to England, but the plane never showed up at the rendezvous point. The second time, in early May, was to be by train to Switzerland, but an Allied bombing raid destroyed sections of the railroad track, so escape was impossible. In his diary, Stern wrote, "It was obvious that the invasion was to follow close upon this large scale destruction of bridges and railroads. So we decided to wait for our liberation."

His last place of refuge was at the secluded home of M. Tits, next door to an insane asylum with "no neighbors able to see into the yard," allowing him and his comrades a rare chance to spend extended time outdoors. The family had a young daughter named Dorrine, whom Stern recalled "went out of her way to make us comfortable," and a son, Joseph, whom Stern found "a bit eccentric but a good fellow." He stayed there for 16 days; it was his longest sojourn during his life on the run. On the morning of May 27, 1944, Stern was still in bed when "there was a loud noise downstairs and people coming up the stairs. The next minute there were three Jerries in my room and I looked down the muzzle of a Mauser pistol. I jumped out of bed while one was wildly shouting, 'Jude! Jude!' [Jew! Jew!] at me." The Underground had frequently told Stern that he would be shot when captured, so when the soldiers took him out into the yard, he assumed the worst. "After about 15 or 20 minutes—it seemed like forever—we heard the siren of a patrol van. We were all put into it, the entire family and us. We were taken to Gestapo headquarters where we saw the rest of my crew; they had been picked up the night before."

The captives immediately suspected they had been betrayed by a member of the Underground, someone who not only knew of their location but the fact that Stern was Jewish. They focused their suspicions on a partisan who had been captured with them and was put into jail "but really," Stern recalled, "to protect him from the rest of the people." In confirmation of their intuition, Stern recalled, "That man was hung at the end of the war."

Taken to a prison, the Americans were initially housed together, but on May 30, they were split up. Stern found himself in a cell with three Belgian patriots. In his journal, he would write, "Here I was doubly lucky, for I could manage French pretty well, having studied it in school and speaking nothing but French for three months in Belgium." One of the Belgians had spent a year in England and spoke English well enough that communication was even easier. The patriots were kind to Stern, sharing extra socks and underwear, as well as stories of the Underground's activities.

After one week, the prisoners were rousted at 3:00 in the morning and placed on lorries, packed in so tight that "if your hands were up they stayed up and if they were down they stayed down. You couldn't even

Stern (first row, third from left) with the crew of his B-17; he served as the navigator. They were downed over Holland in March 1944.

scratch your nose." They were taken to Namur, a classic European fortress city dominated by La Citadelle, which was situated on a plateau with spectacular views of the countryside. La Citadelle was also notorious during the war as the site of many executions by the occupying Germans.

One hundred and fifty prisoners were herded into one large room of the fortress and for the next four days, their rations were only bread and water. Then they were broken up into small groups and placed in a prison block. That's when Stern learned the reason for the sudden transfer; the Allies had launched the Normandy Invasion, and the Germans were looking for a more secure place to hold their captives. "We were all very excited and happy," he would write in his journal, sensing their liberation was at hand.

Once in the prison block, the prisoners' diet got upgraded: potatoes, bread, ersatz coffee, a weekly "treat" of some pressed cottage cheese and every two weeks a half-pint of preserved cherries. The food came not from the Germans but from the local Red Cross and a charity organization called Secours d'Hiver. Considering his captive state, Stern was not uncomfortable. "I met many interesting people in prison," he wrote, "and it was an experience I shall never forget. I was very impressed and surprised by the cleanliness of the prisons I had been in."

Nevertheless, he was "very glad and relieved" on July 20 when the Kommandant of La Citadelle told him and his fellow soldiers that they would leave that day for a prisoner of war camp in Germany. The reason: "On July 15, which happened to be my 21st birthday, I was taken out in the courtyard and 14 of my Belgian friends were shot, one at a time, by a firing squad. And the Kommandant of the prison standing next to me—he had been my interrogator—kept nudging me and saying, 'You're next unless you tell me what I want to know.' Five days later, he gave up on us."

The fact was, Stern recalled in his interview, "We didn't know anything. People in the underground along the way had never given us any names. They [the Germans] knew more about my group than I did. They even told me the name of my father, my girlfriend, the bases I had been at in the States."

Stern spent the next nine days in transit to his final destination of the war. In Frankfurt, he got a chance to write a letter to his family, his first communication with them since he was downed. He was then separated from the other men in his crew; as the only surviving officer, he was off to his own stalag. "We thought it wouldn't be long before we were released, but it turned out to be quite a while," he later recalled. The last train ride took four days, passing through Berlin during an Allied bombing raid.

On July 29, Stern arrived at Stalag Luft I, near the town of Barth on the Baltic coast. Stalag Luft I opened in October 1942 as a camp for British RAF officers, but when the Red Cross visited in February 1943, they found two American noncom officers. By the following January, 507 officers were detained there; in April, that number swelled to 3,463 inmates. By September 1944, a month after Stern's arrival, nearly six thousand POWs were crowded into the camp. In May 1945, when it was liberated, 7,717 Americans and 1,427 Britons were returned to military control.

At the time Stern arrived, Stalag Luft I consisted of three compounds: South and West, in which American officers and British officers and enlisted men were housed, and a newer compound, North I, assigned to the growing number of American officers. Two more compounds on the north end were eventually constructed, but North I was considered the choicest accommodations. It had once housed personnel of the Hitler Youth and featured a communal mess hall, indoor latrines and running water taps. In the other barracks, the prisoners had to cook over a communal stove in the center of the room and use latrines housed separately.

Stern recalls many communal activities at the camp. "The boys put on plays, musical concerts, and we saw a couple of old movies." They were allowed to go on swimming parties, to play rugby, softball, and volleyball. "We had a library, which got better as time went on." Amazingly, the Jews in the camp were allowed to hold services every Saturday.

Stern was first quartered in a tent with seven other men; there were 25 such temporary structures. The men used a communal stove for cooking and the nearby barracks for "daily necessities." He soon moved into a barracks with 16 men to a room. The camp was rapidly filling up; as Stern recalls, 69 bombers went down the day his was shot down. On December 10, he received his first letter from home and "for the first time since I had been shot down I was on the verge of tears."

On January 17, 1945, Stern and most of the Jewish officers, about 200 men, were segregated into one barracks area of North I. Although he liked his new living arrangements better for the separate mess hall— he no longer had to cook where he slept—Stern also feared the worst, that he and the other prisoners were about to be transported to one of the concentration camps "where we would be put to death with the rest of the Jews." That didn't happen, because on that same day, the Red Army unleashed a major offensive across the Vistula River in Poland. "They [the Russians] started to move toward us," Stern recalled, "and I think the Germans in the prison camp saw the handwriting on the wall and started to leave us alone religiously."

In the segregated barracks, there were a number of prisoners, though Stern was not among them, who spoke Yiddish. It was close enough to German to permit more communication with the guards, and those prisoners "could do a lot of trading. So we made out pretty good at that point." They needed help, because the Red Cross parcels, each weighing about 11 pounds and containing Spam, tuna fish, instant coffee (a recent invention), bars of soap, and cigarettes, had stopped coming. Deliveries had been slowing for months, and the men had been dividing them in halves, then quarters. After Christmas, no more arrived. That cold winter, their one daily meal was usually a stew: "dehydrated vegetables, very little meat (horse, ass, oxen) and beaucoup water. We got a loaf of bread for every seven men. It was very heavy German bread; it was 50 percent sawdust." Stern recalled, "We all lost quite a bit of weight during that period."

On March 27, the Red Cross packages started coming again, and then the prisoners made a startling discovery. The parcels were housed in a warehouse at a nearby flak school, where the German Army held instructions in how to fire antiaircraft guns. Starving civilians were raiding the warehouse for the food in the Red Cross bundles. After Colonel Hubert Zemke, the Senior Allied Officer at Stalag Luft I, informed his men of the thefts, "he took all of us from the North Compound, which was about 2,000 of us, and we marched to the flak school and fought off the German civilians." The men strapped the packages into bundles of four and "as weak as we were, we put them on our shoulders and we carried them back to the camp." Each man wound up with seven packages, "and we made pigs out of ourselves."

Every POW camp had its own homemade radios, kept secret from the guards, to pick up news of the outside world. In April, the men learned of the death of President Roosevelt, "followed by good war news, which nobody either heard or understood or cared much about. We were naturally very sad about Roosevelt's passing. He was a fine president." On April 15, there were reports of attacks on Leipzig, and two weeks later, Stern wrote in his journal, "April 29, Germany is falling to bits and most of Berlin is in Allied hands. Hitler is in Berlin and pro- poses to stay there according to the news. Russians and Americans have officially linked up and last night we heard the big guns. We are pretty sure that this time it wasn't practice." On April 30, he wrote: "Many German Volkssturm soldiers [Germany's late-war, ragtag army of teenagers and elderly men] left here last night. Russians not more than 45 miles from here and probably a lot less."

The prisoners were ordered to dig foxholes outside their barracks in case of shelling or any stray bullets. Stern wrote, "The flak school was blown up around noon. We expect the Russians momentarily. At last the end is in sight and it is about time, God knows." Later that

Stern's prisoner of war identification card. He was known by his captors to be Jewish but was not singled out for punishment.

evening, he wrote, "Tonight we really saw the end of the war here. The Jerry is really drunk and is leaving tonite, taking with him several thousand of our Red Cross parcels. Good riddance to bad rubbish." The camp was now under Zemke's command. Stern noted optimistically, "If we live thru the next 12 hours, we should be on our way home within 2 days." On May 1, he wrote, "Still here, but the Jerry has left. We are awaiting deliverance. Tonight the Russians arrived. We heard Adolph Hitler is DEAD in Berlin." The men were able to get *The Hit Parade* on the radio, and the first song they heard was Cole Porter's "Don't Fence Me In."

They stayed at the camp for another two weeks; Russian troops had driven in several cows, and the men butchered them. "We had steaks for breakfast and hamburg for dinner. It allowed us to gain back a little of the weight we had lost in the last year." On May 13, the 8th Air Force arrived and put the American prisoners on planes. "I don't remember very much about the trip," Stern admitted. "I remember they took us down over the Ruhr Valley and showed us some of the bombed-out cities—Cologne, so forth." They were

flown to Camp Lucky Strike, one of the so-called cigarette camps—
including Camp Old Gold and Camp Philip Morris—that had
originally been set up around Le Havre, France, for incoming troops
to the European Theater. By the war's end, they were used for
departing soldiers and especially for liberated POWs. "It was a city
of tents," Stern recalled in his interview. "There were streets
between the rows of tents and on each corner there was a 20-gallon
can—a garbage can, but it was clean. And it was full of eggnog. We
each had a canteen cup we dipped in, and we drank eggnog from
morning to night. Liver and steaks for dinner. They tried to fatten
us up so the people back home would never see us the way we
looked." Stern got to have lunch with General Dwight Eisenhower
when he visited the camp. Stern and a couple of pals commandeered
a jeep and drove down to Paris—"We couldn't go home without
seeing Paris." They were there for the first anniversary of D-Day.
"When we had our fill of whatever—I won't say whatever is," he
said with a grin, "we went back to Camp Lucky Strike and a few
days later we got on board a Coast Guard ship at Le Havre." It was
a five-day trip back to the States. The actor Victor Mature, who was
serving in the Coast Guard, was on board, acting as chief petty officer in charge of mess.

While in Stalag Luft I, Stern kept busy by writing in his journal,
composing poetry, and compiling lists. The first list in his journal was
titled FOODS I WANT TO EAT, which included "Roast Duck or
Turkey," "Toll House Cookies," and "Milk & Cream (Lots)." Things I
Must Do On Return Home was a short list:

Get Married & Start Family.
Try to Get In Touch with Other Members of Crew.
Visit New York City and Wally Kast.
Join Book-of-the-Month Club.

Not surprisingly, the next list, a longer one, is Books I Wish to
Acquire, which included the novels *Christ in Concrete*, *Les Misérables*,
Marjorie Kinan Rawlings's *Cross Creek* and *The Yearling*, Dostoevsky's
Crime and Punishment and *The Possessed*, as well as the Koran and
Oracles of Nostradamus. Stern listed the camp's rations by grams, and he

fantasized about the Ideal Red Cross Parcel, which was another way to list foods he longed for (he subtitled the list "Wishful thinking").

The poetry reflects his experiences, both pre-detention and inside the barbed wire. It's somehow earnest and hard-bitten, too. The best poem is a new set of lyrics to the popular song "Thanks for the Memory," best known as Bob Hope's signature tune. Its final verse:

> *Thanks for the memory*
> *Of days we had to stay—in Stalag Luft I-A*
> *The cabbage stew that had to do*
> *'Till Red Cross Parcel Day—how thankful we were.*

CHAPTER SIX

WAR'S CONSEQUENCES

EVEN THE MOST BATTLE-HARDENED AMERICAN SOLDIERS SERVING IN THE European Theater of World War II were stunned by the discovery of concentration camps in the waning days of the war. One Army private, James Dorris, was among the first to see the horrors of Dachau, and nothing in his training or realm of personal experience could have prepared him for the experience. As an interesting counterpoint, we include the memories of John Dolibois, an American soldier who, fluent in German, was assigned the daunting task of determining who among the Nazi leadership should be tried at Nuremberg in the fall of 1945. We close with the story of Denton Crocker, Jr., a young man, still in high school, who dreamed of serving his country in war. A student of history and current events, he persuaded his parents to allow him to join the army. His story is a poignant reminder of a soldier's commitment to put himself in harm's way in service to a higher ideal.

JAMES DORRIS:
THE LIBERATOR

*"This is what hell is like. In my mind I imagined the devil
himself coming up out of the ground."*

J AMES DORRIS CAME LATE TO THE EUROPEAN THEATER IN
World War II, but he wasn't spared one of the most horrify-
ing experiences that any American soldier lived through in
that conflict.

He was eighteen in 1943, attending the University of Chattanooga
as an engineering student, when he was drafted. During his basic
training at Fort McClellan, Alabama he took a test for the Army
Specialized Training Program and was slotted to be an engineer. But
with the invasion of Europe underway, the Army decided it needed
more bodies for the infantry, and that's where Dorris wound up. He
was made a BAR (Browning Automatic Rifle) man in the 222nd
Regiment.

They landed in Marseilles late in 1944; the weather was chilly and
damp, and when his unit tried to set up camp outside of town, they
had trouble finding wood for warming fires, the countryside had been
so cleanly stripped. They were soon loaded onto railroad cars left over
from World War I, the famed "40 and 8s, which could hold either forty
men or eight horses. "It seemed like we spent a week on those cars,"
he recalled in a 2003 interview. They made candles by scraping wax off

their ration boxes. Near Strasbourg, on the German border, they were transferred to trucks.

Those first few weeks, they seemed to be constantly on the move, mostly following the Rhine River. New Year's Eve found them in a captured chateau, where they celebrated at midnight by firing their guns, which prompted a loud reply from nearby German troops. "We got a lot of noise going on there," he recalled, "but no one was hurt."

They met many grateful French civilians. He spoke a little French, so he was able to communicate better than most of his comrades. One family was so thankful they gave him a drink from a bottle of schnapps. Dorris was not an experienced drinker, and when he tossed down the liquor, tears sprang to his eyes. The mother of the family mistook his reaction and began weeping in sympathy.

They began to encounter German troops in the Hart Mountains. Dorris had one close shave when a sniper picked off four of his buddies and barely missed him. He watched as artillery obliterated the shooter's position. Shrapnel from a tank round wounded him, and he was sent to a hospital for ten days. "The only bad thing about the infantry," he said, "is you know you're going to be there until you're wounded and/or you get killed."

The stress of battle did strange things to his perception. "You're so concentrating on getting to a certain point," he recalled, "your eyes are trained for any kind of movement." That intense focus on movement brought him up short one day in the mountains, when he sat down to eat his rations and suddenly realized he was sitting right next to a dead German soldier. This happened two or three other times; he would be right on top of a corpse before he realized it. "A lot of the time I felt like this poor guy didn't want to be fighting any more than I did, but he was doing his job."

His unit went through Würzburg, searching house by house for any stray combatants. He recalled soldiers hiding in cellars or sewers from the advance search teams and then popping back up to try to ambush the troops coming through town.

Munich was their next destination, but they were diverted to Dachau. They didn't go through the town, which Dorris had heard was "a beautiful city." Instead, they came upon something else.

"We were going in single files down each side of the road, and then you could smell this terrible odor. It was so sickening that at first I wouldn't take a deep breath. I would just breathe as little as I could. I knew right away it was burned bodies and hair. Once you smell something like that, you never forget it. We got to the camp. There were forty boxcars, like we had ridden going up to the front. Little tiny boxcars that were absolutely packed with bodies. These were prisoners; as the Americans kept attacking the camps, [the Germans] kept moving them. We found out later these people had been put on these boxcars at least ten days before without food or water, nothing. By the time they had got to the camps, the German guards just opened the doors and machine gunned anyone who was still alive.

"Well, the bodies just fell out on the pavement. We found one man alive out of the forty boxcars. When we got in the [40 and 8s], I think they put about forty of us; there were sixty or more in these cars. They were packed in there so tightly that they had to stand. It's just hard to imagine the misery.

"When we went in there, it was April 29, and it was very cold, damp, cloudy, the most miserable day. And I can just imagine what these poor people being jammed in these cars went through."

The gate of the camp was guarded by two German shepherd dogs that had been abandoned but were still chained up, "just going crazy trying to get loose to attack us, growling and snarling." They shot the dogs and continued into the camp. Around the perimeter was a concrete wall about fourteen feet high with guard towers. About fifteen feet inside that wall, there was a high wire fence charged with electricity. Dorris's lieutenant told him to patrol the area between the wall and the fence and not to let anyone out. They knew the people in the camp would be terribly diseased and didn't want anyone to leave without getting medical attention first.

"So I started walking down this passageway," Dorris recalled, "and the first thing I saw was this man who had been so horribly beaten that his eye was lying out on his cheek. I didn't know if he was a prisoner or a guard or what." Inside the camp he found a series of barracks buildings, and in front of them were about 200 prisoners, "just standing there with shocked looks on their faces. In front of them was a long pile of naked bodies of people who had died in the barracks, and they were waiting to be taken to the crematory. These people were just standing there looking at me, not saying a word."

One man broke ranks and started running, seeming to be picking something off the ground. Three more took off after him, caught him, and began beating him, trying to get his hands open. Dorris was so stunned he didn't know what to do, but he realized, "This is what hell is like. In my mind I imagined the devil himself coming up out of the ground. And I looked up in the sky and I said, 'God, get me out of this place.' I felt so helpless, I was all alone, and I didn't know what to do with all this."

A man approached him and asked him in German if he had a cigarette. He did have three or four packs, but he was afraid that if he gave the man one cigarette, he might have a riot on his hands for the rest. He told him he didn't, and the man held up his hand, as if to say, "One moment." He came back shortly with a rusty can, and inside it was a cigarette butt about an inch long. He offered it to Dorris and said, "This is in thanks for liberating us." Dorris recalled, "Well, I wanted to cry, and I thanked him profusely. And I had a complete change from the way I felt. The way I felt a few minutes before, despairing, to the way I felt then, it was just no comparison."

Dorris spent the night in the guards' barracks. "That was a weird feeling, sleeping in that bed," he recalled. The Allies brought in food and began feeding the starving prisoners. The next morning Dorris's unit headed east toward Munich.

In Munich they encountered no resistance, but plenty of citizens welcoming them with champagne and food. In early May, they were occupying a town in Austria, about thirty miles from the Brenner Pass through the Alps into Italy. He and two buddies were in a private home they had taken over, relaxing, one of them fooling around with a German gun he had confiscated. It went off, and Dorris took a bullet in his leg. He had to undergo surgery to close the wound, and when he came to, the soldier in the next bed said, "Hey, the war is over."

Thousands of soldiers came home from Europe that year with souvenirs of their experience. But the memento that Dorris cared most about saving disappeared when he went into the hospital. The Army took all of his clothes, including his combat jacket, and he never saw them again. Inside that jacket was a small rusty can with an inch-long cigarette stub, a reminder of James Dorris's encounter with a total stranger, who offered him a modest gift of gratitude.

JOHN DOLIBOIS:
CONFIDANT TO THE NAZIS

"I knew then I was in for an exciting experience."

ORN IN LUXEMBOURG, JOHN DOLIBOIS EMIGRATED TO America at the tender age of thirteen. He displayed a remarkable facility for learning English but retained his fluency in German, which came in very handy in his wartime career as an interrogator of some of the Third Reich's leading war criminals.

Dolibois was born in 1918, three weeks after the Armistice that ended World War I, in a suburb of Luxembourg City, the capital of the Grand Duchy of Luxembourg, a tiny country nestled between Germany and Belgium. He was the youngest of eight children, and ten days after his birth his mother died, a victim of the Spanish influenza pandemic that swept the world that year.

An American soldier, Albert Ernest Felton, had been billeted in the Dolibois home as a member of the Army of Occupation, and John's nineteen-year-old sister Maria fell in love with him. The family was so taken with Felton that when John was born, he was given the same middle name as Maria's sweetheart. But with their mother's death, it fell to Maria to take care of her infant brother and her father, so the romance was thwarted and the soldier returned to his home in Akron, Ohio. Nevertheless, for the next ten years, the two kept up a steady correspondence, and in 1929, Felton returned to Luxembourg to ask for her hand in marriage. She gave it, and they moved back to Akron.

Two years later, John's father, growing concerned about the political situation in neighboring Germany and fearing for his youngest son's future, decided to emigrate to America. All of John's older siblings were married and settled down with their own families, and they chose to remain in their homeland. John's father decided to take his son to Akron, Ohio, where they could live with Maria and Albert.

Of course John didn't speak English, so his teachers at Findlay Elementary School decided to put him in with the kindergarteners. When John had picked up sufficient English, he was promoted to the third grade, within three months. By the end of that semester, he was in the sixth grade with children more or less his own age. "English was my best subject," Dolibois recalled in a 2003 interview.

Dolibois attended Akron's North High School and worked nights at a gas station, where he could study and only be interrupted by the occasional customer. A week before graduation, he had a quite welcome interruption when he met a young woman named Winnie Englehart. They went out for the first time on his graduation night. Dolibois was not only president of his class but also its valedictorian. "I managed to make quite an impression on my first date," Dolibois recalled.

In the summer of 1938, Dolibois persuaded Winnie to attend Miami University with him in Oxford, Ohio; he already had obtained a scholarship to that state school. She entered Miami a semester behind him but made up the difference by going to summer school so that they could both graduate in June 1942. Dolibois pledged the Beta Theta Pi fraternity, founded at Miami, and became president of the chapter.

In the wake of America's entry into the war in December 1941, the college's rules banning married students were suspended. Dolibois and Winnie made what the school called a "Miami merger" by marrying on January 17, 1942, in St. Mary's Church in Oxford.

That November he was drafted and ordered to report to Fort Thomas, Kentucky. When a young Pfc. interviewed him to determine a possible "occupation specialty," Dolibois told the soldier that he was born in Luxembourg, spoke French and German fluently, and would like to get into military intelligence. "Did you ever drive a truck?" asked the Pfc. "No, but I speak German fluently," Dolibois answered. As he recalled, "I wasn't going to give up so easily."

He was placed on a troop train to nearby Fort Knox, and the Army made a tank driver out of him. He soon learned how to drive every vehicle in the armored force and how to fire every weapon. He also qualified for Officer Candidate School, and in 1943 he received his commission in mechanized cavalry from General George S. Patton, then the commanding officer of the Eighth Armored Corps.

Dolibois already had had a run-in with Patton during OCS. "I got my first demerits from Patton," he recalled. If a recruit got twenty-one demerits, he was kicked out of the program, but at the end of nine weeks Dolibois and one other recruit, David Delpino from the Philippines, were the only two soldiers who had not received any. When the sergeant in charge of their barracks announced that the mid-term inspection would be conducted by Patton, a notorious stickler, Dolibois and Delpino were determined to keep their records clean. Delpino was tripped up when Patton asked him how many pairs of socks were in his footlocker; Delpino guessed wrong. The final part of the inspection was of each recruit's rifle. Dolibois had spent hours cleaning his. Patton inspected it, finding not a speck of dirt. When he tossed it back to Dolibois, a nickel that was used to hold the unloaded gun's spring in place fell out and landed at Dolibois's feet. Patton asked Dolibois, "Heads or tails?" Dolibois dipped his head to see the coin and said, "Tails, sir." Patton said, "Two demerits, moving in ranks without permission." As Dolibois recalled, "I caught a glimpse of a smile on his face as he moved on, and behind him our sergeant winked at me and said, 'I told you— everybody gets demerits when General Patton makes inspection.' "

After OCS, Dolibois expected to be shipped overseas, but he was sent to Camp Chaffee, Arkansas, and made a second lieutenant in the mechanized cavalry. At that point, assuming he might be in Arkansas for some time, training soldiers, he and Winnie decided to start a family, and she moved to Arkansas. In the spring of 1944, eighteen months into his military career, with Winnie expecting their first child, Dolibois's life took a dramatic turn when he received classified orders to ship out immediately to Washington, D.C., where he would learn his final destination. He barely had time to leave Winnie a note.

In Washington, he was put on a bus for Camp Ritchie, in the Catoctin Mountains of northern Maryland, near the Pennsylvania border. Ritchie was a secret military intelligence training center, and Dolibois was assigned to become an IPW (Interrogator, Prisoners of War). His major

*Dolibois in Europe, shortly after he was
promoted to captain, in 1946.*

at Miami was psychology, and the Army taught him the psychology of interrogation; he also learned about the organization of the German Army, technical terms for its weapons, and the history behind the rise of National Socialism. As always, Dolibois was a quick study, and he was soon assigned to train others in the art of interrogation.

In his interview, Dolibois explained that there are two levels of interrogation. One is tactical: quizzing soldiers taken prisoner in the course of a battle, finding out about their unit and what plans they knew about for that sector of the battlefield. The other level is strategic: learning the overall battle plan of the enemy. Strategic interrogation involves senior officers, officials high up in the government, or scientists.

Winnie joined him at Ritchie, where their first son, John Michael, was born on May 14—appropriately enough, Mother's Day. After ten months at Ritchie, Dolibois was shipped overseas, arriving in France in April 1945. His assignment was with a unit called 6824 DIC (Detailed Interrogation Center) in the northern French town of Revin. Their headquarters was a former hunting lodge in the Ardennes Forest.

With the German Army in full retreat, there were daily captures or surrenders of officers who had had personal contact with Hitler, Himmler, and other high-ranking officials, and Dolibois was assigned to interview them. He was given a driver, and he traveled anywhere there were prisoners to be questioned on a strategic level. Preliminary interrogation teams would locate a specific prisoner, and then Dolibois would talk to him. The Allies were especially interested in finding Werner Heisenberg, a Nobel Prize–winning physicist who was believed to be working for Hitler on atomic research, but as it happened, he was actually in Switzerland, and not involved in the German war effort.

In late April 1945, when Dolibois found out that his old unit, the 16th Armored Division, was attached to Patton's Third Army and headed for Czechoslovakia, he decided to look them up. In Czechoslovakia, he met a surrendered German officer who belonged to an intelligence unit very much like Dolibois's; they had been gathering information about the Russians. According to Dolibois, the Germans preferred to surrender to Americans rather than the advancing Russians, and this officer was happy to tell the Americans the location of his duty station, which was similar to the Allies' converted hunting lodge back in France. The officer took Dolibois to the station, and Colonel W.W. Holters, the unit's commanding officer, immediately surrendered. The Allies loaded the station's documents onto a 2½-ton truck. Holters got into Dolibois's jeep with him and his driver for the trip back to Revin.

During the drive, Holters asked Dolibois if he knew about a nearby stud farm where the famed show horses, the Lipizzaner stallions, were being bred. Holters loved the horses and was afraid of what would happen if they fell into hands of Russian soldiers and Polish DPs, who were becoming more numerous in the area. Following Holters's instructions, they made a detour to the horse farm. "It was quite a sight to arrive there on a May morning," Dolibois recalled, "the last day of the war, the day before VE Day, this vast meadow with 100 mares and stallions." He reported the location on his field telephone. A colonel sent a tank battalion to surround the farm, and the horses were rounded up. Patton, who, according to Dolibois, couldn't understand why the Germans would assign 58 able-bodied men to train horses to dance, nevertheless put the horses under protection of the U.S. Army, and his "rescue" of the horses added luster to his legend. John Dolibois was proud to report that he was the first American to see the Lipizzaners.

Dolibois and his driver and Holters headed on to Revin, unaware at the time that the war was coming to an end. He recalled, "Oddly enough, I [drove] through Rheims the day that General Alfred Jodl was signing the surrender documents, and I didn't even know it." It was only when they arrived in Revin that they found out that peace was a reality. On May 10, he was able to participate in a small victory parade through the town.

A week or two later, Dolibois's commanding officer, Major Ivo Giannini, informed him that he was going to be transferred to another unit about which Giannini knew nothing. "In fact," Dolibois recalled, "he said it was located in a place he had never heard of, called Luxembourg." His new duty station was the Central Continental Prisoner of War Enclosure No. 32, military code name "Ashcan," in a little spa resort called Mondorf. Dolibois knew the town well; his family vacationed there when he was a boy. Ashcan, in fact, was the town's hotel, the Palace, which before the war featured a swimming pool, mineral springs, and manicured gardens; Luxembourgers would go there "to take the cure."

He arrived at the Palace, a five-story structure, to find it surrounded by a barbed wire fence ten feet high, topped by electrified wire. A machine gun tower sat at each corner, camouflage nets hung everywhere, and the whole compound was brightly illuminated with klieg lights. When he asked the sergeant of the guard what was going on in there, the man replied, "Look, Lieutenant, I've been here three weeks and I still haven't been inside. All I know is to get inside you have to have a pass signed by God—and somebody has to verify the signature."

In his room, Dolibois had begun to unpack his bags when there was a knock on his door. He figured it was one of the other officers coming to introduce himself and explain the setup. Instead, he opened the door to the surprise of his life: a man whom he described in his interview as "about five feet ten tall this way [holding his right hand above his head] and about five feet ten this way [holding his hands apart horizontally]." Clicking his heels, the large man introduced himself as *Reichsmarschall* Hermann Goering. "I gave a very poor representation of an intelligence officer," Dolibois recalled. "I stood there with my mouth open." But he quickly collected his wits and asked the one-time leader of Hitler's armed forces inside. Goering had seen Dolibois arrive and was curious about who this American was. "Are you by any chance the welfare officer?" he asked. Dolibois almost said that he was an intelligence officer, but "in a rare moment of intuition, I said, 'Yes, I'll see to it that you get treated properly.'"

"I knew then," Dolibois told his interviewer, "I was in for an exciting experience."

He soon learned more about Ashcan, which was a special interrogation center for high-ranking Nazis to determine the composition of the first group to be tried that fall at the Nuremberg War Crimes Trials. Although he had been trained at Camp Ritchie, Dolibois recalled, "I learned that we really knew very little about the Nazi organization." He didn't really know the duties of "these Nazi leaders with these high-sounding titles." He didn't know that much about the SS or the SA, the paramilitary organizations of the Third Reich. He had to find out who ran the concentration camps.

"We didn't really know who the arch criminals were," he said. "Before we could bring them to trial, we really had to know more about them—their personalities, their characteristics, and who was responsible for what crimes against humanity." That was why they were all brought together in a top-secret location in the summer of 1945. Dolibois was one of five interrogators stationed there, all of them trained at Ritchie. The guards at Ashcan were members of the 391st Antiaircraft Battalion, soldiers who fought in North Africa and Germany, specially trained to be the guard element for this prison, though they remained outside the hotel. To operate the installation, forty-two German civilian POWs had been selected from various camps; they included cooks, bakers, electricians, carpenters, and hotel managers.

The prisoners were housed on the hotel's third and fourth floors. The plush furniture in each room was replaced with a cot, straw mattress, and one small table. The Allied intelligence officers were housed on the first floor, while the second floor was left empty, as a buffer zone. On the ground floor were the hotel's dining room and lounge; a large verandah bordered the front of the hotel. The prisoners were free to move about the hotel and visit each other; they could walk in the hotel's garden and sit on the verandah. Their freedom was all by design; "we wanted them to talk to each other, to visit each other, to get into arguments, to stimulate conversation, because that helped interrogation."

Dolibois and his fellow interrogators were working for the Nazi War Crimes Commission. The Commission would send them questionnaires to be used "for prisoners they were interested in," and at the daily staff meetings at Ashcan, the interrogators would decide which of them was going to use the questionnaire on the appropriate prisoner. When Dolibois reported his conversation with Goering to his commanding officer, the CO advised him to keep up his front, that he would learn more from the prisoners by posing as their welfare officer. "It'll be your job," he was told, "to visit the prisoners in their rooms, look out for their welfare, make sure they have what they need. Talk to them, win their confidence, listen to their gossip." Each of the interrogators had about a dozen regular prisoners they questioned, but because all the German prisoners knew Dolibois as the welfare officer, he got to know each of them pretty well.

"I got all the gossip," he recalled. "Everybody was out to save his own neck. Everybody was out for his own interest. To stress how important they were. Or, if they were smart, how unimportant they were. That they didn't know anything. That they had nothing to say. We capitalized on all of that."

One way of learning about the prisoners was through the outgoing mail. Some of them wrote letters to General Dwight Eisenhower, General Patton, or President Harry Truman; it was the interrogators' job to translate them into English. Admiral Karl Dönitz, head of the German Navy, wrote to Truman to complain that he wasn't getting treatment worthy of a five-star admiral. The prisoners were permitted to write to their parents, their wives, their children, Dolibois recalled, and "of course we read those letters to gather information about them."

The prisoners fell into three distinct cliques, which usually ate together in the dining room and sat together on the verandah. The first consisted of members of the German General Staff, the elite military command of the German Army. The highest ranking was General Field Marshal Wilhelm Keitel, equivalent to the American Chairman of the Joint Chiefs of Staff. Under Keitel was Alfred Jodl, and under him were Walter Warlimont, General of the Artillery, and Field Marshal Albert Kesselring. The admirals, like Dönitz, in this clique wore a broad red stripe down the side of their trousers. Goering was over them all, sporting a title he gave himself with Hitler's approval: Reichsmarschall.

The second group was the "Nazi criminal element," the most notorious being Julius Streicher, the Third Reich's most virulent anti-Semite. Proud of his bigotry, Streicher called himself "the leading racist of Germany." Streicher published *Der Stuermer*, a magazine that contained scurrilous and often pornographic stories and cartoons about Jews designed to stir up racial hatred. Hans Frank, the so-called Butcher of Poland, who sent millions to concentration camps, was in this group, as was Baldur von Schirach, the man in charge of the Hitler Youth, and Robert Ley, the Labor Front leader who saw to it that five million Europeans were forced into labor for Nazi Germany. The criminal element, said Dolibois, "wanted nothing to do with the generals, whom they blamed for losing the war. The generals wanted nothing to do with the Nazis, whom they blamed for the atrocities and the concentration camps, of which the generals claimed they did not approve."

The third category included the bureaucrats and statesman: Franz von Papen, Admiral Nicholas von Horthy, and other officials. Some had been in government before Hitler came to power, and when he took over, they joined the Nazi Party as what Dolibois called "political opportunists."

In all, there were 86 prisoners staying in Ashcan. Dolibois and his cohorts didn't bother to interrogate quite a few of them, such as military aides to Goering, Keitel, and Jodl, men who were taken prisoner at the same time as their bosses. They offered no value from a military intelligence standpoint. On August 12, after sifting through all of the interrogation reports and analyses, the War Crimes Commission settled on 22 men to be tried at the first session of the Nuremberg War Crimes Trial. These were transferred to Nuremberg and placed in the war prisoners' wing of the prison there. The remaining prisoners at Ashcan were divided into witnesses for the prosecution or witnesses for the defense.

In a second phase, Dolibois interrogated German military officers at another site in Germany, a Military Intelligence Service Center in Oberursel. These men were not considered criminals of war; this interrogation would be the basis for a history of the German General Staff. At this time, Robert Ley wrote to Dolibois from Nuremberg, offering important information if Dolibois would come to him. Dolibois sensed that Ley wanted to open up to him because he had won the Nazi's confidence. He was sent to Nuremberg to talk to Ley, but he resented Ley's luring him to Nuremberg; "I wanted nothing more to do with the Nazis," he recalled.

Colonel Burton Andrus, the head of Ashcan, now head of the prison in Nuremberg, pulled strings to keep Dolibois in Nuremberg, making him deputy commandant of the prison. Once Dolibois got there, the prison psychiatrist, Major Douglas Kelly, who couldn't speak German, asked him to help administer Rorschach tests, but Dolibois tired of that and pulled some strings himself to get transferred back to Oberursel.

That fall, he did sit in on some of the Nuremberg trials and saw Goering and Hess testify. Eventually, he moved away from intelligence work and became a motor pool officer. His new assignment had nothing to do with Nazis or interrogation techniques. He simply drove all over Germany and Austria, gathering parts for his motor pool, putting over 10,000 miles on a jeep that was painted with the name of his first son, Johnny Mike. In June 1946, Dolibois had accumulated enough points to come home to Winnie and his son.

Dolibois chronicled his life in a 1989 memoir titled *Pattern of Circles*. The title refers not only to his return to Luxembourg for his memorable experiences at Ashcan. After the war, he and Winnie went back to

Oxford, Ohio, where he accepted a position with the university, eventually becoming its vice president for university relations. In 1981, shortly after he retired from Miami, he came back to Luxembourg once more, this time as ambassador representing the United States. President Ronald Reagan had made Dolibois the first naturalized American citizen to return to his home country as an ambassador.

DENTON WINSLOW CROCKER, JR.: A PATRIOT FOR HIS TIME

"I still believe that individual freedom is the most important thing in the world and I am willing to die defending that idea."

E ARLY IN THE MORNING OF OCTOBER 19, 1964, A SEVENTEEN-year-old high school senior ran away from his home in Saratoga Springs, New York, to join the Army. Denton Crocker, Jr., known to his family as Mogie, was an excellent student, a popular young man whose affection for his three younger siblings was matched by his consuming interest in history and current events. He had been closely following developments in Southeast Asia and was convinced that he had a role to play in helping the South Vietnamese in their struggle against their Communist neighbors to the north.

Denton Crocker, named after his father, was born in Ithaca, New York, where his father was working toward a Ph.D. in zoology at Cornell. Denton Sr. had served in the Army in World War II as a scientist, working to eradicate malaria-transmitting mosquitoes in the South Pacific islands. (His story is told in *Voices of War*, the first volume of stories from the Veterans History Project.) The Crocker family moved several times as Denton Sr. obtained academic positions at Amherst College in Massachusetts and Colby College in Maine. In 1960, they settled in Saratoga Springs, where Denton taught biology at Skidmore College.

"We were a family secure in our love for each other," wife and mother Jean-Marie Crocker wrote, "stimulated by the academic community of which we were a part, strengthened by the ideals and traditions that enlarged our concerns. We thought the private happenings of our lives were merely parallel to the rush of crises and events in the years after World War II. Instead, one day we woke to find that those events had overcome us."

Denton Jr. got his nickname, "Mogie," as an infant. His mother recalled, "Fair and blue-eyed, early full of smiles and laughter, he kicked and cried lustily with spells of colic, demanding attention. 'A regular mogul,' his father said, bending his dark head over him lovingly. In a few months he outgrew the colic, but the nickname 'Mogie' was permanent."

When the family was living in Maine, one of young Mogie's best friends was a boy named Frank Dietz. "Frank's father was a fighter pilot recently returned from Korea," Jean-Marie recalled, "stationed with the Air Force Reserve Officers Training Corps at Colby. His stern, forceful presence verified his deeds as a flier and defender, making him a hero to six-year-old Mogie."

The Crockers did not own a television when Mogie and his younger sister Carol were growing up in the 1950s, and Mogie took an early interest in reading. "Soon he was reading junior editions of history recommended for children several years older," Jean-Marie recalled. He used his allowance to collect miniature cowboys, Indians, and Revolutionary and Civil War soldiers, and he reenacted stories he'd read. He made another friend in Peter Pfeiffer, whose wealthy father bought him miniature soldiers from an exclusive New York toy shop.

One day, the two boys burst into the Crocker kitchen to confront Mogie's mother. "The Communists in Hungary threw babies and caught them on their swords!" Mogie cried out. When Jean-Marie demurred, the boys claimed it must have been true, that they had read it in a magazine at Peter's house, and then they went off to play.

A year later, at the age of ten, Mogie decided that he wanted to be an Air Force pilot when he grew up. That November, an eye exam revealed that Denton Jr. had inherited his father's nearsightedness, and he would have to wear corrective eyeglasses for the rest of his life. On the way home from his exam, he told his mother soberly that he would not be able to be a flier.

By the time he reached the seventh grade, Mogie had the reading skills and comprehension of a junior in college. In junior high school, he wrote an editorial for the student magazine on the formation of the

United Nations Security Council and the difficulties of dealing with the Soviet Union in that organization. He continued to be fascinated by American history, devouring a large book on the American Revolution his father's parents had given him. He would call his mother into his room to show her illustrations of maps, uniforms, and armaments; he would discuss military strategy and extol the heroic names of that long-ago conflict.

By his freshman year in high school, he had acquired the six volumes of Winston Churchill's *The Second World War*, studying them more intently than anything assigned to him at school. In his preface, Churchill wrote of the events at Munich in 1938, at the conference in which Churchill's predecessor, Neville Chamberlain, capitulated to Hitler's demands to annex parts of Czechoslovakia as a guarantee for "peace in our time."

"There never was a war more easy to stop," Churchill wrote. "It is my earnest hope that pondering upon the past may give guidance in days to come, to enable a new generation to repair some of the errors of former years." Mogie's book report stated that "the author widened my life by giving me a sort of life strategy. When you are confronted with a problem, obtain all the information you can get on the problem and solve it as fast as possible. Due to his upbringing and schooling Churchill could think politically and militarily at the same time. The inability of Americans to think in such a way is mainly responsible for the Soviet control of Eastern Europe."

Mogie was thrilled with the election of John F. Kennedy to the presidency in 1960. He saw the vibrant young president as someone with a sense of history and a steadfast attitude toward the worldwide expansion of communism. In the winter of 1962–63, as trouble began brewing in Southeast Asia, Mogie watched with great interest as President Kennedy spoke of the "extremely serious" situation in Vietnam by averring, "We are anxious for peace in that area and we are assisting the government against this subterranean war."

In August 1963, during a speech to the new class of midshipmen at the Naval Academy in Annapolis, Kennedy said, "I hope you realize how great is the dependence of our country upon the men who serve in our armed forces." Kennedy had already ordered the expansion of the Army's Special Forces, the elite soldiers trained to fight in less conventional conditions. "Mogie," reported his mother, "who valued physical fitness, who welcomed the rigors of weather and risk, read the spate of newspaper and magazine articles on military training for guerrilla-type missions, mentally tested himself, and dreamed of valiant exploits. His father gave him several of his World War II manuals on survival. "The practical competence and self-reliance that they taught affirmed the importance of the individual," Jean-Marie wrote. "It was a concept that suited Mogie naturally."

Next on his reading list was a history of World War I, "a volume," Jean-Marie remembered, "that recalled the grievous battles at Ypres, the Somme, Verdun, Meuse-Argonne, Belleau Wood, and Chateau-Thierry. Ten million men had died, another twenty million were wounded; yet an occasional aura of romance survived the slaughter in tales of lone and daring aviators, and soldiers like George C. Marshall, George S. Patton, and Douglas MacArthur, who lived to serve their country through World War II and after."

Mogie read with special interest about the Treaty of Versailles and the roots of the rise to power of Hitler. "It seemed that Mogie learned too much and too early of war," Jean-Marie wrote.

In the spring of 1964, she and her husband met with their son's high school guidance counselor to discuss Mogie's future. "He says he'd like to go to West Point," the counselor said. "Oh, that wouldn't be right for him," Jean-Marie quickly replied. "He's too independent, really not suited for that." Mogie had already wondered aloud to her whether the draft would affect his ability to attend college, and she had tried to assure him that with his academic achievements (he had tested in the top 2 percent nationally), he could attend virtually any school and get a deferment from military service.

That summer Mogie confided to his sister Carol that he wanted to join the Navy, but he knew his parents wouldn't let him. He did talk to Jean-Marie about enlisting in the Army before he went to college. "You know you and Daddy could save a lot of money if I went into the service before college!" he told her. But his reasons went beyond the monetary. "He refused to leave the risks of military service to those too poor or ill-equipped to go to college," Jean-Marie wrote. "He believed absolutely that service to one's country was an obligation, regardless of the current need in Vietnam, and he wanted to fulfill that obligation before starting college."

At age 15, Denton Crocker, Jr., was already a student of history who was following unfolding events in Southeast Asia with great interest.

"October in 1964," Jean-Marie Crocker wrote, "was a continuation of summer ease, endless days of gentle sunshine, of unusual drought, only gradually diminishing in warmth and light." On the 18th, a Sunday afternoon, she planted tulip bulbs in her back garden, while across the alley bordering their yard, Mogie raked leaves for a neighbor.

Twenty-six hours later, Jean-Marie and Denton were frantic with worry. Their son had left for school that morning but never showed up there. Their immediate suspicions were confirmed when they found a letter in a drawer of his desk. It read:

> After weeks of thought I have come to the decision that I must run away and join the service. Please do not search for me! It will only cause many people a lot of useless trouble as I will fight my way out if anyone tries to capture me. Believe me when I say that nothing except my own conscience has made me do this. You both have been wonderful parents and although I loathe school it contributed very little in my decision. What did make me decide to run away was a combination of reasons, which I will list.
>
> I wanted to join the service this year which I knew you would never allow. My reasons for wanting for join were:
>
> 1. A realization that without military forces S.E. Asia would collapse. I wanted to and still want to help the Vietnamese to keep their freedom.
>
> 2. Even if I was not sent to Vietnam I could still use my military training in helping freedom-loving peoples after I was discharged.
>
> 3. I wanted to spare you the expense of sending me to college, which I know I am not ready for.
>
> I wanted to earn my own way in the world while helping people at the same time. I still believe that individual freedom is the most important thing in the world and I am willing to die defending that idea.
>
> Don't be too upset by my running away and don't pay attention to the jerks who may try to say you're bad parents. I will write to you as soon as I am eighteen, at which time you could not get me out of the service. My main concern in running away was how it would affect you, so please don't worry.
>
> Try to understand my decision.
>
> Love,
>
> Mogie

Denton and Jean-Marie had no communication with their son for three months. On January 16, 1965, Mogie called home. He was without a job and had to give his cigarette lighter as security to a hotel desk clerk to make the phone call. And yet he would not tell his parents where he was unless they would agree to sign for his enlistment. His father agreed, asking that he stay home for one month first. "For Dent," Jean-Marie wrote, "it was an honor-bound agreement. For me, it represented a retreat from which I hoped to gain time."

Mogie was in New York City, at a hotel run by the Young Men's Christian Association. He had been in Montreal and New York City, trying without success to enlist, taking odd jobs, selling his meager possessions to stay afloat. After a few more phone calls, arrangements were made to wire him money, and he agreed to take an early morning bus to Albany.

Once his son was home, Denton Crocker made a last-ditch effort to sway him from his decision. "How would you like to go to England for a year?" he asked Mogie one evening as the three of them sat around the dinner table. "It was an extravagant, heartfelt gesture, a financial impossibility unless we went into debt," Jean-Marie recalled. "Once, it would have been all that Mogie could wish. Now, caught by surprise, he weighed the possibility. 'Well, thanks,' he answered after a bit, 'but I know that once I got there I'd just try to get to the Congo.'"

It was his parents' turn to be caught off guard. They knew of the struggle between the Congolese Army and Communist-supported rebels, and that mercenaries from England and other European countries were flocking to that African nation in support of the Army. "We were astounded," she wrote, "that his personal battleground extended to that angry continent. That possibility never occurred to us."

During Mogie's disappearance, Jean-Marie had spoken with Sergeant Madigan, an Army recruiter at the local post office, in hopes of exploring leads on where her son might try to enlist. The sergeant came to the Crocker house one Saturday in February to talk with Mogie. "Apparently he had been made acquainted with our academic background," Jean-Marie recalled, "for at once he began to outline the various school and training programs that would be available to Mogie in the Army. In response Mogie announced bluntly that he was only interested in the paratroops." Even when Madigan described the rigors of his own infantry training in the tropics, Mogie seemed unfazed. Madigan agreed to take him to Albany on Monday for a physical exam.

On February 22, the principal of Mogie's high school called his parents to tell them that in the statewide Regents' Scholarship Examination

Mogie took in the fall, he finished tops in the school. Later Denton and Jean-Marie found that he finished fourth in the county. Mogie wasn't interested. He had set his sights on joining the Special Forces, but when he found out that he had to be eighteen to do that—and he wasn't going to turn eighteen until June—he decided on the paratroopers.

On Saturday, March 13, Sergeant Madigan came to the Crocker home with Mogie's enlistment papers. Two days later, Denton Crocker, Jr., was off to Fort Dix for induction into the U.S. Army.

The first message from him, scrawled on a postcard, read in part: "After five days of orientation we have started Basic Training. The days have been long and we get little sleep, but nothing really difficult has started yet."

He completed basic on June 3, 1965, his eighteenth birthday. On leave he came home and spoke to his parents of the men in his outfit: "the habitual AWOLs, who would do anything to get discharged; the occasional college-educated draftee hoping to find a safe assignment; the disruptive drunks returning to the barracks on weekends; and the proud boys from Appalachia who resented the Johnson administration's effort to help their families become part of the 'Great Society.'"

Some of his fellow recruits, noting his fondness for reading, couldn't understand what he was doing in the Army. When he told them that he was going into Advanced Infantry Training and the paratroops, they were even more bewildered. "They ask me why I want to be a 'line animal,'" Mogie said with a chuckle.

Then he told them of a recruit who had lost his leave pass. "He was all ready, his shoes shined and everything, but he lay down on his bunk because he was tired. The sergeant came in and saw him and cancelled his pass. It didn't seem fair. He won't have another chance to get home."

That summer, Jean-Marie had taken ill with a respiratory ailment. She theorized it was a reaction to Mogie's absence. The morning after he described life in the barracks, he sat by her bed and talked to her about how excited he was by the prospect of going to Vietnam. Although he would be eligible in six months for officer training, he told her that he had decided against a military career. "It's too hard on a family," he told her. "I think it caused a lot of stresses in the Dietz family. I'll do my time and then get into something else." He wasn't sure that he still wanted to go to college after his hitch in the Army. He had been thinking about joining the Peace Corps.

Crocker at age 17. He read Churchill's history of World War II and later wrote "the author widened my life by giving me a sort of life strategy."

Later that summer, Denton and Jean-Marie took the younger children for an extended vacation. They drove south, camping along the Delaware coast. They found a campground near Colonial Williamsburg, and for three days they toured the town's 18th-century buildings. "Mogie's commitment in our country's current crisis," she wrote, "lent a special vividness to the abundant symbols and evidence of this earlier brave history that he cherished. Almost shyly we were beginning to realize that we had raised a patriot for our time."

While the Crockers were in Williamsburg, Mogie had completed his first week of paratroop training at Fort Benning in Georgia. He received his wings on September 13, and not long afterwards he told Denton and Jean-Marie that he expected to be off to California and would join the 173rd Airborne Brigade on Okinawa for jungle training. He assumed that he would be in Vietnam soon after that.

Jean-Marie needed to talk with someone about her growing anxiety, and she went to Ben Holmes, the pastor of Bethesda Episcopal, the church the Crocker family attended in Saratoga Springs. "I recalled my agonized fears when Dent was overseas in World War II," Jean-Marie wrote. (They had been engaged when he was serving in the South Pacific.) "[Holmes] shook his head and told me that it would be different, more difficult, having Mogie overseas. My involvement as a mother brought a far more complex responsibility and response than the single-minded love of a twenty-year-old girl."

Not long after that, the family was watching television coverage of Vietnam, and they saw the 173rd Airborne setting up tents outside Saigon. They looked in vain for a shot of Mogie. Two days later, he called from Travis Air Force Base in California, to say he had been delayed in leaving.

They then began receiving postcards from Mogie: from Guam, Wake Island, and finally one from Clark Air Force Base in the Philippines. Denton had been stationed for a time at Clark in 1944. "For me," Jean-Marie wrote, "having waited for mail through World War II, it was a reminder of the peculiar, repetitive power of outside events."

His first letter from Vietnam was dated September 29, 1965. "One of the amazing things here," he wrote, "is the peaceful look of the country, even though pill boxes and bunkers manned by RVN [Republic of Vietnam] troops are all over the place." In his second letter, he sent the red, white, and blue patch of the Screaming Eagles, the 101st Airborne Division. Jean-Marie taped it to the framed corner of Mogie's high school picture, "where its small fierceness contrasted with his smiling face." Mogie reported his disappointment at not being assigned duty as an infantry soldier; instead he was made an armorer in the company headquarters. Jean-Marie was relieved.

In a letter to his father postmarked October 31, Mogie expressed outrage over antiwar demonstrations in the United States:

> What is taking place in America that causes men like Saul Bellow and John Hersey to support these people? It would seem that we are in a period corresponding to the pathetic decade prior to 1939, when intellectuals supported the appeasement of Nazi Germany. Certainly there are mistakes and wrongs committed in Vietnam;

however, these are dwarfed by the good I have personally seen being done. The belief I have in our present policy has been completely confirmed by what I have seen here, and after talking with my friends Cai, Toi and Honcho, I am of a mind to extend for another year when the time comes. My chief worry is that these pacifist bleatings might effect even a small change in government policy at a time when we appear close to success.

A letter postmarked November 24, again to his father, addressed the similarity in their war experiences:

It must be a strange feeling after having gone through the Second War in a similar area to have me undergo a like experience 20 years later. For you the danger was greater, our country being up against a more powerful foe. However, you will not be surprised when I tell you my situation is much like the stories you used to tell me, minus the air attacks. The terrain, people, animals, and vegetation are remarkably alike. Thus I suppose these events bring us closer together. Understandably you feel worry for me as your folks worried for you. Worry, however, serves no purpose and is best put aside as much as possible. As I have written before, I am probably as safe as I would be racing around in my friends' cars back home.

On Christmas Eve that year they got a letter from him describing a field mission he was assigned to. His unit hadn't encountered any Vietcong but did destroy an enemy base and its supplies.

In January 1966, he wrote of his frustration at being assigned to a supply job in a rear area at Phan Rang. "I think perhaps you will understand my disappointment when you see that there is little sense in being over here unless one faces the main objective, the destruction of the VC. Certainly one feels no sense of accomplishment when one's friends are facing all the dangers. Because of this situation I am transferring to the line or elsewhere upon return of the unit."

A few weeks later, he wrote to tell about a book he had been reading, *The Letters of James Agee to Father Flye*. Agee, the author of *Let Us Now Praise Famous Men* and *A Death in the Family*, corresponded for many years with Flye, a priest he met in 1918 at a private school ten-year-old Agee was attending. Mogie wrote:

> The whole book was so tragic, especially in recording the struggle Agee had in finding time and energy to battle against what could be called his own weakness. The depression Agee wrote of was quite appropriate considering my mood during the last month or so. As I wrote before, this comes from being forced to do a job I consider of negligible importance and which is absolutely an absurd task to give someone trained as an infantry man. I can assure you I would never have joined the Army if I had thought they would give me the job of a bloody clerk.

In the same letter Mogie outlines the "main types" of men he had met in the army. The officer types were "mainly decent in their technical duties but over 50 percent are not intelligent enough, or perhaps I should say ambitious enough, to comprehend the political and deeper military aspects of the conflict." As for the NCOs, "many of whom are tops, I believe if it were not for them the unit could not function, and they have my real respect."

The third type were the EM (enlisted men),

> Who can be further divided as the killers, the average Joes and the duds. (I'm part of the last as far as this job goes.) The killers are the chaps who like to fight and are here simply for that reason. In a battle these chaps are great—in camp a major discipline problem. The average GI is the simplest. He tries to "get over" on the Army and in battle follows orders but no more than that. This type comprises the majority of the EM. Supply is considered a "getting over" job, and in turn I try to get over even more because I detest it. (Not a very mature attitude but I can't help myself.) The dud is just that.
>
> Remaining is a tiny minority, which I have given no name and from which two good friends of mine are. I also consider myself basically from this group. This minority consists of the intelligent, the unconventional, gung ho, ruthless, and for lack of a better term, patriotically motivated soldier.

Classifying people in groups is repugnant, and when classifying individuals I feel it is utterly absurd. Also this has been rather egotistical of me. However, I needed to get some of this off my chest and also I believe you might understand a little bit more of what the war seems like to me as far as it concerns the Army. By this I mean the organization.

Well, I hope no censor reads this.

In April came news that Mogie had indeed been reassigned to a Recondo (reconnaissance) platoon. "We are supposed to be the elite of the elite," he wrote. "We have been given black berets with the recondo patch on the left side and black and white scarves." Jean-Marie recalled, "His happy pride in his new outfit could not penetrate the sickening sense of danger that dulled my feelings. When Dent came home from work he read the letter silently."

A letter from Mogie to Jean-Marie dated May 16, 1966, announced that "our operation here on the Cambodian border has been quite a success. No doubt you will read about it or hear about it on the news." He said that his unit had been involved in two other operations since he last wrote, and complained that he hadn't received any mail in a long time, adding, "I may take a 15-day leave to Tokyo to keep from cracking up, so if you or Dad want anything special from Japan please write very soon."

Jean-Marie was "sick with apprehension." She knew her son had "been through something very terrible." "He sounds bitter and queer," his sister Carol announced when she read the letter. Denton immediately replied to Mogie: "I hope you are finding the strength to combat the various tests to which I imagine you are being subjected— boredom, physical exhaustion, fear, killing—as well as sights of poverty, starvation, and cruelties of war generally. I can not really fully imagine the course of a day on patrol and what it must feel like. In that we can't share your experience with you or relieve your stress, all we can do is send you our love which we feel most deeply."

Later, Jean-Marie inadvertently discovered among papers on Denton's bureau a *Newsweek* article his mother had mailed to him at the college. It described in intense detail what Mogie's outfit was going through as part of an operation nicknamed the checkerboard.

Denton Crocker, Sr. at Camp Pickett,
Virginia in 1942. He served in the
Pacific Theater as a scientist.

According to the article, the various patrol units of the 101st Airborne "steadily [moved] from one topographical square to the next—in constant radio contact with battalion headquarters." The commander of the battalion, Lt. Col. Emerson, nicknamed The Gunfighter, played his units "like checker pieces, hoping to jump or block the enemy." The strategy was "a fast-moving, exhausting, subtle style of war." Each soldier carried two cans of meat rations and 21/2 pounds of rice, enough for five days. Emerson said, "I try to get my men to sustain themselves for five days without re-supply. My effort is to try to beat the damned guerrilla at his own game."

Mogie's next letter, postmarked May 19 and addressed to both Denton and Jean-Marie, was brief. It read, in part, "I am now in the

3rd Field Hospital in Saigon with a minor infection in my leg. This is unfortunate but at least I am getting good chow and sleep in a bed now. There is really very little to write about. I've been reading a lot, everything from Anton Chekhov to Donald Fleming and am trying to catch up on current events."

A letter dated May 25 was next to arrive. It read in full:

> Just a note to let you know I'm just about over whatever it was I had and should be out of the hospital in a few days.
>
> As you can guess, I'm doing very little except reading, listening to the radio, and sleeping.
>
> I really don't know what to ask about concerning things at home as I haven't had any news in quite awhile so I'll say goodbye now and write again as soon as my situation changes.

On June 4, the Saturday of Commencement Weekend at the college, Jean-Marie was home early in the afternoon, expecting Denton to return from running some errands. She stepped out on the front porch and saw their car pull in front of the house next door.

"Suddenly I was aware that Ben Holmes was walking across the street with someone. I thought that he had an odd expression on his face, was perhaps joking with Dent. Then I realized that he was with two Army men. The world changed shape.

"I ran down the steps, reaching first a short, young man and, seizing his lapels, I implored him.

'No, not my beautiful boy. Don't say it!'

"He stood quietly and simply said, 'Yes.'

"I tried to ask what happened, and the young lieutenant replied:

'He died of wounds from small arms fire.'

"In an effort to contradict him I replied that Mogie had been in the hospital with an infection, not wounds, and that he had written that he was getting better. The officer repeated that he had died at 2:15 am on June fourth of wounds suffered in combat.

"Ben tried to lead us toward the house, and for the first time in that brief but eternal interval I saw Dent clearly. He was ashen, drained of all life and vitality. I walked a few steps toward him to put my arms around him and said, 'We'll be all right.' Then we all went into the house."

Denton Crocker, Jr., 18 years old, at Fort Benning, where he underwent paratroop training in the summer of 1965 before shipping out to Vietnam.

In the house, the Army men repeated that Mogie had died at 2:15 on the morning of June 4, Vietnam time. Jean-Marie wrote, "He had died in the afternoon of June third our time, his nineteenth birthday, while I picked lilacs in the sun."

The Army suggested that he be buried at Arlington National Cemetery. Jean-Marie would write,

"The growing realization that Mogie would not have sought any greater honor than to die for his country began to comfort us. Awesome though that concept was to us, it was in the tradition of everything he cherished in history and in his personal devotion to goodness and courage. Burial at Arlington would be a perpetual tribute to him.

"Although Ben had suggested the possible consolation of being able to visit Mogie's grave, if it were nearer home, a corner of my heart knew that, if he were buried near us, I would want to claw the ground to retrieve the warmth of him. Perhaps at Arlington I could more easily leave him to rest in the company of heroes, where bravery was demanded of mothers, also."

A few weeks later, a high school buddy of Mogie's shared a letter he had received from his friend. It was written around the same time as Mogie's last communication to his parents.

Duff,

As you can see by the salutation I am no longer forthright and legible, the reason being my nerves are shot and I can no longer print. Actually this isn't completely true. My nerves are shot but I can print.

At present I am malingering in a Saigon hospital with an unknown disease (possibly bubonic plague—the doctors actually dismissed this possibility) which I am almost cured of. I should be back to my unit shortly.

Since I last wrote which is several months, a number of exciting but terribly unpleasant events have occurred, the worst of which was being pinned down by two Chinese machine guns firing 900 rd. per min. (C Co. later captured them) and having my best friend killed more or less beside me. Also I'm being put in for some sort of decoration (maybe red, white and blue bunting or possibly an addition or subtraction by a plastic surgeon). Anyway someday I may tell you the whole story if my nerves aren't completely gone by then. Actually the latter is just wishful thinking in false hope they will take me off the line.

I was fantastically religious for a while, sending up various and sundry prayers, mainly concerned with trying to stay alive.

In August, a letter arrived at the Crocker house from Mogie's commanding officer, Captain Walter R. Brown, who outlined the circumstances of Mogie's death. Their company had been given the mission of securing a position for an artillery battery near Dak To. Mogie's platoon was to take the high ground. "Denton was killed," wrote Capt. Brown, "by automatic weapons fire as he bravely and fearlessly joined his fellow troopers in an assault against the enemy position to save his fellow platoon members." Brown told Denton and Jean-Marie that Mogie's death was "quick and I hope without pain." He also enclosed some personal items of Mogie's that the Army wouldn't have ordinarily sent back.

In a box accompanying the letter were a roll of undeveloped film, a journal kept during the first week of Mogie's tour, a battery-run shaver, two kimono-like garments of black-and-white satin embroidered in red, a white sport shirt, and a set of woven green-and-black striped placemats and napkins. Also there were some papers: his certificate of training as a light infantryman from Fort Dix, his diploma from completing the Airborne Course at Fort Benning; his orders to go overseas; his promotion to Private First Class, and the document awarding him the Combat Infantryman Badge.

They developed the film and loaded the slides into their projector, hoping for one last look at their lost son. There were shots of mist-shrouded mountains, a laden ox cart, bicycles, a Vietnamese work detail, an exotic temple, and along a road, clusters of curious, smiling Vietnamese children—but nothing of Mogie. Denton even thought to look for a glimpse of Mogie in the rear-view mirror of the jeep from which the pictures were taken, but no luck.

"The sensation of viewing bits of Vietnam through Mogie's eyes, in vignettes selected for his camera lens, was powerful," Jean-Marie wrote. They had several large prints made and kept them in a drawer in the living room, "where we could look at them from time to time, as we struggled to comprehend our unalterable link to that distant country."

Nearly thirty years after her son was killed in Vietnam, Jean-Marie Crocker wrote a detailed memoir of his life and times, titled *Son of the Cold War*. The quotes in this story, including those from Denton Crocker Jr.'s letters, are all contained in that work, as is this observation:

"For Dent and me, remembering the handsome little boy playing soldiers on the floor, remembering the many passionate enthusiasms that enriched his brief life beyond ordinary expectation, it almost seemed that the end had been predestined. In my days of joy, I had predicted that Mogie would do something 'fabulous.' He had fulfilled my prophecy, but his actions would forever astound and awe us."

TELL US YOUR STORY

EVERY VETERAN HAS A STORY TO TELL, AND THE MISSION OF THE Library of Congress Veterans History Project is to collect and preserve those wartime stories from men and women who served in all branches of military service: the Air Force, Army, Coast Guard, Marine Corps, Navy, and Merchant Marine, with an emphasis on World War I, World War II, and the Korean, Vietnam, and Persian Gulf Wars. The project also documents the contributions of civilians, such as war industry workers and medical volunteers, who served in support of the armed forces.

All over the country, communities are honoring our veterans. With its heavy reliance on volunteers, the Veterans History Project is a wonderful way for communities to get involved in recording history and to share in our collective appreciation for the sacrifices of our armed services in wartime. We are particularly eager to capture the memories of World War II veterans of all ranks. Most of them are now in their 80s, and their stories must be recorded soon. We want to urge veterans and families of deceased veterans of that war, World War I, Korea, Vietnam, and the Persian Gulf to share their stories and ensure that the human experiences in these conflicts are recorded in this significant archive.

A visit to the Veterans History Project's web site, at *www.loc.gov/vets*, will provide you with all the information you need to conduct interviews of your own and help contribute to this national effort. As the moving stories in this volume make clear, the contributions of millions of ordinary Americans helped preserve this country's ideals. Without donning a uniform or shipping out to a foreign land, you can now make your own contribution to honoring their sacrifice and patriotism. Few things have been more rewarding to me as Librarian of Congress than my own experience of interviewing veterans for this project, and I know this is true of many others here at the nation's library.

The focus of the project is on audio and video recordings of personal wartime experiences. Written memoirs and diaries, as well as collections of letters and photographs that tell the veteran's or civilian's story, are also welcome. Maps, home movies, drawings, and other documents may be included as well. The Veterans History Project does not collect or accept objects such as medals, uniforms, or other memorabilia.

How to Participate
The Veterans History Project encourages contributions from ordinary citizens. You may be a veteran, be related to one, or know one with an existing collection of written materials that fit our criteria. Or you may want to record the memories of a veteran, either on videotape or audiotape. The VHP can help you with guidelines and tips. We will send you the necessary forms for donating materials to the project or you can obtain them through our web site.

What Happens to Your Materials
After you submit the interview, with the required Biographical Data and Release Forms, the interview and other documents will be preserved according to professional archival standards. Certain information from the participants' Biographical Data Forms will be presented to the public in the project's online database. The materials will be available to researchers, educators, family members, and others at the American Folklife Center in the Library of Congress.

James H. Billington
The Librarian of Congress

For more information about the Veterans History Project, please contact:

The Veterans History Project
American Folklife Center
Library of Congress
101 Independence Ave., SE
Washington, DC 20540-4615
www.loc.gov/vets

RESOURCES

Military History Centers

Each of the service branches maintains a history center containing a reference collection of books, documents, published unit histories, photographs, medals, and artifacts. The addresses and web sites for these centers are listed below.

United States Air Force
Air Force History Support Office
AFHSO/HOS
Reference and Analysis Division
200 McChord Street, Box 94
Bolling AFB, DC 20332-1111
Telephone: (202) 404-2261
Web site: http://www.airforcehistory.hq.af.mil/

U.S. Air Force Historical Research Agency
600 Chennault Circle
Building 1405
Maxwell AFB, AL 36112-6424
Telephone: (334) 953-2395
Web site: http://www.au.af.mil/au/afhra/

U.S. Air Force Museum
1100 Spaatz Street
Wright-Patterson AFB, OH 45433-7102
Telephone: (937) 255-3286
Web site: http://www.wpafb.af.mil/museum/

United States Army
U.S. Army Center of Military History Building 35
102 Fourth Avenue

Fort McNair, DC 20319-5058
Telephone: (202) 685-2733
Web site: http://www.army.mil/cmh-pg/default.htm

U.S. Army Military History Institute
Carlisle Barracks, PA 17013-5008
Telephone: (717) 245-3611
Web site: http://carlisle-www.army.mil/usamhi/

United States Coast Guard
U.S. Coast Guard Historian's Office
United States Coast Guard Headquarters
Room B-717
2100 Second St., SW
Washington, DC 20953
Telephone: (202) 267-2596
Web site: http://www.uscg.mil/hq/g-cp/history/collect.html

Coast Guard Museum
U.S. Coast Guard Academy
15 Mohegan Avenue
New London, CT 06320-8511
Telephone: (860) 444-8511
Web site: http://www.uscg.mil/hq/g-cp/museum/MuseumInfo.html

United States Marine Corps History Division
Marine Corps Educaion Command
Marine Corps University
3094 Upshur Avenue
Quantico, VA 22134
Web site: http://hqinet001.hqmc.usmc.mil/HD/

Marine Corps Air-Ground Museum
Marine Corps Combat Development Command
2014 Anderson Avenue
Quantico, VA 22134-5002
Telephone: (703) 784-2607
Web site: http://hqinet001.hqmc.usmc.mil/HD/Home_Page.htm

United States Navy
Naval Historical Center
Washington Navy Yard
Building 57
805 Kidder Breese Street, SE
Washington Navy Yard, DC 20374-5060
Telephone: (202) 433-3634
Web site: http://www.history.navy.mil/

LOCATING MILITARY SERVICE RECORDS
INDIVIDUAL PERSONNEL FILES
The National Archives and Records Administration (NARA) is the official repository for records of military personnel who have been discharged from the U.S. Air Force, Army, Marine Corps, Navy, and Coast Guard.

A veteran (or next of kin) may request his or her individual military personnel file (201 file) by sending a request to the National Personnel Records Center, Military Records Facility, 9700 Page Boulevard, St. Louis, MO 63132-5100.

Additional information about the contents of these personnel files, instructions for submitting a request, and a downloadable PDF copy of the request form may be found on the National Personnel Records Center home page of the National Archives and Records Administration web site (http://www.archives.gov/facilities/mo/st_louis/military_personnel_records.html).

Personnel records of civilians who worked for the various branches of the military are also held by the National Personnel Records Center. The address to write for these records is National Personnel Records Center, Civilian Records Facility, 111 Winnebago Street, St. Louis, MO 63118-4199.

CONTRIBUTORS

RAFFI BAHADARIAN was born in 1977 in Beirut, Lebanon. He enlisted in the Marines in 1996 and served in the Iraq War. He lives in California.

ASA BALL was born in 1928 in Hamilton County, Tennessee. He served from 1950 to 1952 in the Army during the Korean War. He died in 2005.

RAYMOND BRITTAIN was born in 1921 in San Diego, California. He served with the Navy in the Pacific Theater during World War II. He lives in Wyoming.

RUTH DELORIS BUCKLEY was born in 1918 in Prescott, Wisconsin. She enlisted in the Army Nurse Corps, and served in North Africa and the European Theater during World War II, from 1940 to 1946. She died in 1991.

RHONDA CORNUM was born in 1954 in Dayton, Ohio. She enlisted in the Army in 1978, and served in the Persian Gulf War. She is stationed in Germany.

DENTON WINSLOW CROCKER, JR. was born in 1947 in Ithaca, New York. In 1965, he enlisted in the Army and served in Vietnam from September 1965 until his death there in June 1966.

DODSON MOORE CURRY was born in 1922 in Birmingham, Alabama. He served in the Army during the Korean War, from 1952 to 1954. He lives in Alabama.

EUGENE CURTIN was born in 1889 in Williamsport, Pennsylvania. During World War I he was attached to the British Expeditionary Force as a physician from 1917 to 1919. He died in 1951.

RICHARD DELEON was born in 1944 in New York City. He served in the Army during the Vietnam War. He lives in New York.

JOHN DOLIBOIS was born in 1918 in Luxembourg. He enlisted in the Army in 1942, and served in the European Theater of World War II until 1946. He lives in Ohio.

JAMES DORRIS was born in 1924 in Chattanooga, Tennessee. He served in the Army in the European Theater of World War II. He lives in Tennessee.

ROBERT FRANKLIN DUNNING was born in 1920 in Brooklyn, New York. He enlisted in the Army in 1941 and served in Europe, Africa, and the Middle East during World War II. He left the service in 1946, and currently resides in Massachusetts.

HILLIE JOHN FRANZ was born in 1894 in Bernardo, Texas. He served in the Army in World War I from 1918 to 1919. He died in 1982.

JULIA GRABNER HASKELL was born in 1945 in New York City. She served in the Army Nurse Corps during the Vietnam War from 1968 to 1969. She lives in Indiana.

ALBERT HASSENZAHL was born in 1920 in Toledo, Ohio. He served between 1942 and 1945 with the Army in the European Theater of World War II. He lives in Michigan.

NORMAN IKARI was born in 1919 in Seattle, Washington. He served in the Army from 1942 to 1945 in the European Theater during World War II. He lives in Maryland.

ROGER DEAN INGVALSON was born in 1928 in Austin, Minnesota. He served in the Air Force from 1950 to 1976, serving in Vietnam. He lives in Tennessee.

DARLENE ISKRA was born in 1952 in San Francisco, California. From 1979 to 2000 she served in the Navy, including a tour of duty during the Persian Gulf War. She lives in Maryland.

JOHANN KASTEN IV was born in 1916 in Honolulu, Hawaii. He served in the Army from 1943 to 1945 in the European Theater of World War II. He lives in the Philippine Islands.

YEIICHI KELLY KUWAYAMA was born in 1918 in New York City. He was drafted into the Army and served in the European Theater during World War II, from 1941 to 1945. He lives in Washington, D.C.

FRANCES LIBERTY was born in 1923 in Plattsburgh, New York. She served in the Army Nurse Corps from 1943 to 1946 and from 1951 to 1971, with tours of duty in the European Theater of World War II, in Korea, and in Vietnam. She died in 2004.

HAROLD LIPPARD was born in 1921 in Statesville, North Carolina. He served in the Navy and Navy Reserves from 1944 to 1956, doing a tour of duty in the Pacific Theater of World War II. He lives in Tennessee.

JOSÉ MARES was born in 1932 in Prescott, Arizona. He served in the Army from 1949 to 1971, with a tour of duty in the Korean War. He lives in Georgia.

JOHN MCCAIN was born in 1936 in the Panama Canal Zone. He served in the Navy from 1958 to 1981, with a tour of duty in the Vietnam War. In 1982 he was elected to the U.S. House of Representatives for the First Congressional District of Arizona. In 1986, he was elected to the United States Senate to represent Arizona.

GILES MCCOY was born in 1926 in St. Louis, Missouri. He served in the Marines in the Pacific Theater of World War II from 1944 to 1946. He lives in Florida.

ROBERT POWELL was born in 1920 in Wilcoe, West Virginia. He served in the Army Air Force from 1942 to 1944, with a tour of duty in the European Theater of World War II. He lives in Georgia.

AUGUSTUS PRINCE was born in 1924 in Philadelphia, Pennsylvania. He served in the Navy in the Pacific Theater of World War II from 1944 to 1945. He lives in Florida.

PHILIP THOMAS RANDAZZO was born in 1946 in Gross Pointe, Michigan. He served in the Army from 1967 to 1969 during the Vietnam War. He lives in Michigan.

CHARLES REMSBURG was born in 1925 in Highland Park, Michigan. He served in the Army between 1943 and 1946 in the European Theater of World War II. He lives in Michigan.

HAROLD RILEY was born in 1894 in Minneapolis, Minnesota. He served from 1917 to 1919 in the French Army and the U.S. Army Air Corps during World War I. He died in 1975.

KENNETH RAY RODGERS was born in 1951 in Mayfield, Kentucky. He served in the Army from 1968 to 1970 and 1977 to 1996, with tours of duty in Vietnam and the Persian Gulf War. He lives in Kentucky.

JOHN STENSBY was born in 1920 in Hales Corner, Wisconsin. He served in the Army from 1939 to 1960, and was in the Pacific Theater during World War II. He lives in Wisconsin.

MILTON STERN was born in 1923 in Buffalo, New York. During World War II he served in the European Theater with the Army Air Corps from 1942 to 1945. He lives in New Jersey.

JOHN SUDYK was born in 1922 in Hinckley, Ohio. He served in the Army from 1942 to 1945, with a tour of duty in the European Theater of World War II. He lives in Ohio.

WENDY MARIE WAMSLEY TAINES was born in 1971 in South Bend, Indiana. She served in the Army from 1990 to 1991 during the Persian Gulf War. She lives in California.

CAROLYN HISAKO TANAKA was born in 1935 in Santa Maria, California. From 1966 to 1968, she served as a nurse in the Army, stationed for 18 months in Vietnam. She lives in California.

BERTRAN WALLACE was born in 1918 in Waco, Texas. He was in the Army from 1942 to 1978, serving in both World War II and Korea. He lives in Florida.

ACKNOWLEDGMENTS

T HE STAFF OF THE VETERANS HISTORY PROJECT, WITH THEIR TIRELESS devotion to preserving the stories of thousands of veterans, made this book possible. Chief among my colleagues for this book were Diane Kresh, Sarah Rouse, Eileen Simon, and Anneliesa Clump Behrend. Thanks also to Peter Bartis, Donna Borden, Tanya Brown, Christy Chason, Tracey Dodson, Ellen Donnelly, Sheila Dyer, Talia Gibas, Vicki Govro, Megan Harris, Neil Huntley, Geanie Jackson, Danielle Johnson, Jeff Lofton, Matt McCrady, Heather McCaw, Rachel Mears, Nancy Mitchell, Monica Mohindra, Debra Murphy, Shantee Owens, Robert Patrick, Alexa Potter, Sarah Reeder, Angela Reid-Ampey, Sandra Savage, Carrie Schneider, Tim Schurtter, Taru Spiegel, Aron Swan, James Taylor, Roisin Wisneski, and Lee Woodman. Many thanks to Betsy Miller, Moryma Aydelott, Morgan Cundiff, Glenn Gardner, Corey Keith, and Nate Trail of the Library of Congress's Network Development Team for their stellar work on the Veterans History Project's web site. The interviewers whose work graced these pages (their subjects are in parentheses) are Rebekah E. Adams (John Stensby), Robert Babcock (Robert Powell), Brenda Beter (Bertran Wallace), Naomi Casasanta (Julia Grabner Haskell), Mary Ann Donahue (Wendy Wamsley Taines), Janet B. Hammond (Raymond Brittain), Alice Healy (Milton Stern), Michele Kelly (John McCain), Judith Kent (Giles McCoy, Augustus Prince), Robert Landry (Frances Liberty), Kathy Lang (John Dolibois), Tony Mavredes (Asa Ball), Cathleen McLoughlin (Richard DeLeon), Tony Mavredes (Asa Ball), Rachel Mears (Darlene Iskra), Calvin Ninomiya (Norman Ikari, Yeiichi Kuwayama), Larry Ordner (Kenneth Rodgers), James B. Pachucki (Philip Randazzo), Dorothy M. Schneider (Raffi Bahadarian), Tom Swope (John Sudyk), Michael Lloyd Willie (James Dorris, Roger Ingvalson, Harold Lippard, José Mares), and Brad Winchester (Rhonda Cornum). Special thanks to Lisa Thomas for her editorial support on matters big and small. Ralph Eubanks and Aimee Hess of the Library's Publishing Office offered invaluable encouragement. No one's support means more to me than that of my wife, Barbara Humphrys. I dedicate my work on this book to Joe Volk, a veteran with his own story to tell, and Maureen Humphrys, in gratitude for her energetic work on behalf of veterans.

INDEX

ILLUSTRATIONS CREDITS

ABOUT THE AUTHOR

Tom Wiener is the historian of the Library of Congress Veterans History Project, the largest archive of wartime veterans' experiences in the United States. He is the editor of *Voices of War: Stories of Service from the Home Front and the Front Lines* (National Geographic Books, 2004) and the author of two other books. He lives in Washington, D.C.

Voices of War: Stories of Service from the Home Front and the Front Lines is available wherever books are sold.